Thinking Through Education

Thinking Through Pedagogy for Primary and Early Years

Thinking Through Education

Thinking Through Pedagogy for Primary and Early Years

Tony Eaude

LearningMatters

First published in 2011 by Learning Matters Ltd

British Library Cataloguing in Publication Data
A CIP record for this book is available from the British Library.

ISBN: 978 0 85725 063 6

This book is also available in the following ebook formats:
Adobe ebook ISBN: 978 0 85725 066 7
EPUB ebook ISBN: 978 0 85725 065 0
Kindle   ISBN: 978 0 85725 067 4

Cover design by Toucan
Project management by Deer Park Productions, Tavistock, Devon
Typeset by PDQ Typesetting Ltd, Newcastle-under-Lyme, Staffordshire
Printed and bound in Great Britain by Bell & Bain Ltd, Glasgow

Learning Matters Ltd
20 Cathedral Yard
Exeter EX1 1HB
Tel: 01392 215560
info@learningmatters.co.uk
www.learningmatters.co.uk

Contents

About the author

Dr Tony Eaude has been a teacher and headteacher for over 30 years, working initially in a special school and then in suburban, new town and multicultural primary schools. He completed a master's degree in Educational Research Methodology and a doctorate on how teachers of young children understand spiritual development, both at the University of Oxford, where he is a Research Fellow in the Department of Education.

He works as an independent research consultant, evaluating educational programmes, leading training, teaching at Masters' level at the Institute of Education, London and Westminster Institute, Oxford Brookes University and writing for both teachers and academic audiences. He continues to teach young children in an urban primary school.

Other publications which Tony Eaude has written include three short books, one as co-author, in a series for parents, several booklets for teachers, including *New Perspectives on Spiritual Development and Values Education – Developing Positive Attitudes*. His book *Children's Spiritual, Moral, Social and Cultural Development – Primary and Early Years* is published by Learning Matters. He has also written a range of academic and practical articles on related subjects.

More details of Tony Eaude's work can be seen on www.edperspectives.org.uk. He welcomes comments and feedback on this book and can be contacted on tony.eaude@education.ox.ac.uk.

Acknowledgements

This book is the result of many years of working with thoughtful colleagues, especially those in the schools where I have been privileged to teach, and of teaching young children, many of whom have helped me to learn more about the many different routes into learning. I wish to thank them all, too numerous to name.

I should like to thank the school whose statement of aims I have used in Chapter 1 for permission to do so; and those who were kind enough to read and comment on specific chapters or sections; Geerthi Ahilan, Jane Godby, Lucy Gething and Nick Swarbrick. Their ideas were very helpful, in terms of content and style. And, in particular, Jude Egan, who has listened, commented and encouraged me, with patience, wisdom and love, as well as guiding me over many years to understand more deeply the importance of emotional processes, of relationships and of stories and how these are interlinked and affect us all.

The extract on pages 16–18 is © TLRP Teaching and Learning Research Programme. Every effort has been made to trace the copyright holders and to obtain their permission for the use of copyright material. The publisher and author will gladly receive any information enabling them to rectify any error or omission in subsequent editions.

Introduction

This book, the first in the series called Thinking Through Education, explores pedagogy for those working with young children. Pedagogy is usually associated only with teachers. However, this text will suggest that pedagogy applies, in different ways, to all of those who support children's learning – referred to as educators – considering, later, what is distinctive about teachers.

The term 'pedagogy' remains unfamiliar in the English educational system, as indicated by the title Alexander's 2004 article, 'Still no pedagogy?'. However, his view (2004, page 11) that it *is what one needs to know, and the skills one needs to command, in order to make and justify the many kinds of decisions of which teaching is constituted* is a good starting point. Chapter 1 of this book examines this in more depth, drawing especially on the findings of the Teaching and Learning Research Project (TLRP, 2006). One issue explored throughout the book is to what extent primary and Early Years education has features distinctive from other phases, and from each other; and what these are. This indicates that pedagogy is more complicated and interesting than teaching in terms of transmitting subject knowledge, or the mechanics of planning and assessment, important though these are; and goes far beyond simplistic appeals to 'what works'. So, it is an ideal area for 'thinking through'.

Who is this book for?
This book is primarily for those:

- training to gain Qualified Teacher Status (QTS) to work as a teacher in primary or nursery schools or other Early Years settings, so that it refers to the Standards for Achieving QTS (TDA, 2007);
- studying on courses such as education studies and early childhood studies, so that it refers to the QAA Benchmark Standards (QAA, 2007a, b).

However, you may already work in an Early Years setting or a school, in one of many other roles such as a nursery nurse, learning mentor or teacher. Whoever you are, it will be valuable for you to continue to think through pedagogy throughout your professional life.

For many reasons, how children are educated may change substantially in the next 20 to 30 years. This calls for flexible, committed and thoughtful professionals, able to adapt to changing circumstances and expectations, but conscious of how children learn best and the values and the models that adults present. The importance of these stretches beyond the profession, so you might even be a governor or a parent.

Let me say a few words about myself. I have taught for about 35 years in special, primary and first schools and, more recently, on courses for teachers. I was the head teacher of a first school for nine years and am now a researcher who also teaches in a primary school. My particular interest is in young children's spiritual, moral, social and cultural development. I believe that education has the power to transform lives, but too often schools fail to do so. The reasons cannot be understood without considering the wider context in which children learn and the beliefs that we, individually and as a society, have about children, learning and schools.

This book tries to help you think through how you can enhance young children's learning. Although this book concentrates on children up to the age of 11, I do not define what I mean exactly by 'young children', because children's learning is so varied that educators should draw ideas from different traditions and Key Stages in thinking through what is appropriate for their children.

Using 'you' reflects my belief that knowledge is created, not transmitted; and that most learning is reciprocal, requiring the learner's active engagement. These ideas are explained during the course of the book, but, briefly, they suggest that the answer to important questions does not lie 'out there', in a book, a policy or anywhere else. Rather, we learn by constructing and refining our understanding, encountering new experiences and ideas, sometimes directly, sometimes through conversation, sometimes through books, films and other media, and incorporating these into new understanding. So, what I call 'thinking through' involves you being engaged with what these may mean for you in your own context. You will be encouraged to take the long view and challenged to think 'outside the box'.

Although I draw on research, inevitably my own views and interests will be evident. In particular, I shall suggest what pedagogy 'looks like' when practised by an expert and how you can work towards this. This involves challenging many current assumptions, for example about the aims of education, the most valuable types of learning and how to enable these. Naturally, I hope to persuade you that these ideas are right, but you may disagree. More important is to engage your interest, so that you think deeply about key ideas and questions – and add your own. This involves you using a range of skills – to be explained – to examine your assumptions and think differently, sometimes laterally and usually more broadly, about concepts such as learning and knowledge and how this might, and can, apply to your own context and practice. I hope that this approach will help you to engage with the questions raised, to think of examples, to challenge my, and your, ideas, to recognise the benefits of 'thinking through...' pedagogy; and above all to enhance children's learning and lives.

What does 'thinking through' involve?

As we shall see, pedagogy is complicated and fascinating. Courses on using a new piece of software or athletics or teaching phonics help mainly with *what* to teach. I am encouraging you to think through the much harder question of *how* to enhance children's learning. This entails examining – and re-examining – our assumptions on what we often take for granted about children and schools, about learning and knowledge. It requires a willingness to ask questions, be creative and open-minded and understand ideas and concepts in new ways – rather than simply doing as one is told or looking for simple answers, since thought is linked to action and our beliefs and actions affect each other. Let me give an example.

I wonder what image comes to mind when you read the words 'think through'. My guess is probably of someone – most likely a man, probably middle-aged or older – sitting on his own at a desk, perhaps touching his head and looking worried. I may be wrong. You may have imagined a cook adapting a recipe by adding herbs and spices, tasting the casserole from time to time. Or a parent and toddler reading, discussing and laughing at a picture book. Or a group of four-year-olds rearranging a pile of bricks and jumping up and down with enthusiasm at successfully completing a task they planned together.

Are all of these thinking? Is thinking only a cerebral process? How does 'thinking' relate to action?

We tend to imagine thinking as a solitary activity, separate from action. Yet, much of our best thinking occurs through sharing ideas with other people; and success in most activities requires constant reflection on what is happening and how best to adapt one's approach. Moreover, many good ideas emerge as we work them out in practice; or in the 'spaces' when we stop focusing directly. Schön (1987) makes the distinction between reflection *in* action and reflection *on* action – about what is happening and what has happened. Since working with children is a practical and often unpredictable activity, reflection in action is an essential part of understanding what is happening and adapting our actions and expectations. But because it also relies on knowledge and understanding, reflection on action can help us realise why one lesson worked, or one group of children responded well, and another not; and decide what to do differently next time.

How are the skills involved in 'thinking through' presented in the QTS and QAA Standards?

The Professional Standards for QTS (TDA, 2007) are in three sections. These are:

- professional attributes;
- professional knowledge and understanding;
- professional skills.

Interestingly, the Standards neither consider explicitly what is meant by 'professional' nor specify attributes as such, but we will explore these. The knowledge and understanding relate mainly to the content of what is required to achieve the Standards.

Skills highlighted include demonstrating positive values, attitudes and behaviour, communicating effectively, recognising and respecting other people's contributions, reflecting on practice, identifying priorities, being creative and constructively critical and acting upon advice and feedback. Those more specifically associated with pedagogy include planning for progression, designing opportunities, assessing learning needs and evaluating the impact of teaching.

The Quality Assurance Agency Benchmark Standards set out what is required for students to complete degree programmes in education studies (QAA, 2007a) and early childhood studies (QAA, 2007b), respectively. Different courses will have varying content, but the two sets of Standards highlight skills to use and develop in reading this book.. To give one example, Education Studies

 is concerned with understanding how people develop and learn through their lives, and the nature of knowledge and critical engagement with ways of knowing and understanding. It offers intellectually rigorous analysis of educational processes, systems and approaches and their cultural, societal, political, historical and economic contexts...[Courses] all include critique of current policies and practice and challenge assumptions.

(QAA, 2007a, page 1)

Among the skills highlighted for Education Studies (QAA, 2007a, pages 4–5) are:

- application, including considering different dimensions of education, accommodating new ideas, analysing complex situations and using examples;
- reflection, including reflecting on one's own values, development and practice, questioning concepts and theories, and interrogating assumptions;
- working with others and analysing, synthesising, evaluating and identifying problems and solutions.

The Benchmark Standards for Early Childhood Studies (QAA, 2007b, pages 5–7) highlight a long list of similar skills, adding observing, generating and exploring hypotheses, taking and evaluating different perspectives, integrating and demonstrating. Some are subject-specific, some generic, that is not directly related to the subject matter of the course, though QAA (2007b, page 5) recognises that *this distinction is a fairly artificial one since the distinction...is not clear-cut*. All the skills you will be expected to use during your course, and subsequently, are interlinked. However, Table 1 highlights 14 which will help as you read, on your course and in the classroom – and then as you apply these to your practice. I refer to specific skills at particular points, indicating those which are most important at the start and end of each chapter and in each critical thinking exercise – but keep thinking all the time.

Table 1 Critical thinking skills

Observe	what you have seen (and heard and felt) yourself, other adults and children do
Explore	what sense one can make of these observations
Analyse	what reasons there may be for these actions
Consider	the factors which influence these actions
Interpret	people's motivation and the consequences of their actions
Illustrate	your views by using examples
Compare	different actions, people and contexts
Articulate	your beliefs and assumptions (in speech or in writing)
Challenge	your own and other people's assumptions
Discuss	with other people – tutors, other students, teachers – the issues raised
Imagine	how you might act differently and the consequences of this
Synthesise	these ideas to decide what you might do differently
Identify	what you have to do, or to avoid, to make your plans successful
Experiment	with different approaches, but keep observing, exploring, considering, imagining…

Using these skills in reading this book

Each chapter starts with a box to highlight the critical thinking skills, from the list above, most valuable in reading what follows and those aspects of the Standards and Benchmarks to which it is most relevant. Each chapter includes at least one case study, key ideas and questions and critical thinking exercises, with further reading recommended at the end. Each exercise includes a series of questions to prompt your thinking and is followed by a commentary on the issues raised, linking these to ideas raised elsewhere in the book. The ideas and discussion are drawn from policy and research drawn from disciplines related to education, such as psychology, sociology and philosophy. The last section of this introduction provides a brief overview of the main themes, to help you see the ground to be covered.

This is presented, as far as possible, in simple language. To gain maximum benefit, I suggest that you read slowly, maybe in small sections, using the skills outlined above. If possible, discuss the issues with other people, either as part of your course, in your school or separately. Learning works better as a social, interactive process than as an individual, isolated one. A book such as this can only touch the surface of these complicated issues; and at times will, inevitably, oversimplify. However, I hope that you will be encouraged to read the Further readings to probe deeper. A particularly rich source is the recent Cambridge Primary Review (Alexander, 2010), on which I draw extensively, though at times critically.

The case studies and examples are drawn from Early Years settings and primary school classrooms and from different subject areas and groups of children such as those with special educational needs, English as an additional language and the gifted and talented. These raise the questions I see as especially pertinent to encourage you to think through what pedagogy involves and the practical implications. However, thinking through will raise others. I can provide examples and ideas, but only you can supply two essentials: a knowledge of the context in which you work and your own questions. For ease of reading, all schools and settings are referred to as 'schools'.

Many issues raised are contested. For example, you may disagree strongly (with me or others) about the purposes and aims of primary education; or about whether certain aspects are appropriate especially for young children or possible in the current educational climate. Frequently, we shall encounter one policy or aim contradicting or making difficult another. However, a belief that an emphasis on the basics entails too little time spent on the arts or that creativity is inhibited by focusing on test scores does not mean that one is right, the other wrong. Rather, this demonstrates a reality of classroom life – constantly trying to steer a passage between these often unresolved tensions and conflicting expectations. Asking the right questions matters more than agreeing. Be prepared to defend and, if need be, change your views.

While pedagogy is shaped by one's beliefs, there will always be expectations from government, Ofsted, the local authority, head teachers and other colleagues, and you have to take account of these, often involving compromise. Educators always have to balance theory and practice, idealism and pragmatism. All sorts of pressures prevent us from thinking deeply about how best to enable children to learn – other people's expectations, our own doubts about how to cope, the busy-ness of classroom life, commitments outside school. However, I shall suggest that professionalism involves making your own judgements, not just doing what you are told, and moving beyond unthinking compliance. Underlying this is a belief that how adults think about children and education is more important in enhancing children's learning than specific techniques or programmes.

Working with young children requires enormous skill, sensitivity and expertise. Experts make what is difficult look easy, but because teaching is a practical activity, what this involves is hard to pin down. Much is what Polanyi (cited in Schön, 1987, page 22) calls 'tacit knowledge', acquired mainly by experience. This book tries to help you articulate tacit knowledge and assumptions – your own and other people's – and enrich your theoretical understanding, to synthesise these and identify the practical implications.

Linking theory and practice: an overview of this book
I am encouraging you to look beyond the present, to 'take the long view', to think through the practical implications of the issues raised. I expect (and hope) that you will constantly say 'but, if that's the case, then…'. In particular, you may feel that some of the ideas and implications are unrealistic for you to implement as an inexperienced educator, though I shall suggest that much of what you can do to build up expertise

can be achieved in relatively simple ways; and gradually. So, it may help to know what will be discussed, though never entirely resolved. In this section, I outline briefly the content of each chapter to provide an overview of the main ideas considered. You might like to think of this as like the picture on the box of a jigsaw, to guide you in assembling the pieces.

Chapters 1 and 2 provide a historical background, to help you to recognise that the assumptions and practices often taken for granted in the current educational climate are not the only ones possible and to imagine possible alternatives. Chapter 1 opens up the discussion on what is meant by pedagogy, as the range of practices and the underlying range of understandings involved in educating children. This indicates that pedagogy can only be understood within a particular context and that the purpose and aims of education and how children learn should be the first consideration in thinking through what constitutes effective pedagogy. It goes on to discuss the features of professionalism, suggesting that the level of autonomy is one important, though contested, aspect and that judgment based on professional expertise is vital, while leaving open what this consists of.

Chapter 2 shows that teaching methods have always been a matter of debate, depending on a society's answers to questions such as 'what is education for?' and 'what do we value?' This is intended to demonstrate that an education system depends on, though it also helps shape, its social and cultural context; and that the current assumptions about education, pedagogy and childhood are not the only ones possible. This is illustrated by a discussion of different traditions of pedagogy for young children, drawing historical and international comparisons. In particular, policy and practice in English education in the period before and after 1988 and the rationale and assumptions behind these are explored. This indicates how policy often draws on different theories and traditions, resulting in a range of tensions between policies and with educators' beliefs about the best way to enhance children's learning.

Chapters 3 and 4 offer a brief consideration of theoretical issues related to young children's learning, drawing especially on the insights of psychology and sociology of education. This is to help you to explore and interpret what occurs as children learn and to articulate and analyse your own beliefs about learning and teaching. Chapter 3 looks at young children's learning and development, showing how cognition and emotion, the conscious and unconscious, the formal and informal aspects of learning are more intertwined than is often recognised. The importance of children's prior experience and of social and cultural influences and of agency and engagement are introduced, as are less direct influences such as example and story. Chapter 4 examines some key concepts, such as knowledge, intelligence, and ability, whose meaning is often taken for granted, but shape our thinking about children and pedagogy. This is illustrated with reference to ideas such 'gifted and talented' and emotional intelligence. This emphasises how knowledge is created and integrated into existing patterns of understanding, both individually and through social interactions, involving processes such as feedback and dialogue, habituation and metacognition.

Chapters 5 and 6 explore what constitutes successful learning, in the long term, and the conditions which encourage this. This is to prompt you to identify and analyse what attributes and qualities matter most and discuss the best type of environment in which to develop these. Chapter 5 starts by considering the attributes of successful learners, of any age. It continues by examining what helps to build children's self-concept, sense of self-as-a-learner and motivation; and what enhances or inhibits these. The role of reward, punishment and praise are considered. In particular, we explore why some children find it so hard to engage with learning, drawing on the idea of cultural capital to suggest that the types of knowledge and activity most valued in school should be re-considered. Chapter 6 explores why the learning environment matters and what an inclusive environment entails, emphasising relationships and expectations. Expectations on educators, both within-school and external, affect this, but it is argued that young children's learning attributes are often fostered, or inhibited, by little, everyday actions. A balance of safety and challenge, of space and pace, of breadth and focus are presented as key elements of what young children need, recognising that this balance will vary according to the children's age, their prior experience and the type of activity.

Chapters 7 and 8 move into the more practical implications of what enhances children's learning and how adults can encourage this. This encourages you to challenge some basic assumptions and consider how these may relate to your own specific role. Chapter 7 starts by questioning the idea of 'the basics', emphasising the importance of breadth and balance. We then go on to examine the types of activity, experience and interaction which enhance young children's learning, exploring in particular play, first hand experience and the expressive arts and humanities, both in themselves and as ways of engaging children's interest and confidence and developing their linguistic, mathematical and scientific skills. This is developed further in Chapter 8 which discusses scaffolding and feedback to emphasise adult–child interactions and how these can best support successful learning. The importance of dialogue and of a learning community, and to what extent, and how, young children can learn to work as experts is considered.

Chapters 9, 10 and 11 focus more on the educator's role, relating the discussion about children's learning to your own development, both now and in the future. This is to encourage you to synthesise the ideas in previous chapters and to imagine the future implications for you and how you might, where appropriate, experiment with new approaches. Chapter 9 considers the link between assessment, planning and pedagogy. It suggests a broad view of assessment, as how one discovers the child's current understanding, presenting this as one of the teacher's main skills, done both in-the-moment and separately, and as the basis for planning. This must offer some flexibility to enable children to pursue their interests and adults to respond to these, reflecting the emphasis on agency, feedback and reciprocity. Chapter 10 explores how you can build up your own expertise. This starts with what expertise working with young children 'looks like' and what is distinctive about the expert teacher, notably fluidity and confidence to depart from predetermined formulae. It then considers continuing professional development and how best to build up your expertise, emphasising that this is a gradual and collaborative process.

Chapter 11 is more speculative, about how to prepare for a future in which none of us know the challenges ahead, in the light of technological and cultural change. In particular, we consider how pedagogy may involve using a more varied range of learning opportunities than at present, since education is much broader than schooling. The argument is made that:

- the subject-specific knowledge required changes more than knowledge about learning;
- pedagogical skills need to be selected from a repertoire and adapted according to the age of the children, the social, cultural and school context and the subject area; and
- professional attributes and values are what vary least with changes of time and place; and
- pedagogy is at the heart of school improvement;

re-emphasising the importance of adaptability, of professional judgment and of constantly thinking through pedagogy.

Further Reading

QAA (Quality Assurance Agency for Higher Education) (2007a) Education Studies Benchmark Statement www.qaa.ac.uk/academicinfrastructure/benchmark/honours/Education07.pdf

QAA (Quality Assurance Agency for Higher Education) (2007b) Early Childhood Studies Benchmark Statement www.qaa.ac.uk/academicinfrastructure/benchmark/statements/EarlyChildhoodStudies07.pdf

Training and Development Agency (TDA) (2007) Professional Standards for Teachers – Qualified Teacher Status www.tda.gov.uk/upload/resources/pdf/s/standards_qts.pdf

1 Revealing assumptions about learning and teaching

Chapter Focus

The critical thinking exercises in this chapter focus on:

⊙ **analysing** widely held assumptions and beliefs related to pedagogy and effectiveness;
⊙ **challenging** these, and your own, assumptions;
⊙ **considering** the link between pedagogy and aims;
⊙ **identifying** key features of professionalism and how this affects personal beliefs and policy expectations.

The key ideas discussed are: **pedagogy, context, effectiveness, professionalism**

This chapter is particularly relevant to QTS Standards: **3 a,b**, **7 a**, **8**, **26 b** and to Knowledge and Understanding and Application (*Education Studies*) and Subject knowledge and Subject skills (*Early Childhood Studies*)

Introduction

This chapter introduces several themes and ideas discussed in greater detail subsequently. It starts by exploring different meanings ascribed to 'pedagogy', drawing especially on the Teaching and Learning Research Programme (TLRP, 2006) to emphasise that one should focus initially on how children learn rather than what adults do, though later chapters explore the interaction between these. Discussion of effectiveness leads into a consideration of the purposes and aims of education and the idea of what professionalism entails. This is the basis of the view that pedagogy for young children must take account of:

• children's differing backgrounds and prior experience;
• the varied and complex ways in which children learn;
• the multiple, sometimes conflicting, aims of education;
• assumptions made about children and learning;

showing that many current assumptions, often unexamined, are not the only ones possible.

CASE STUDY

I taught a series of lessons each week on science, focusing on forces, to a class of eight- and nine-year-olds. In groups of three or four, the children conducted simple experiments – for example, rolling different items down ramps and making parachutes – to explore concepts such as friction and gravity, recording these simply and then discussing the results as a class.

The children were not familiar with such an approach. They enjoyed the experiments, gradually learning to plan these more systematically. They were keen at first to work with their friends, but got used to working with others, since I ensured that the groups kept changing. Accurate observation and, especially, recording they found difficult, but practice helped with the first and a worksheet to encourage them to draw or write exactly what they saw with the second. Most children enjoyed and benefited from the whole-group discussion, though some found it hard to listen to others and some were reluctant to join in. Rules to encourage them to listen and participate were helpful, especially at first.

This description inevitably tidies what happened. At times, there were balls rolling over the floor, interrupting other groups. Some children complained at working with others, though they got used to it. The recording, at times, was unsystematic, though when the children became familiar with what was expected, this improved significantly. The whole-class discussion was rather dominated by me initially, but most of the children became more confident in explaining their thinking. They showed a wide range of understanding, with some demonstrating remarkable insight and explaining ideas more accessibly than I could; and others whose understanding remained at a simpler level.

This case study illustrates how complex learning is in a fairly ordinary series of lessons, rather than how science should be taught, showing some difficulties the children encountered, what seemed to help them most and what changed as time passed. The challenges were not just cognitive, related to science. Some were organisational, as in controlling the experiments and recording the results. Some were social, such as the groupings, and listening and speaking in a large group. Some were emotional, like being uncertain about whether their ideas were acceptable. Especially for young children, these are closely interrelated. The experiments were what most children enjoyed best. The practical activity led to most children being engaged and active, though a few remained tentative. The structure of setting clear expectations and rules helped to limit the range of possibilities and to enable a thoughtful discussion, though often they found too much freedom a challenge. Working both in small groups and coming together as a large group meant that they learned from each other. Indeed, children explaining what they thought had happened seemed to improve the understanding of both the person talking and those listening. Over time, the children became more used to what was expected and the rules, in some respects, could be interpreted more flexibly. Much of the discipline they showed resulted from what the activity demanded, rather than being externally imposed. Practice, building on previous feedback, led to more accurate observation and recording and enhanced the discussions.

We return to these themes in future chapters. Some ideas, such as agency and self-concept, may sound complex, others like rules and groups more familiar. Some are general, others more specific to a particular situation. You may have identified others. However, they are all part of the detailed tapestry of pedagogy.

Key idea: **Pedagogy**

> **Doesn't teaching just involve common sense?**
>
> The TLRP is a large-scale, cross-phase project, which provides a good starting point to think about pedagogy. This identifies ten principles, set out in the next section, and suggests that three fundamental changes applicable to all ages are required.
>
> 1. *Learning processes, as distinct from learning contexts, do not fundamentally change as children become adults, with the interventions of teachers or trainers most effective when planned in response to how learners are learning. So we [TLRP] have retained 'pedagogy'. The term 'pedagogy' also has the advantage of highlighting the contingent nature of effective teaching, i.e. the interventions of teachers or trainers are most effective when they are planned in response to how learners are learning.*
>
> 2. *The conception of what is to be learned needs to be broadened beyond the notions of curricula and subjects associated with schools.*
>
> 3. *More prominence needs to be given to the importance of learning relationships.*

As we shall see, the first of these is more controversial than it may appear. Several reports and researchers (e.g. Anning, 1991; Ball, 1994; Siraj-Blatchford, 1999) suggest that Early Years pedagogy has distinctive features. The second reflects the many (often-overlooked) opportunities outside school to support children's learning in school and, importantly, to learn in ways other than those available, or valued, in school – ranging from football training to the Brownies and from reciting the Quran to computer games. In emphasising relationships, the third takes account of the interactive and social nature of learning.

Critical thinking exercise 1: exploring what pedagogy means

The Oxford English Dictionary (OED) defines 'pedagogy' as *the art or science of teaching; teaching.*

Watkins and Mortimore (1999, page 3) describe pedagogy as *any conscious activity by one person designed to enhance learning in another.*

We have already read Alexander's definition (2004, page 11) that it *is what one needs to know, and the skills one needs to command, in order to make and justify the many kinds of decisions of which teaching is constituted.*

A **Consider** whether teaching is just applied common sense and, if not, why not.

B **Compare** the advantages and difficulties of a narrow definition, such as that of the OED, and broader ones, such as the others.

C **Articulate** and **discuss** (preferably with someone arguing each case) to what extent teaching is an art, a craft or science. It may be best to **identify** the features of each and match them to what you have **observed** a teacher (of young children) doing.

Comment

Many parents and politicians – and some educators – are suspicious of educational theory, arguing that teaching is largely applied common sense. Every so often, a politician becomes a teacher for a few days. Imagine this happening for an engineer or a surgeon! Or a proposal is brought forward suggesting that the amount of training required, especially to work with under-fives, is minimal. After all, one might say, *it's not rocket science, they're only small children.* But this book paints a picture of:

- pedagogy as far more complicated than rocket science;
- educating young children as more challenging and crucial, because they are unpredictable and the foundations of tomorrow's society.

The reluctance of English teachers and policy-makers to discuss pedagogy seems to be related to a suspicion of theory, saying that theory makes everything too complicated and we need only to know 'what works'. However, 'what works' in one situation may not in another, and is, logically, associated with what one wants to achieve. This is behind my attempt to help you understand better how and why children (and we) act, react and interact. What seems common sense may not be borne out by experience and research. Research often reveals that the ordinary is complicated, exposing that what may seem obvious may not be so. For instance, you will have a view of what children should know by a certain age, but I will encourage you to question ideas as basic as what it means to know something and what is worth knowing. More practically, you probably think that feedback works best when it is positive. Yes, but we shall see that some types are more beneficial than others.

The OED definition focuses on the act of teaching, rather than the broader context within which teaching occurs. This may lead to a view of pedagogy, based on notions of instruction and transmission, which fails to capture the complexity of the different elements involved. Watkins and Mortimore's definition broadens out to include interaction and relationship, though I shall question whether pedagogy includes only conscious activity. Alexander's definition moves into the arena of knowledge and skills and the underlying rationale for these, recognising the complex range of decisions required. This is reflected in the TDA Standards' emphasis on professional attributes, knowledge and understanding and skills. The picture that I shall try to create is even broader, reflecting:

- the Cambridge Primary Review's emphasis on a repertoire to deal with the inherently unpredictable nature of learning and of teaching;
- the TLRP's emphasis on relationships.

This suggests that all of these definitions focus too much on cognition rather than the close interaction of social and emotional influences and the wider development of the 'whole child'. This is why judgement, based on a range of attributes, knowledge and understanding and skills, matters so much, especially with young children.

One long-standing debate is whether education is an art, a craft or a science. Those who see it as a science may emphasise the link between objectives and outcomes, the use of evidence and the value of being systematic. Those advocating for it as an art could cite the elements of playing to, or with, an audience and creativity, both in planning and adapting activities and in original means of presentation. The features of a craft are more practical, often with tasks involving design and adaptation, and an approach where the skills and theory are learned from someone more experienced, in view of the recognition of *uncertainty and the limits of predictability* (Watkins and Mortimore, 1999, page 2). Pedagogy seems to require the systematic approach of the scientist, the imagination of an artist and the practical wisdom associated with a craft.

Alexander (2008, page 36) highlights two main approaches to teaching: didactic and exploratory. In the first, the teacher is largely in control, while the latter places the learner centre-stage. Alexander refines this categorisation (page 79), drawing on his major study of primary education in five countries, *Culture and Pedagogy* (2000), with six versions of teaching. These are:

- transmission;
- negotiation;
- initiation;
- facilitation;
- acceleration;
- technology.

While the following summary does not do justice to the (rather complicated) discussion of this (2008, pages 78–81), it provides some clues as to why transmission as the main strategy is inappropriate, especially for very young children. Transmission involves primarily passing on information, with this tending to reduce the opportunities for reflective, deeper understanding. As Desforges (1995, page 129) comments *direct instruction is best used for knowledge transmission, for showing, telling, modelling and demonstrating. It is never, on its own, sufficient to ensure deeper understanding, problem solving or creativity.* And, I would add, the less children are familiar with, or used to processing, the language used, the less effective it is – though enabling them to do so is part of the educator's role.

Negotiation involves a different type of relationship where the teacher is not the main source of knowledge, but encourages the child to be an active agent in learning, with the classroom more like a workshop and the educator like a more experienced partner in learning. Initiation involves introducing children to how to work in a particular discipline, for example as a mathematician, an artist, or a reader – like the children learning science in the case study. This requires specific ways to use materials, to talk, to think and to judge success. This overlaps in some respects with facilitation, where the educator's main role is to enable rather than direct the child and draw on his or her learning strategies. Acceleration, in contrast, draws on Russian thinking and practice, notably that of Vygotsky, to argue that the teacher has a much more proactive role in leading the child into areas of learning, outpacing (natural) development. Teaching as a technology involves economy and pace based on standardised procedures and materials, an approach associated especially with eastern and central European pedagogy (see Alexander, 2008, page 81).

We shall discuss most of these in more detail. However, for now, it is worth noting that these reflect differing views of learning and of children. Each may be appropriate in particular situations, which is why expert teachers require a repertoire of approaches. But, as we shall see, 'effectiveness' depends on what one seeks to achieve; and 'what works' with one age group or class may not do so with another.

Key idea: **Context**

To what extent can one generalise about pedagogy?

The title of Jerome Bruner's book, *In Search of Pedagogy* (2006), reminds us that understanding how children learn, and to apply this in practice, always entails search. There is no one right approach to pedagogy, regardless of circumstances, however tempting it is to believe in simple solutions. As we shall see, anyone new to being an educator will wish to start by keeping things simple. But becoming more expert involves both recognising different levels of complexity and building up your expertise. This requires imagination, reflection, adaptation, practice and reappraisal, building on your experience and taking account of your theories and beliefs.

We all have theories which influence our expectations and actions, whether we like it or not. How we understand children and their minds, and concepts such as intelligence and ability, affect our interactions with them. For example, to treat a four-year-old as a 'non-reader' rather than someone not yet able to make sense of text alters how we view their learning; or to describe a nine-year-old as 'bright' may suggest that ability is largely inherited. Unless we examine, revise and elaborate our theories in the light of research and experience, we are like architects who overlook modern ideas on design.

The learning needs of a three-year-old and those of a ten-year-old differ, as do those of a child with dyslexia and a talented musician. We are all different. Teaching a class in a mixed-age rural primary school and working as a nursery nurse in a large inner-city nursery present contrasting challenges and opportunities. The knowledge and skills required to teach art or science may vary from those needed to encourage communication, language and literacy or physical development. In considering to what extent general principles about pedagogy apply, these always have to take account of, and be applied to, the particular circumstances in which you work – the neighbourhood, the school, the class, the individual child. However, many attributes of educators and the features of a learning environment to enhance learning – whether one is four years old, or 24, or 54 – are similar. So to what extent can one generalise about pedagogy, since classrooms are complex, often unpredictable, places?

Critical thinking exercise 2: are there general principles of effective pedagogy?

Consider the following summary of the TLRP's evidence-informed pedagogic principles and, especially, whether any of the points in **bold** surprise you.

1. **Effective pedagogy equips learners for life in its broadest sense.** Learning should aim to help individuals and groups to develop the intellectual, personal and social resources that will enable them to participate as active citizens, contribute to economic development and flourish as individuals in a diverse and changing society. This means adopting a broad conception of worthwhile learning outcomes and taking seriously issues of equity and social justice for all.

2. **Effective pedagogy engages with valued forms of knowledge.** Pedagogy should engage learners with the big ideas, key skills and processes, modes of discourse, ways of thinking and practising, attitudes and relationships, which are the most valued learning processes and outcomes in particular contexts. They need to understand what constitutes quality, standards and expertise in different settings.

3. **Effective pedagogy recognises the importance of prior experience and learning.** Pedagogy should take account of what the learner knows already in

/continued

Critical thinking exercise 2 – continued

order for them, and those who support their learning, to plan their next steps. This includes building on prior learning but also taking account of the personal and cultural experiences of different groups of learners.

4. **Effective pedagogy requires learning to be scaffolded.** Teachers, trainers and all those, including peers, who support the learning of others, should provide activities, cultures and structures of intellectual, social and emotional support to help learners to move forward in their learning. When these supports are removed the learning needs to be secure.

5. **Effective pedagogy needs assessment to be congruent with learning.** Assessment should be designed and implemented with the goal of achieving maximum validity both in terms of learning outcomes and learning processes. It should help to advance learning as well as determine whether learning has occurred.

6. **Effective pedagogy promotes the active engagement of the learner.** A chief goal of learning should be the promotion of learners' independence and autonomy. This involves acquiring a repertoire of learning strategies and practices, developing positive learning dispositions, and having the will and confidence to become agents in their own learning.

7. **Effective pedagogy fosters both individual and social processes and outcomes**. Learners should be encouraged and helped to build relationships and communication with others for learning purposes, in order to assist the mutual construction of knowledge and enhance the achievements of individuals and groups. Consulting learners about their learning and giving them a voice is both an expectation and a right.

8. **Effective pedagogy recognises the significance of informal learning.** Informal learning, such as learning out of school or away from the workplace, should be recognised as at least as significant as formal learning and should therefore be valued and appropriately utilised in formal processes.

9. **Effective pedagogy depends on the learning of all those who support the learning of others.** The need for lecturers, teachers, trainers and co-workers to learn continuously in order to develop their knowledge and skill, and adapt and develop their roles, especially through practice-based inquiry, should be recognised and supported.

10. **Effective pedagogy demands consistent policy frameworks with support for learning as their primary focus.** Organisational and system level policies need to recognise the fundamental importance of continual learning – for individual, team, organisational and system success – and be designed to create effective learning environments for all learners.

/continued

> **Critical thinking exercise 2** – continued
>
> A **Identify** to what extent the emphasis is on the learner or the teacher (or other adult). Why does you think this is?
>
> B Select one principle and **illustrate** this with what a school you know does for one specific child. For example, if you chose number 3, how does the school build (or not) on his or her prior learning? Or, if you picked number 7, what does the school do which encourages or inhibits both individual and social processes and outcomes? Be specific and **challenge** what may seem to be the case at first glance.
>
> C Choose a different principle and **consider** the implications for you as an educator. If number 2, what sorts of knowledge are regarded as most important? Are these always what you value most? If number 8, how do you as an educator, or the school, show that you take account of informal learning? **Articulate** both positive aspects and those with which you are less comfortable.

Comment

Although these principles look simple, we shall see that the policy context, both national and local, raises both opportunities and challenges in implementing them. For example, the curriculum, as taught, may encourage or inhibit the active engagement of the learner; and prescribed assessment methods may, or may not, help to enhance learning as well as determine what the child has learned.

'Learner' or 'learning' appear in eight of the principles; and 'teacher' or 'teaching' in none, suggesting that the educators' main focus should be on learning. Simon (1981) relates the neglect of pedagogical studies in England to the public – that is independent – schools' concern with character formation rather than intellectual development. My view is that a major reason has been too great an emphasis on schooling and on teaching based on instruction and the transmission of knowledge. Learning is such a multifaceted and puzzling process, extending far beyond schooling, that pedagogy must take account of wherever and however learning occurs.

Looking in detail at the implications for a child, or for an educator, one sees that, in practice, many factors may make it hard for the individual educator to put these principles into action. Some result from policy and external expectations, others from trying to relate to a large group of children and cater for their differing needs and interests. It is therefore difficult to separate 'pedagogy' from aspects such as curriculum, timetables and assessment. So, our discussion touches on this, but always with a view to how you, as an educator, can apply appropriate principles within the classroom. Since education is a practical activity, you will be concerned with what to do. I shall suggest some practical actions, but this is mainly to help you think through how you can gradually build up a wider repertoire of 'tools' to enhance children's learning. Active learning involves, as we shall see, making one's own sense of the situation.

Rather than definitive answers, the TLRP principles therefore provide a good basis for asking further questions about pedagogy and how this is applicable in your own context, such as:

- to what extent has primary education a pedagogy distinct from that of secondary or further education?
- should 'Early Years' pedagogy be seen as distinct from that for primary education?
- are there are distinct pedagogies for separate disciplines such as mathematics, art or geography?

We shall address all these questions.

Key idea: **Effectiveness**

How can one judge effectiveness?

Each of the TLRP's ten principles starts with the word 'effective'. However, this term only makes sense in relation to what one tries to achieve. For example, if you teach multiplication, effectiveness can be assessed by whether children reach the right answer. But how this is done may affect, in many ways, other aspects which may, or may not, matter – the children's ability to apply this to practical situations, their sense of achievement, their happiness, their long-term attitude to maths, their motivation. Short-term and long-term success may not necessarily be associated, for example if immediate high performance leads to resentment; or, conversely, if experiment, error and reflection lead to a deeper understanding of number patterns. Children will react differently. And the purposes and aims of education – its broader social function and the more immediate intentions of those running schools, respectively – are rarely simple.

Alexander (2010, especially pages 174–202) argues that aims and principles must precede the detail of curriculum and pedagogy and that the National Curriculum and assessment procedures have become detached from a coherent set of aims or principles. In Chapter 2, we look at the extent to which the aims set out in the 1988 Act reflect the actual priorities of policy-makers and those inspecting schools. Recognising that your own aims are unlikely to match exactly those set out in national or school policy – though hopefully there will be a significant overlap – let us look at two sets of aims.

Critical thinking exercise 3: what are the aims of primary education?

Consider the aims of education set out in these two passages. The first is drawn from the Rose Report on the Primary Curriculum (DSCF, 2009, from paragraphs 1.20 and 1.21).

/continued

Critical thinking exercise 3 – continued

Discussion with headteachers and schools has found strong support for these three easily remembered aims (originally set out for secondary education) and their applicability to the primary curriculum:
enabling all children to become:
- *successful learners who enjoy learning, make progress and achieve;*
- *confident individuals who are able to live safe, healthy and fulfilling lives; and*
- *responsible citizens who make a positive contribution to society.*

A **Consider** and **discuss** to what extent this reflects:

- what you believe. In particular, think what is missed out. Are there aspects which need to be emphasised more for very young children?
- what those judging schools or teachers currently deem most important, especially in terms of inspection or what parents are looking for in a school.

The second is from the prospectus of a Church of England primary school:

The school is a happy place which welcomes all.

Our ethos is based on Christian principles within a multi-faith and multi-cultural community.

Our aim is for our children to:
- *discover the joy of learning and creativity*
- *care for and respect everyone in the school community*
- *appreciate the wider world*
- *achieve their unique potential*

We offer strong leadership, outward looking teachers and excellent support staff within a stimulating and nurturing environment.
We have high expectations of our children in their learning and behaviour.
We work in partnership with families and other schools to provide the best possible education for all our children.

B **Explore** to what extent this reflects and emphasises:

- the same or different aims as the Rose Review above;
- distinctive aspects of the school's foundation and community;

C **Identify** aspects of both statements which may, or may not, be especially applicable to the under-fives, remembering that the Rose Review was looking at primary education and this school is for 5–11-year-olds.

Comment

Such statements of aims often seem unexceptionable, because their wording is so general. You probably looked at the Rose Review aims and found them perfectly reasonable. However, they do not lead to specific priorities as much as the school prospectus does for its own community. Aims are never simple, because they are multiple and interrelated (see White, 2010). So you may wish, like those in the school above, to help children *discover the joy of learning and creativity*, but find that the opportunities for creativity are limited. Or you may be in a school which does not mention community cohesion much, but contributes to it nevertheless. Although it may be tempting to ignore statements of aims, they articulate a framework of aspirations which can both help to remind you of your own beliefs and act as a way of judging your own pedagogy against a set of more general principles. Your own beliefs must take account of national and local aims and take account of school policies and schemes of work, quite apart your own knowledge of particular children. You are likely to agree with some parts and disagree with, or be more doubtful about, others; a good reason for thinking through what you are trying to achieve.

Jackson et al. (1993) conclude that what teachers really value is always evident in what they do rather than what they say. So, at national level, the priority given to children with special educational needs should be judged by how their needs are actually met, for example the types of school available, the resources allocated and training provided for teachers and other staff. Similarly, at school level, how particular children's needs are assessed and met, for example through specific equipment, resources, additional support and liaison with parents matters more than the school claiming to be 'inclusive'. And this is evident at classroom level in the detail of how a child is sensitively integrated, with whom he or she is grouped, how success is celebrated and challenges addressed.

Let us consider the broader purposes behind schooling. For example, the public schools' concern with character development was linked to the administration of the British Empire, in the nineteenth century. In contrast to the United States, the churches in England have had a substantial involvement in education, with the nurturing of religious faith a strong motivation for this, especially the Roman Catholic Church, with the Church of England tending to have a somewhat wider remit. The Education Act of 1870, which formed the basis of compulsory education, was intended in part to raise levels of literacy and numeracy, in part to prepare children for their place in society – whether at work or at home. But it was also designed to ensure that children were looked after while their parents were at work and the long tradition of providing school lunches indicates an enduring concern with children's health, especially those living in poverty. Similar concerns are evident in the last twenty years, with the focus on the skills required for employment, the recent extension of breakfast clubs, after-school care and other initiatives outside school hours.

In other countries, the school's role is seen rather differently. For example, in Alexander's words (2010, pages 64–5), *while in other European countries, such as France and Finland, there are clear divisions of responsibility, with parents doing the caring and socialising, and schools doing the schooling, these divisions have always been blurred and controversial in England.* And, in Ofsted's (2003, page 5), *much more importance is attached in Finland and Denmark to the way six-year-olds develop as people, rather than what they should know and be able to do. Although literacy and numeracy and other areas of learning are important..., personal and social development, learning to learn, developing self-control and preparation for school are given a higher priority.* This reminds us that education is not the same as schooling; and that the aims of schools, and educators, always depend on the broader social and cultural context.

So, the purposes of education are multi-faceted, including:

- children's personal self-fulfilment and well-being;
- the needs of parents;
- the needs of employers;
- the wider need for social order and control.

The relative importance ascribed to these varies depending on the age of the child and historical, social and cultural assumptions about what education is for. You will have your own beliefs about such questions. In the busy life of the classroom and schools, it is easy to forget these sorts of question. You could not spend your whole time thinking about them. But one hallmark of a professional is to keep at the back of your mind, and from time to time revisit explicitly, beliefs and assumptions on questions as fundamental as *how does what I am doing accord with my aims?, how do these children learn best?* and *what factors influence how this particular child is learning?* As I was trying to, over time, with the science lessons described in the case study.

Key idea: **Professionalism**

What qualities are needed to work with young children?

Moyles (2004) describes passion, paradox and professionalism as integral elements of working with children under seven. She paints a picture where passion and professionalism are necessary, but often challenged by paradoxes inherent in the system. So, understanding what professionalism entails helps educators sustain their passion and live with the often paradoxical, or conflicting, demands on them. This theme runs through this book, primarily because pedagogy involves judgement, often in complicated situations, requiring the knowledge associated with being a professional.

Passion is essential for many reasons, among them that;

- *young children are pre-programmed to ensure that potential carers respond favourably to them* (Moyles, page 11);
- *the very nature of the work demands strong feelings towards both protecting and supporting young children and engaging empathetically with [the] wider family and community aspects of the child's life* (page 11);
- *this passion [as 'work enthusiast'] is part of the nature of professionalism within and outside education and, as such, is continuously challenged within the current climate of accountability* (page 10).

Passion helps to enhance the child's learning, promote partnership with those around the child and sustain the educator's own professionalism. Moyles indicates that, even in China, with a clear distinction between 'care' and 'education' roles, the ability to care for children, communicate with families and ensure children's educational welfare and happiness, rather than academic aspects, was paramount in appraisal of both those who 'care' and those who 'educate'.

Moyles sets out (pages 14–15) some of the paradoxes of working with young children, such as:

- the need to balance one's knowledge of child development with the imposition of common standards;
- the challenge of encouraging discipline and high standards of behaviour, when (some) parents and other members of society are *not always models of…socially acceptable behaviours*;
- the low level of salaries set against high expectations of 'professionalism'.

This makes it *easy to feel disempowered and inadequate [which] can readily reduce any appropriate passion* (page 15).

What professionalism entails is disputed, with Alexander (2010, pages 450–1) summarising different views. However, I argue for a 'classical' view that, to be useful, this must include various traits or features. Otherwise, almost any activity can lay claim to being a profession.

Critical thinking exercise 4: what does professionalism entail?

Among the typical characteristics of a profession highlighted by John (2008, page 12) are:

- mastery of a knowledge base requiring a long period of training;
- tasks that are inherently valuable to society;
- a desire to prioritise the client's welfare;
- a high level of autonomy;
- a code of ethics to guide practice.

/continued

Critical thinking exercise 4 – continued

A **Discuss** to what extent this reflects how doctors and lawyers are seen? Are any of these more or less applicable for a doctor or a lawyer than a teacher or a physiotherapist? And, if so, why?

B **Identify** which of these separate teachers from other, less qualified support staff.

C **Consider** whether you would highlight any other characteristics of teacher professionalism.

Comment

This is a surprisingly hard exercise. We tend to have a vague idea of what being a professional means. It implies an enhanced status and usually level of salary, especially for the older, more prestigious professions such as medicine and the law. For newer professions, especially those sometimes disparagingly called the 'caring' professions, often mostly made up of women, neither of these apply to anything like the same extent.

Osborn (2008, especially page 76) argues that changes since 1988 (to be described in Chapter 2) resulted in professionalism changing from being based on trust, with accountability being personal and moral, to being seen as the fulfilment of a contract to deliver, with external accountability, mainly through measurable outcomes such as test scores. She associates this with education being seen as a commodity and argues that the result is less confidence, fulfilment and spontaneity in teaching. Osborn presents this contractual approach as leading to a restricted, rather than extended, professionalism, where teachers expect, and are expected, to conform to external expectations rather than make their own judgements. This is closer to the French model of professionalism (similar to that in Belgium, Italy, Spain and Portugal) where teachers do not expect to be autonomous, as opposed to the Scandinavian model (similar to that in England) where teachers have a wide range of duties and are encouraged to take a 'holistic' approach (Osborn, 2008, page 78). Despite recent efforts to agree a Code of Ethics, for instance by the General Teaching Council (GTC), this has not led to a consensus on what professionalism involves.

Professionalism may be defined by what one should not do. For example, occasionally doctors are struck off or teachers banned for committing serious offences. This is, often, uncontroversial, but one area of dispute on the GTC's draft Code of Ethics was to what extent teachers' actions matter when not at work. You may think that teachers should not go on strike because they are professionals, or that they should – still a matter which sharply divides the profession. However, a professional must try to ensure that the client's best interests are served. While it may not always be obvious whether the client is the child or the parents/carers, the child's best interests should be paramount, even if there is disagreement about what these are. Professionalism involves taking the long and the broad view – not just doing whatever seems easiest in the short term or responding to individual requests without recognising the consequences for others.

It would be impossible, in my view, to argue that other groups, such as teaching assistants or caretakers, are not engaged in tasks valuable to society or do not wish to prioritise the children's welfare. One feature of teachers-as-professionals seems to be the degree of autonomy that they have. As with other professions, to what extent external control is appropriate remains a matter of contention. This is linked to the extent to which teachers have a *mastery of a knowledge base requiring a long period of training*. If teaching is just applied common sense, it is hard to see what this knowledge base consists of. If we cannot identify what constitutes expertise in a teacher, then how can we argue that the role is significantly different from a technician's? As the QTS Standards emphasise, 'professional' knowledge and understanding, skills and attributes are essential to becoming, and developing as, a teacher. Chapter 10 considers what is distinctive about these, especially in working with young children.

Conclusion

This chapter has introduced some of the complexities associated with pedagogy. The critical thinking exercises will have helped you:

- ⊙ **identify** different definitions of pedagogy, asking in what respects it is a science, a craft or an art;
- ⊙ **consider** to what extent there are general principles of pedagogy, and how these must be applied to specific contexts;
- ⊙ **discuss** how the principles of 'effective' pedagogy must logically be linked to the aims of education and objectives to be met;
- ⊙ **explore** what professionalism entails, recognising that the attributes, knowledge and understanding and skills involved may vary for different ages and groups.

You may have started to articulate and challenge some 'common-sense' assumptions – yours, mine and other people's – and to identify possible practical difficulties and opportunities. Future chapters will explore these further, starting with an overview of different traditions of pedagogy for young children.

Further Reading

Alexander, R (ed) (2010) *Children, their World, their Education – Final report and recommendations of the Cambridge Primary Review.* Abingdon: Routledge Chapter 12 'What is primary education for?' is a detailed and interesting discussion of issues raised in this and the next chapter, though the Review's remit did not include Early Years.

/continued

Moyles, J (2004) *Passion, Paradox and Professionalism in Early Years Education* pages 9–24 of Wragg, EC (ed) *The RoutledgeFalmer Reader in Teaching and Learning.* London: RoutledgeFalmer

An interesting chapter about how three elements complement, and conflict with, each other with an emphasis on the Early Years, but also applicable to those working with older children.

Teaching and Learning Research Programme (TLRP, 2006) *Improving Teaching and Learning in Schools.*

The summary of the lessons of this large project, well worth exploring in more detail.

Watkins, C and Mortimore, P (1999) *Pedagogy: What do we know?* pages 1–19 of Mortimore, P (ed) *Understanding Pedagogy and its Impact on Learning.* London: Paul Chapman Publishing

A fairly short, but thought-provoking, discussion of key themes on pedagogy in more detail than is possible here.

2 Exploring the historical, cultural and political context of pedagogy

Chapter Focus

The critical thinking exercises in this chapter focus on:

⊙ **articulating** the assumptions behind different traditions of educating young children;
⊙ **comparing** how educational policy has developed before and since 1988, to ask how these impact on pedagogy;
⊙ **considering** key ideas such as entitlement and accountability;
⊙ **describing** changes within and outside education and **interpreting** how these have affected children's lives and their approach to learning.

The key ideas discussed are: **tradition, entitlement, accountability, autonomy, standards, well-being**

This chapter is particularly relevant to QTS Standards: **5**, **10**, **18** and to Knowledge and Understanding and Reflection (*Education Studies*) and Subject knowledge and Subject skills (*Early Childhood Studies*)

Introduction

This chapter explores approaches to pedagogy in the past and in other countries to show that those currently prevalent are not universal. It starts by describing three traditions, and their influence on primary and Early Years education in England before and since 1988. A discussion of the concerns which the 1988 Act and subsequent policies tried to address shows how these contain (often conflicting) elements of these traditions. The third exercise considers the consequences for professional accountability and autonomy and the last how social, cultural and political change in the last 30 to 40 years – roughly an adult working life – has affected how children are viewed and their attitudes and responses. Alternative views are presented to encourage you to keep thinking through pedagogy in a climate focused on performance and a culture where other possibilities are often forgotten.

CASE STUDY

Descriptions of Victorian elementary classrooms such as Speed (1983) highlight that the rooms were often crowded, with boys and girls in separate classes or schools. The teaching was heavily based on rote learning and drill, with a strong emphasis on reading, writing and arithmetic, along with religious instruction and, for girls, needlework and, for boys, technical skills. Children were expected to listen, to copy and to be obedient, with discipline severe for those who did not. The teacher, often poorly qualified, was judged on a narrow set of outcomes. Children's attendance was often poor, with prizes given for good attendance and punishment for those who had been absent. Parents were, largely, excluded.

Reggio Emilia is a town in northern Italy associated with an educational approach involving centres for children from three months to three years old and infant schools for children from three to six years old. Central to its philosophy are beliefs that:
- children are powerful and articulate learners, with the relationship between educator and child reciprocal;
- the expressive arts have a vital role in children's learning;
- the relationship between school, family and community are central.

These two descriptions reflect contrasting views of young children and of pedagogy. In the Victorian classroom, the children were seen as 'empty vessels' to be filled, by repetition and coercion if need be. Pedagogy consisted largely of rote learning to ensure conformity, with content largely determined for, rather than by, the teacher and outcomes closely monitored by inspectors. Edwards et al. (cited in Hart et al., 2004, page 257) describe the cornerstone of the Reggio Emilia approach as *the image of children as rich, strong and powerful... They have potential, plasticity, the desire to grow, curiosity, the ability to be amazed and the desire to relate to other people and to communicate.* Pedagogy is based more on children's interests, and interaction between child and adult, drawing on the child's experiences and involving the whole community.

These two examples represent extremes of what might be called 'traditional' and 'progressive' pedagogy. However, we shall see that this characterisation is too simple. Alexander (2008, page 102) suggests that English primary education is best seen not as a pendulum where 'traditional' replaces 'progressive' pedagogy, but as an amalgam of different traditions and assumptions about teaching, many of them deep-rooted in our ideas of education and of children. So, we shall see some surprising continuities and that much of what we, as educators, may wish to do is constrained not just by external expectations, but by our own, and our culture's, remarkably enduring beliefs about pedagogy.

Key idea: **Tradition**

What can we learn from traditions of pedagogy?

The word 'tradition' may sound rather stuffy and rigid, conjuring up the heavy hand of authority or looking back to old certainties, rather than forward to new possibilities. However, in Macintyre's (1999, page 222) words, *traditions, when vital, embody continuities of conflict.* What I describe as traditions are broad trends of thought and practice, rather than what you might observe in a pure form in any one time or place. They are like beaches where the shoreline is constantly re-sculpted but an overall continuity is retained.

Traditions of pedagogy encapsulate a wisdom without which we run the risk of losing a sense of historical perspective and so being vulnerable to the appeal of the latest fashion. They enable us to draw on the often hidden lessons of the past. As Hannah Arendt wrote of her friend Walter Benjamin (Benjamin, 1999, pages 54–5:

 (his) thinking delves into the depths of the past – but not in order to resuscitate it the way it was and to contribute to the renewal of extinct ages. What guides this thinking is the conviction that … some things 'suffer a sea-change' and survive in new crystallized forms and shapes that remain immune to the elements, as though they waited only for the pearl diver who one day will come down to them and bring them up into the world of the living – as 'thought fragments,' as something 'rich and strange'.

So, as you read, look out for 'pearls', for thought fragments, since the lessons of other eras and cultures are too easily overlooked.

Critical thinking exercise 1: three traditions of educating young children

Blyth (1998, vol 2, pages 20–43) identified three main approaches to young children's education:

- *elementary – ensuring that children are equipped for adult life, especially that of work;*
- *preparatory – preparing children for the next (and, usually implicitly, more important) phase of schooling;*
- *developmental – treating childhood as a time with value in its own right.*

/continued

Critical thinking exercise 1 – continued

A **Compare** the underlying assumptions of each of these traditions about:
- childhood and children;
- the role of schools.

B **Illustrate** how these traditions vary in relation to the purposes and aims of education.

C **Consider** the implications of each for how teachers are expected to work.

Comment

These ideas may sound uncontroversial. After all, surely educating young children is about all three: preparing for adult life, getting ready for secondary school, and developing at their own pace. However, let us look more closely at how these worked out in practice to understand the assumptions behind them.

The elementary tradition stemmed from the growth of schooling for the poor in the seventeenth century but grew out of industrialisation, becoming the dominant approach in the late nineteenth and early twentieth centuries when legislation resulted in almost universal schooling for children of primary age. It was based on educating most children only to a certain level, appropriate to what they would need in adult life. Elementary schools had a low status, being mostly for children who would work in unskilled or semi-skilled jobs. While some children might be selected for grammar school, based on the results of an IQ test, with others going if their parents could afford to pay, most left at the age of 14 to go straight into the world of work. As in the description of the Victorian classroom, the child tended to be seen as 'an empty vessel' to be filled. The curriculum was largely based on the 3Rs (reading, writing and 'rithmetic), religious instruction and a limited range of subjects. The teachers, often with a low level of qualifications, taught large classes. Pedagogy was based on rote learning, the transmission of factual knowledge and the acquisition of those skills deemed useful for adult life.

The preparatory tradition was linked to the rise of prestigious schools, both independent and grammar, for older children, which expanded rapidly in the nineteenth century. These were intended to equip children for high-status, broadly middle-class, jobs. The purpose of schools for younger children was mainly to ensure that they were prepared for the next stage of schooling, with a curriculum that concentrated on the 3Rs, but often with a strong emphasis on character education, notably through sport, and providing a grounding in academic subjects such as history, geography and the classics. The teachers, often university graduates, but many without teaching qualifications, taught small classes. Pedagogy varied, but was based on a mixture of transmission and the acquisition of skills and qualities necessary for when 'real education' started at the next school.

The developmental tradition's roots lie within romanticism, stemming from the ideas of educators in Western Europe, such as Rousseau, Froebel and Montessori and, subsequently in America, Dewey. It views the child as like a seed to be nurtured and education as an unfolding of natural abilities – as reflected in the term 'kindergarten', (children's garden). This has been very influential in the education of children under the age of five in England and slightly older in other European countries; and, following the Plowden Report in 1967 (HMSO, 1967), primary schools in England. The developmental tradition tends to emphasise learning through activity and discovery, often following the individual child's own interests, and breadth of experience especially through play and the arts, with less emphasis on the 3Rs and content. The teachers, increasingly trained at colleges of education, but struggling to gain the status of a profession, taught classes usually smaller than in elementary, but larger than preparatory, schools. Pedagogy tended to be based on the belief that experience will lead to learning, with the teacher's role more as a facilitator, usually accompanied by a belief in educating 'the whole child'.

These traditions were based on differing assumptions about childhood, which affect how children were viewed and the priorities of schools. Elementary schools valued conformity and provided a limited curriculum. The preparatory tradition emphasised children as not-yet-adults and focused on 'the basics' to enable a later broadening of interests. The developmental tradition saw children as active learners requiring a broad range of experiences, placing little emphasis on measurable outcomes. These beliefs, inevitably, affected how teachers viewed their role. In the elementary and preparatory traditions, this was to focus on the 3Rs, with the teacher usually relying on a series of readers or textbooks and on phonics and regular practice in arithmetic. In the developmental tradition, this involved a broader and less clearly defined structure, including more time spent on the expressive arts with the teacher facilitating children to follow their own interests, for instance in choosing their own books and areas to investigate.

Key idea: **Entitlement**

What was the rationale for the National Curriculum and subsequent policies?
Until 1988, there was a broad consensus that the detail of the curriculum should be decided locally, with local education authorities influential, but in practice usually being under the control of head teachers and often individual teachers. The detail of how to teach was not seen as anything to do with politicians. For instance, no major legislation was introduced after 1944 directly related to the curriculum or pedagogy for young children until 1988.

Always very influential with under-fives, the thinking behind the developmental tradition became increasingly influential in primary schools in the 1960s and 70s. However, Her

Majesty's Inspectorate (HMI) in 1978 reported that only 5 per cent of classrooms were fully 'exploratory' and three-quarters used what HMI called 'didactic' methods' (see Alexander, 2010, page 30); and the ORACLE project (see Galton et al., 1980), gathering evidence in 1975–80, indicated that, in practice, most schools and teachers spent most of the time on English and mathematics. However, a growing concern that schools were not meeting the needs of the economy and calls for greater accountability were expressed in Prime Minister Callaghan's 1976 Ruskin speech. The perception of politicians and the press was that a *laissez-faire* approach, with more emphasis on thematic work than systematic teaching, was common.

The main rationale for the National Curriculum was that there was too much inconsistency in children's experiences, teaching and outcomes. In particular, this was based on a belief that too many children were leaving primary school without having achieved sufficiently high standards in English and mathematics, having spent too much time on inadequately planned topic work. Linked to this was a belief that many children were receiving a significantly worse range of experiences than others. For example, the Swann Report (DES, 1985) highlighted the underachievement of minority ethnic children and there was widespread concern about the attainment of children in disadvantaged areas. So, the 1988 Education Reform Act was a conscious attempt to break with the approach of the previous 20 years, to ensure that all children received their entitlement to a similar pattern of education and that standards of attainment were raised.

Critical thinking exercise 2: entitlement and standards

In 1987 the Department of Education and Science…issued a consultation document that set out the rationale for a National Curriculum…which essentially identified four broad purposes:

- *introducing an entitlement for pupils to a broad and balanced curriculum;*
- *setting standards for pupil attainment and to support school accountability;*
- *improving continuity and coherence within the curriculum; and*
- *aiding public understanding of the work of schools.*

(House of Commons, 2009, page 10, para 14)

A **Compare** the possible advantages and disadvantages of:
- having a National Curriculum or not;
- of the National Curriculum being relatively brief or very detailed;
- detailed strategies which prescribe how teachers should teach.

B **Consider** the consequences of an emphasis on standards on what, and how, teachers are likely to teach.

/continued

Critical thinking exercise 2 – continued

C **Discuss** whether an emphasis on measurable outcomes in literacy and numeracy makes it easier or harder to:

- provide a broad and balanced curriculum;
- encourage creativity;
- include a wider range of children in mainstream classes.

Comment

It is probably hard for you to imagine an education system without a National Curriculum. One main rationale for a National Curriculum is to ensure educational entitlement, regardless of where children live or their background in terms of class, language or gender. So, entitlement is strongly linked to equity, ensuring that children in Preston, Penzance or Peterborough have the same opportunities; and that the needs of those with English as an additional language or specific gifts or learning difficulties are catered for. While a wide variety of quality or of resources exists, and other policies encouraging comparisons and competition between schools may make it harder for some to provide this, such entitlement remains an aspiration rather than a reality; but an important aspiration nevertheless.

From the outset, the National Curriculum suffered from curriculum overload. This resulted both from subject groups all wanting detailed content to be covered and, subsequently, from new strands or subjects such as environmental awareness and health and citizenship being added. Each may have been worthwhile, but there was a marked reluctance to drop anything. So, the National Curriculum, based on subjects, grew unwieldy and content-heavy. This was much more so in primary schools than with younger children, with the Early Years curriculum based more on areas of learning, with less prescription of the detail of pedagogy. The Dearing Review, in 1993, proposed that 20 per cent of curriculum time should be at the school's discretion. The Rose Review in 2009 supported a change to the primary curriculum to base it more on 'areas of learning', with the Cambridge Primary Review in 2009 proposing a restructuring based on domains of learning. However, attempts since 1988 to slim down the National Curriculum have encountered significant challenges.

The rhetoric of 'leaving teaching methods to the teacher' survived the introduction of the National Curriculum. However, the 'Three Wise Men' report (Alexander et al., 1992) called in 1992 for a mixture of whole-class, group and individual work. From 1998, the National Literacy and Numeracy Strategies were introduced, backed by a massive investment in professional development and materials. They recommended an approach based on a lesson format which remains familiar today, with an introduction, group or individual work and a plenary, and clearly defined learning objectives. Less obviously, they effectively created literacy and numeracy as separate 'subjects' taking up much of the timetable and foundation subjects being covered in less depth, often in the afternoons. Although not statutory, the Strategies were widely seen as obligatory, at least in that those not adopting them left themselves open to criticism, especially with the increased emphasis on test scores. The value of the Strategies remains the source of debate, though teachers were more positive about the Numeracy Strategy. The two strategies were amalgamated in 2003 into the Primary National Strategy. From 2011, the Strategies are to be abolished, though at this stage it is unclear what, if anything, will replace them.

Excellence and Enjoyment (DfES, 2003) was a reaction to concerns about too great an emphasis on literacy and numeracy, compounded by how inspections focused on these, leading to a narrowing of children's experiences. This called for more enjoyment and breadth, arguing that this was consistent with higher standards, although the emphasis, notably through inspection, on results meant that its message was interpreted as 'make learning more enjoyable but not to the detriment of standards'.

Soon afterwards, Every Child Matters (ECM) (DCSF, 2004) was introduced, an initiative which affected not just education but a wide range of government policy, mainly as a response to concerns about child safety. It was concerned with children's well-being, with these five main outcomes:

- *being healthy*: good physical and mental health and living a healthy 'lifestyle';
- *staying safe*: being protected from harm and neglect;
- *enjoying and achieving*: getting the most out of life and developing the skills for adulthood;
- *making a positive contribution*: being involved with the community and society and not engaging in anti-social or offending behaviour;
- *economic well-being*: not being prevented by economic disadvantage from achieving their full potential in life.

Every Child Matters was widely welcomed, though some consequences, inevitably, have been questioned. For example, educators may query whether achieving economic well-being is either one of the main aims of education or to what extent schools can help children achieve this. However, ECM led to major changes, for instance increased support for parents/carers, early intervention and child protection and more inter-agency work. This reflects a concern stretching back to the nineteenth century on health and the social conditions in which children grow up.

The emphasis on standards results in the period since 1988 being characterised as the 'standards agenda'. Policy and practice often draw elements, and sometimes contradictory ones, from the three traditions described above. For instance, the standards agenda is based on a view similar to the preparatory tradition, emphasising the core subjects (or 'basics') and skills essential for later schooling and employment; however Excellence and Enjoyment encouraged teachers to engage children's interest by making learning fun and introducing more creativity. Nevertheless, Table 2 outlines some broad differences between the developmental tradition and the standards agenda.

Table 2

Developmental		Standards
local, to the class or school	control	centralised
set largely by the class and/or school	expectations	set externally to the class and/or school
cross-curricular and thematic	curriculum	subject-based, with focus on the core subjects
broadly conceived and usually not measured	outcomes	age-related attainment measured in core subjects
largely child-led	activities	largely adult-directed and closely monitored and inspected
facilitative with learning objectives usually not specified	teaching	direct where the learner is aware of what s/he is supposed to learn
engagement and depth	emphasis	challenge and pace

Subsequent chapters explore to what extent these different elements enhance the attributes of successful learners, especially for young children, and argue that this involves drawing on aspects of both traditions to find the right balance. This will vary in different contexts and areas of learning, requiring informed judgements by a range of adults who know the children well, especially the class teacher.

This discussion shows that different policies may encourage, or require, those in schools to concentrate on outcomes potentially in conflict with each other, if for instance there is a choice to be made between a focus on standards and on the five ECM outcomes. We shall see further tensions between different policies and re-examine several assumptions, often thought to be unproblematic, especially by those who may not have known different approaches. However, first, we consider the implications of these changes for professionalism.

Key ideas: **Autonomy and accountability**

What have been the consequences for professionalism of policy changes since 1988?

Since 1988, education has moved into the political limelight. Quite why is complicated, but key elements were:

- a greater interest in education as a driver of economic growth, allied with, in Ireson et al.'s words (1999, pages 212–13), *the emergence of international studies of education (which) have made governments acutely aware of comparisons of the outputs of different systems;*
- an increased emphasis on consumer – in the case of education parental – choice, linked with the perceived need for more information to enable this and greater political accountability to achieve results;
- a belief that education is the best means of meeting broader social and political aims, such as reducing inequality and encouraging community cohesion.

This led to:

- a significant increase in funding for education and especially a substantial expansion of provision for the under-fives, through initiatives such as Sure Start, although the historic differential of funding in favour of older students remains;
- a greater emphasis on test scores and on inspection, with the introduction of Ofsted after 1993, with the results publicly available to enable schools to be compared and teachers and politicians to be accountable;
- a succession of policies and initiatives, with primary schools, in particular, but increasingly Early Years provision, dominated by a drive to raise standards, but also to address other agendas such as Every Child Matters, inclusion and community cohesion;
- a much greater involvement in the detail of how to teach, not only through the Strategies but in specific areas such as the emphasis on synthetic phonics since the 2006 Rose Review (DfES, 2006).

Critical thinking exercise 3: autonomy, accountability and compliance

Excellence and Enjoyment (DfES, 2003, page 27) states:

> The new Primary Strategy will support teachers and schools across the whole curriculum, building on the lessons of the Literacy and Numeracy Strategies, but moving on to offer teachers more control and flexibility. It will focus on building up teachers' own professionalism and capacity.

A **Consider** to what extent teachers should have autonomy in how they teach; and possible advantages and disadvantages of greater autonomy.

B **Discuss** to whom or what teachers (and other educators) should be accountable.

C **Illustrate** in which respects educators should be compliant with external demands and in which not; and **identify** the consequences for professionalism.

Comment

Barber (2005), one of the architects of the reforms, argues that there were four phases, namely:

- *uninformed autonomy* before 1988;
- a period of *uninformed prescription*, when detailed guidance about the curriculum pedagogy was needed to raise expectations and results;
- a move towards *informed prescription*, when teachers were given greater freedom, based on a clearer structure of what is expected and 'what works';
- an increasing emphasis on *informed autonomy* where teachers have greater

freedom on the basis that they have a securer knowledge of how to achieve the expected results.

This analysis is extremely controversial, both historically and analytically. While teachers had greater autonomy before 1988, the suggestion that this was 'uninformed' is hard to substantiate; and the Cambridge Primary Review describes the current situation as a *culture of compliance*, rather than informed autonomy. This book questions the suggestion that anyone knows 'what works', regardless of context, or that prescription is the best route to autonomy.

In Osborn's view (2008, page 76), *teachers, like pupils, are increasingly being required to respond to a 'performance'-orientated system based on external measures of quality*. The accountability of schools was increased by the introduction of Ofsted (Office for Standards in Education) inspections in 1993. These enabled (however controversially) children (and parents) to be told how well they were doing relative to other children and school results to be compared, based mostly on test results in the core subjects. Moreover, it was accompanied by teachers' performance being regularly monitored by senior colleagues, usually to check that they were abiding by external expectations.

To what extent educators should be autonomous and to whom they should be accountable will always be a matter of debate. Although the government elected in 2010 is committed to less direct involvement in the detail of pedagogy, there seems little doubt that schools and teachers will continue to be held accountable largely on the basis of results, while the implications for professional autonomy remain unclear.

Key idea: **Standards**

> Support for a National Curriculum and the notion of entitlement is high, even among those who are critical of its content. The problem is how best to achieve this entitlement. Many teachers have welcomed the detailed guidance which resulted from the Strategies, both in terms of planning and pedagogy, whereas others have seen it as restricting professional judgement, limiting the range of opportunities for children and teachers and providing more consistency but at the cost of loss of creativity; all issues to which we shall return.

The 'standards agenda' makes test scores the main focus of school and teacher accountability. Testing is assumed to raise standards. However, Harlen (2010, page 512) argues, on the basis of research in the UK and elsewhere, that *evidence of changes in standards of achievement over the years does not support the claim that testing 'drives up standards'*. The emphasis on inspection and monitoring has resulted in what is called 'high-stakes' accountability, where success or otherwise affects the school's viability and the teacher's career prospects. The Cambridge Primary Review calls for a broad view of accountability, not based primarily on test results, but with teachers being accountable to evidence in justifying their decisions, a view in line with the 'extended professionalism' current before 1988.

Campbell and Kyriakides (2000) argue that 'standards' include three different meanings of the term:

- those set by policy-makers;
- those set by teachers when planning;
- those achieved by pupils.

They state that these may not match. Saying that 80 per cent of a group should reach a certain level does not mean they will. Black (2001, p 73) states that *standards can only be raised by improving teaching*. While this is questionable, since changes to the curriculum or social conditions may do so, it indicates that better outcomes result from mainly what learners and educators do differently, rather than from policy-makers just saying that standards should rise.

A second difficulty is that, presumably, all educators and parents want higher standards, but standards of what? Maybe, of how to behave and conduct oneself or of well-being, or across the curriculum or in the expressive arts. However, by emphasising test scores, especially in reading, writing and numeracy, the standards agenda presupposes that such outcome measures are what matter most, often suggesting that this is all that matters, tending to make any discussion about the multiple aims of education superfluous.

These two difficulties might not matter if an emphasis on 'standards' did not affect issues such as inclusion, behaviour, or motivation, creativity or breadth and balance adversely. In future chapters, I shall suggest that the insistent emphasis on raising standards affects all of these.

It would be ridiculous to argue that compliance is never appropriate. For instance, on matters to do with children's safety, whether related to equipment, or health, or residential experiences, compliance seems not only appropriate, but non-compliance unprofessional. Equally, on questions of discrimination, it is both necessary and right to adhere to the law, national and local policies and professional codes of ethics. On questions of pedagogy, it is more open to question whether compliance is appropriate, reflecting the discussion in Chapter 1 on whether teaching is a science, a craft or an art. In a laboratory, a technician would undermine the scientific process if he did not follow procedures. However, no film producer would agree to use only a restricted range of camera angles; and no professional cook would put up with being forbidden to use certain pieces of equipment or vegetables without very good reason. When the expectation of compliance interferes with the child's best interests, it is the responsibility of the professional to exercise judgement. The problem is therefore not one of compliance as such but of unthinking compliance if that interferes with professional judgement.

Key idea: **Well-being**

What has been the impact of social and cultural change on children and on pedagogy?

An education system both reflects, and contributes to, social, cultural and political changes and assumptions. These may result from:

- conscious political choice as in the decision to abolish elementary schools after the Second World War or introduce the National Curriculum; or
- more reactive responses, such as the periodic reviews of teaching methods or the introduction of citizenship, often following a panic about falling standards or moral decline.

It is therefore necessary to understand how social and cultural change has affected young children's lives, attitudes, and well-being.

Mayall (2010) argues that current and future priorities for pedagogy should take account of the changing nature of how childhood is understood in the light of social and cultural change. While some changes discussed below may not seem directly related to pedagogy, they affect the context in which children live and their attitudes to school. Since this is a huge area in which it is easy to make sweeping judgements about whether such changes have been beneficial or otherwise, such judgements are often affected by our own (often nostalgic) view of childhood and beliefs about what is best for children.

Critical thinking exercise 4: social and cultural change

Among the key social and cultural changes in recent years highlighted by Alexander (2010, pages 53–55) are:
- a much improved level of physical health, though greater concern about mental health;
- a higher level of disposable income and possessions for most but not all;
- changing patterns in both the immediate and extended family and communities;
- a rapid change in types, and availability, of technology;
- a less deferential approach to authority.

A **Consider** what has happened in relation to each of these areas and possible benefits and disadvantages of each for young children.

/continued

Critical thinking exercise 4 – continued

B **Articulate** to what extent these may have affected children's views of success and how to achieve it.

C **Identify** how these may have affected young children's approach to learning.

Comment

Most children are physically healthier than 50 years ago, with the worries about undernourishment and disease, especially in deprived areas, expressed by reformers such as the McMillans around 1900 and still a major concern after the Second World War, much less in evidence. Indeed, most current worries about physical health relate to obesity and too sedentary a lifestyle. However, there is greater concern about mental health, most obviously in relation to whether children are happy or overstressed. For instance reports such as that of UNICEF (2007) and books such as Layard (2005), Layard and Dunn (2009) and Palmer (2006) describe children in the UK as among the least happy in comparable countries. This has resulted in a growing concern about children not being able to enjoy childhood, and becoming prematurely adolescent. This is debatable, but it is widely accepted that the greater level of parental and societal concern about possible harm to children has led to adults and children becoming more risk-averse. Moreover, Every Child Matters emphasises a broader notion of well-being than just happiness and the Cambridge Primary Review (see Alexander, 2010, page 197) calls for well-being to include being *wholeheartedly engaged in all kinds of worthwhile activities and relationships*, continuing that *well being thus defined is both a precondition and outcome of successful primary education.*

A second trend has been a rapid increase, for most, in levels of income. Most children have become used to a greater level of material prosperity, although the effect of this has been uneven, with a significant minority of children still growing up in poverty. Wilkinson and Pickett (2009) make a convincing case that greater levels of equality benefit the whole of society, not just those who are poor. Linked to other trends, notably the rise of consumerism, the changing level of disposable income emphasises that success is associated primarily with possessions. For instance, advertising reinforces having the right brand and the cult of celebrity suggests that success is to be seen in terms of money and the result of good looks.

The patterns of family life and the nature of communities have changed significantly in the last 30 to 40 years, often as a result of greater geographical mobility. Many more children now grow up in families where they do not live with both of their birth parents and many do not live close to their extended family. Fewer children grow up in a family where long-term relationships within and beyond their immediate family are the norm. It has, arguably, increased the number of children who come to school unused to predictable and nurturing relationships. The changed composition of communities, especially in urban areas, in relation to ethnicity and culture, has brought both opportunities for greater cross-cultural understanding and challenges in relation to racism and intolerance.

A further trend, especially in the last ten years, is the availability of, and access to, a range of technology, much of it portable, such as mobile phones and iPods. As a result, most children from a young age spend many hours watching television or playing computer games. This provides children with the opportunity to access very quickly a huge range of information and to develop skills at a much faster rate, but may lead to children having less space, a shorter attention span and an impatience with slower ways of thinking and acting. Similarly, the growth of social networking sites may provide the chance to relate to a wider group of friends in new ways, but opens up the possibility of cyberbullying or predatory behaviour.

A subtler trend results from a less deferential approach to authority, for instance shown by how the role and expertise of doctors or teachers are increasingly challenged. This is associated with the greater emphasis on parental choice and children's voice. There is an assumption that parental choice is always a good thing, whereas one person's choice may restrict another's; and those who are educated and powerful are more able to exercise choice than those who are not. 'Children's voice' is linked to the UN Convention on the Rights of the Child (see UNICEF, no date), which spells out that children everywhere have the basic human rights of:

- survival;
- developing to the fullest;
- protection from harmful influences, abuse and exploitation;
- participating fully in family, cultural and social life.

The four core principles of the Convention are:

- non-discrimination;
- devotion to the best interests of the child;
- the right to life, survival and development;
- respect for the views of the child.

Children's participation in the decisions which affect them is often at best superficial. While the extent to which, and how, young children can, and should, participate is a matter of debate, Mayall (2010) calls for children to be seen as social agents who participate actively in both social relations and learning and for a re-consideration of what children can offer to society, rather than seeing them as valued largely in economic terms or their current or later 'usefulness'.

Many of these areas are both under-researched and hard to research because results are heavily influenced by value judgements. Moreover, in Alexander's (2010, page 53) words, *sometimes it must seem to children growing up in Britain today that they cannot win*, as when their lives and enthusiasms are reported it is *all too often in terms of stereotypes*, appearing as *suffering innocents…in a dark and menacing world* or little devils whose behaviour is out of control by adults. However, it seems that young children grow up in a world which:

- is 'busier', so that children have less space, both physical and mental, to play in an unsupervised way, except through using technology, and are, arguably, less used to concentrating for sustained periods of time, especially in groups;
- enables access to a wider range of opportunities, but usually under the supervision of adults, so that leisure, play and sport are increasingly 'scholarised' and under adult control, especially at school (see Mayall, 2010, page 61);
- emphasises individualism, consumerism and, especially for girls, sexualisation, so providing mixed messages about what to aim for, and how to achieve it;
- results in a minority growing up confused about how to conduct themselves, and less aware and/or immediately accepting of the norms of behaviour in social situations.

Such trends affect educators in particular because much of what was previously taken for granted often can no longer be assumed and has to be negotiated or made explicit, both with parents and children. Adults must take account of the social and cultural world outside school, both because, as Brooker (2002, especially Chapter 3) argues, children learn a great deal, and in different ways, at home and, as the TLRP says, *the conception of what is to be learned needs to be broadened beyond the notions of curricula and subjects associated with schools*; and also because the influences on children outside school are so powerful and influential in how they think and act.

This is not simply about more, or less, or different types of homework, or whether children should be discouraged from reading comics; but about the sorts of knowledge valued in school and society and the types of people we wish children to be. And, as with the Reggio Emilia approach, how children can be encouraged to be powerful and articulate learners and the relationship between school, family and community be developed to enable this.

Conclusion

This chapter has considered the current policy climate in a broader historical and international context, showing how policies are like a collage drawn from traditions of practice in educating young children. Approaches to education change over time. Given how social, cultural and political change influences children's lives, priorities are likely to change in the next 30 to 40 years, in ways considered in Chapter 11. So, pedagogy will have to adapt accordingly, with educators prepared to exercise judgement about both purpose and techniques – the why, as well as the how, of pedagogy.

The critical thinking exercises will have helped you:

- ⊙ **compare** the assumptions underlying the main traditions of educating young children;

- ⊙ **identify** the rationale behind the 1988 Education Act and the main changes in assumptions, expectations and practices which followed;
- ⊙ **analyse** how such changes affect, and are affected by, changing views of ideas such as accountability, professionalism and pedagogy;
- ⊙ **discuss** the impact of social and cultural change on children's lives and attitudes, encouraging you to reflect on how this affects their beliefs and approach to school.

In the next chapter, we explore how young children develop and learn, since it is unwise to think how to enhance this without considering how it happens.

Further Reading

Alexander, R (ed) (2010) *Children, their World, their Education – final report and recommendations of the Cambridge Primary Review.* Abingdon: Routledge Section 2 (pages 51–146) discusses in far more detail than is possible here important recent trends related to childhood and children.

Anning, A (1991) *The First Years At School.* Buckingham: Open University Press Chapter 1, 'Histories and Ideologies', provides useful summaries of the history and key figures in the history of education for 4–8-year-olds.

3

Making sense of young children's development

Chapter Focus

The critical thinking exercises in this chapter focus on:

⊙ **observing** and **articulating** some of the many ways in which children learn;
⊙ **interpreting** what is distinctive about young children's approaches to learning;
⊙ **considering** to what extent learning involves individual and social processes;
⊙ **identifying** different aspects of development and how these are linked.

The key ideas discussed are: **agency, reciprocity, internal working models, development, interaction, modelling, narrative, the whole child**

This chapter is particularly relevant to QTS Standards: **10**, **18**, **22**, **25 b**, **26 b** and to Knowledge and Understanding and Reflection (*Education Studies*) and Subject knowledge and Subject skills (*Early Childhood Studies*)

Introduction

This chapter considers how young children learn, recalling that the TLRP saw learning as the basis of effective pedagogy. We look first at how babies and toddlers learn, emphasising making sense of experience, with the next two critical thinking exercises discussing to what extent young children develop through distinct stages and the processes, both unconscious and conscious, involved. The final exercise looks at aspects of development other than the cognitive, indicating that these are all interlinked.

CASE STUDY

Jessica's question somewhat punctured my belief that the lesson had been really successful. Her Year 6 class had been discussing volcanoes, where the lava came from, why they erupted, even the theory of tectonic plates, drawing out from the children what they knew, by some careful questioning and illustrating the process with pictures and analogies. It really seemed that the children's understanding had been enriched. Just before hometime, I asked if anyone had a final question. Tentatively, Jessica, a quiet child, raised her hand and, looking puzzled, said *But what I don't understand is why people make volcanoes in the first place.* Some of the others started to laugh, but I stopped them, said how good it was that she could ask and explained that volcanoes were natural.

I wonder what you think had been going on 'in Jessica's mind'. I imagine that she had been puzzling about this question throughout the lesson, without having much idea what the other children, or I, were talking about. In the excitement (mine and theirs) of demonstrating what we knew, I had assumed a basis of knowledge she (and probably others) did not have. Perhaps, the only redeeming feature was that she felt able to ask the question, even if too late. What is obvious to some children may be a source of confusion to others. Far too often, as educators, we build on a foundation we assume to be there, but which is not.

Key ideas: **Agency and reciprocity**

What can we learn about learning from tiny children?

Think of what a two- or three-year-old has already learned before she starts in a setting outside the home: a range of skills and abilities, usually including physical control, some measure of self-regulation and, most remarkably, how to use language to communicate with other people. While the emerging understanding of how the brain develops provides important insights, the processes involved in how the mind develops remain mysterious. However, Alexander (2010, page 106) offers a good starting point:

> So, how do children develop, think, feel, act and learn? Answering that question lies in part in recognising the intricate and intertwined influences of what used to be called nature and nurture: the interdependence of children's development and the social and cultural environment in which it takes place.

The implications of this are too often forgotten, with the current emphasis on cognition, measurable outcomes and individual processes. This book encourages you to:

- view learning as more than academic achievement;
- think about learning processes more than outcomes;
- recognise that learning is both social and individual;

and realising for example, that intellectual attainment is affected by one's emotional state – and vice versa – and that biological and genetic factors interact with social and cultural ones. Let us start with how babies learn.

Critical thinking exercise 1: a young baby's actions and interactions

Imagine (and if possible **observe**) a young baby's actions.

A **Identify** what she is doing – looking around, sucking, grabbing hold of objects, crying, yawning, sleeping…

/continued

> **Critical thinking exercise 1** – continued
>
> B Try to **interpret** why she is doing these.
>
> C **Consider** what adults do to assist her learning.

Comment

Gerhardt (2004) provides an accessible account of how a baby's brain and development are affected by his or her upbringing. Most obviously, babies are responding to sensation, emotion and external events, exploring what is themselves and what is separate and the range of puzzling sensations and experiences encountered. While it is hard to interpret mental processes with any degree of confidence, research over the last fifty years suggests that babies are much more active seekers for meaning than had been assumed previously. Bruner (1996, pages 71–2) summarises his own research: *infants…were much smarter, more cognitively proactive rather than reactive, more attentive to the immediate social world around them, than had been previously suspected…they seemed to be in search of predictive stability from the start.* Babies' focus is, initially, on themselves and they are able only to explore within their own immediate environment, but they are, from the start, learning creatures, searchers for, and active participants in making, meaning. In Isaacs' words, (1970, page 102) *the thirst for understanding springs from the child's deepest emotional needs and with the intelligent child is a veritable passion. He must know and master the world to make it feel safe.*

The active aspect of learning is often described as agency – which, as Bruner (1996, page 93) suggests, *takes mind to be proactive, problem-oriented, attentionally focussed, selective, constructional, directed to ends.* Though rather a mouthful, this shows that learning is based on attending to, selecting and resolving problems and doing so actively and constructively. Agency involves being engaged with the task in hand. Although the baby's attention span may be short, she can be absorbed in the activity. Without such engagement she will not actively make sense of her experiences. While one can, as we shall see, become over-engaged or over-focused, and much learning occurs without conscious thought, agency and engagement are central to successful learning.

A baby's crying suggests how she is often overwhelmed by primal, biological needs. Maslow's (1968) hierarchy of needs indicates that 'higher-order' mental functions depend on these being met. So, for instance, being creative, focused and productive depends on:

- being known and appreciated by others; which depends on
- feeling safe; which depends on
- not being dominated by physical needs such as hunger or pain.

Physical and emotional distress dominate brain function unless alleviated. A high level of anxiety will lead to 'fight or flight' – aggression or withdrawal – making it harder to regulate one's behaviour consciously.

What and how a baby learns will depend on many factors, some genetic, others depending on prior experience and the specific situation. For instance, Kagan (1994) emphasises the role of temperament, which is largely inherent and unchanging. However, prior experience makes a considerable difference. So, a child who has been ignored when she cries may cry more, or less, or in a different way; and the same child will respond differently, when comfortable, or comforted, from when wet or shouted at. For the purposes of parenting and pedagogy, which factors one can influence, and to what extent, are what matter most.

The interaction between baby and adult through gazing, smiling, talking, touching – the list is endless – is at the root of how the baby makes sense of experience (see Gerhardt, 2004, Chapter 1, for a good summary of the following issues). By about 6 months old, infants can tell if they are being looked at and by about 12 months follow and pay attention to what an adult is looking at. While babies and toddlers gradually learn to regulate their responses, they have many needs – such as for nourishment, warmth, and reassurance – which they cannot meet unassisted. When the baby is hungry, most mothers are attuned to recognising the need and responding appropriately.

Learning to communicate, and then to talk, requires processes which are not simply imitative, but involve reciprocal relationships. Between 18 months and two years of age, children usually start, in their play, to distinguish between reality and pretence. This is the basis of what is called 'theory of mind', by which they understand that other people have beliefs and desires which vary from their own, and so can make inferences about other people's behaviour and motivation. As Fox (2005, page 106) indicates, *knowing that someone else has different beliefs and different desires to yours is fundamental to understanding their actions.* So, while agency involves individual effort, learning is, from the start, reciprocal and interactive, enhanced by responses which are predictable and attuned to the child's needs.

Key idea: **Internal working models**

What can we learn about children's behaviour from understanding early child development?

This is not a book about looking after babies, though the previous section has provided some clues about older children's responses and behaviour from considering how babies learn and develop. In Gerhardt's (2004, page 24) words *unconsciously acquired, non-verbal patterns and expectations … are inscribed in*

/continued

Key idea: **Development** – continued

the brain outside conscious awareness, in the period of infancy and...underpin our behaviour in relationships through life. These help to explain what underlies children's self-concept to which we return in Chapter 5. One of the most important sources in understanding emotional responses and behaviour is attachment theory.

Attachment theory suggests less obvious lessons about the structure of the mind and the role of reciprocity. This stems from Bowlby's work (see 1965 for a short summary) on how babies respond differently to potentially distressing experiences. Put simply, this suggests that 'internal working models' are learned during early infancy through the baby's relationship with the prime carer, usually the mother. These are the basis of how infants learn to act and interact with other people.

Models of attachment may be secure or insecure, with the latter usually divided into avoidant, anxious (or resistant) and disorganised. Those with secure models of attachment can cope better with adversity because they can access a 'secure base'. This both provides emotional support and enables them to be more adventurous and take more risks. Infants with avoidant models explore but take little notice of their mother and are not worried either at her departure or her return, sometimes being more sociable with a stranger. Having learned not to rely on their mother in seeking comfort, they are less prone to express their emotions. Those with anxious models are reluctant to explore in their mother's presence and distressed when she leaves. Reunions lead to the children trying to make contact but resisting her moves to provide comfort, reacting angrily or passively. A small number of children with insecure attachments fit neither of these two categories, showing both avoidant and anxious responses. Known as 'disorganised', such children demonstrate paradoxical behaviour, finding it very hard to maintain a consistent strategy, for example crying loudly but avoiding the mother's comfort, or approaching her without being able to seek comfort and support. They are sometimes thought to have strategies to seek the security they crave but be unable to implement them, having learned that these do not work predictably.

The relative importance of models of attachment and genetic factors and how permanent their effect is remains contentious (see Goldberg, 2000, page 247). However, three main lessons emerge. These are:

- the importance of anxiety in determining behaviour;
- how emotion is processed and patterns of behaviour depend (at least in part) on the internal working models, or models of attachment, learned in infancy;
- that these result reciprocally from the type of interaction between baby and mother, with the mother's emotional attunement (broadly speaking, sensitivity to the baby's emotional state) a key feature of this.

Key idea: **Development**

How do young children's minds differ from adults'?

As Geertz (2001, page 22) writes:

> seeing even the infant and the pre-schooler as active agents bent on mastery of a particular form of life, or developing a workable way of being in the world, demands a rethinking of the entire educational process. It is not so much a matter of providing something the child lacks, as enabling something the child already has: the desire to make sense of self and others, the drive to understand what the devil is going on.

Although his ideas have been misunderstood and challenged in several respects, Piaget remains deeply influential in understanding children's development, especially of cognition. One of his great insights is that knowledge is constructed by the learner, with a conceptual structure which is reshaped as a result of new experience (though not only experience). He saw development as a progression through consecutive, fixed stages of development. As a simple analogy, one cannot build the fourth floor of a block of flats until the first three have been completed. This ran counter to a belief that young children's minds were just like those of adults, only smaller and less capable, or that learning could somehow be transplanted in their minds.

Critical thinking exercise 2: making sense

Gardner writes (1999, page 94) that *humans are deemed the creatures par excellence of communication, who garner meanings through words, pictures, gestures, numbers, musical patterns and a whole host of other symbolic forms.*

A Try to **identify** key ways in which a young child (say between 4 and 8 years old) learns. For instance, what about the role of activity, of listening, of watching…?

B **Discuss** to what extent a young child's mind develops evenly and naturally.

C **Consider** what factors may affect whether young children engage with a task.

Comment

The process of learning is both complicated and multifaceted. For example, it may involve imagining, acting, thinking, talking, memorising, experimenting, practising, imitating, identifying patterns, to name only a few. Drawing on Bruner's work, Gipps and MacGilchrist (1999, pages 50–1) summarise three main views of children, and the learning process, as:

- *imitative learners: the acquisition of know-how*, with pedagogy based on an apprenticeship model, leading the novice into the skilled ways of the expert;
- *learning from didactic exposure; the acquisition of propositional knowledge ('facts')*, with pedagogy based on presenting children with facts, principles and rules to be applied;
- *thinkers: the development of intersubjective exchange*, with pedagogy based on discussion and collaboration so that children become increasingly active participants in their own learning.

All three are necessary but the current emphasis is heavily on the second of these. As Gipps and MacGilchrist (1999, page 47) write, *learning occurs not by recording information but by interpreting it, so that teaching is not seen as direct transfer of knowledge but as an intervention in an on-going knowledge-construction process.* They summarise research findings by saying

66*isolated facts, if learnt, quickly disappear from the memory because they have no meaning and do not fit into the learners' conceptual map. Knowledge learnt in this way is of limited use because it is difficult for it to be applied, generalized or retrieved. Meaning makes learning easier, because the learner knows where to put things in her mental framework, and meaning makes knowledge useful because likely purposes and* 99 *applications are already part of the understanding.*

op.cit., page 47

Let us consider some lessons from research into how brain development, though the mind consists of more than the (physical) brain. One key message is that young children's brains are plastic, constantly changing, as a result of experience. This process builds up the connections essential in how the brain works, though these are later 'pruned'. In David's (2001, page 58) words, *we cannot afford to waste children's time by treating them as if they have no brain or as if their brains need 'filling up' with knowledge simply transmitted (transplanted?) from our adult brains*, given the dynamic interaction of nature and nurture and that the human brain is at its most plastic in the earliest years.

The deep structures of the brain are shaped in early childhood. We have considered internal working models which form part of the earliest and most deeply rooted form of memory – procedural – operating at a pre-conscious or automatic level. These precede more familiar sorts of memory, notably semantic, developing from the end of the first year and enabling information from sources other than direct experience to be incorporated; and episodic which arranges specific events into chronologically ordered accounts and develops in the pre-school years (see Goldberg, 2000, pages 151–2). While most relevant for teachers of very young children, those who teach older children should also remember that deep structures and responses operate independently of conscious thought, especially at times of extreme anxiety, recalling Maslow's hierarchy of needs. So, when a child does not exercise conscious control, it may be that he cannot, not that he will not.

Even experienced learners are always making sense of experience of which our understanding is only partial, always elaborating an incomplete understanding. Learning does not just involve having experiences, but integrating facts and procedures into existing patterns of feelings, understandings and actions. So, learning depends not only on the type of experience but how the learner represents these. Bruner (2006, volume 1, page 69) highlights three main ways of representing experience, which are:

- the enactive, through actions;
- the iconic, through visual means;
- the symbolic, through symbols, especially language.

One respect in which young children's minds differ from those of adults is in their ability to think abstractly. Donaldson (1992, especially Chapter 3) argues that very young children develop from 'point mode', where they can only focus on the here and now, through 'line mode', where they can see themselves as part of a broader notion of time and space, through to the 'construct mode', where they become able to shift their focus of concern outside a specific place or time. Young children's thinking is context-dependent and they only gradually become able to use with confidence the symbolic representation on which adults usually rely.

Adults tend to assume that thinking should precede activity. Yet they are more subtly linked, especially with young children not used to symbolic representation. In Black's (1999, page 121) words, *one of Piaget's principles that still commands acceptance is that we learn by actions, by self-directed problem-solving aimed at trying to control the world and that abstract thought evolves from concrete action.* And, as Bruner writes (1996, page 79), *we seem to be more prone to acting our way into thinking than we are able to think our way explicitly into acting.* When we find a task too abstract, it usually helps to draw a chart or a mind map or make a model, or even to act out a situation. It may help to think about assembling a self-assembly bookshelf. I have to lay it out to visualise how the pieces fit together, before going back to the instructions (and usually taking apart what I've already done). I can't work it out abstractly. Action and thought need to operate in parallel. Young children, especially, need opportunities to do and to draw, not just to talk (let alone write), especially at the limits of their understanding.

Piaget built his theory of developmental stages on experiments designed to see how children understood and responded to particular tasks, concluding that their conceptual development limited them to one way of thinking. This helped show that a child might not yet be ready for certain sorts of task, though it was misused in a belief that children would naturally progress, without support, as they matured. However, Donaldson (1982, especially Chapter 4) demonstrated that a failure to carry out a task may not result from conceptual difficulty, but for other reasons such as not understanding or being interested in the task, or being physically incapable of doing so. For example, when a four-year-old does not engage with an adult reading a book to him, this may result from not realising what is expected. And as a little boy, I had poor fine motor skills. Although I learned to read easily, I found writing incredibly difficult. Being left-handed and having to write with a dip-pen didn't help. This may sound as if it was in the Middle Ages, but it was only about 50 years ago. But I was not physically ready for such a task.

Prior experience, context and physical and cognitive readiness affect how a child engages with a task. Yet, all too often, as adults, we seek to impose meaning, rather than enabling children to find it for themselves. So, how a child responds will depend on her understanding of, or familiarity with, the type of task and she may move back and forward between modes, according to context, and the level of challenge. As they mature, children learn new modes of representation but the old ones are not discarded (unless they are persuaded otherwise).

Key ideas: **Interaction and modelling**

To what extent is learning an individual or a social process?

We talk naturally about children 'developing'. Yet how we understand development affects what we expect of children. This may result in a belief that education matters mainly because of what a child may become rather than what they are in the 'here-and-now'. More practically, it can lead to providing activities and experiences which are too, or insufficiently, challenging. Alexander (2000, page 216), comparing different cultural assumptions, suggests that *in England, development happens, (but) in Russia, schools, parents and the community make it happen.*

Piaget's theories are often criticised as seeing learning as too individual and compartmentalised, though, as Siraj-Blatchford (1999, page 29) writes:

> *[the] part of Piaget's theory which provides an account of the role of social factors in early childhood development has been largely neglected…Piaget argued that adult–child and peer relations influence every aspect of development and that affective and personality development are intimately related to intellectual and moral development.*

Learning is not just an individual activity. Bruner writes (1996, page 93) *we do not learn a way of life, and ways of deploying mind unassisted, unscaffolded, naked before the world.*

> **Critical thinking exercise 3:** social and cultural influences
>
> Donaldson (1992, page 20) writes:
>
> *when we discuss the development of the human mind we are talking about processes of self-transformation: processes by which we turn ourselves into different beings. However…this is not a solitary effort. We are dependent in the most crucial ways on the help of others. And others may hinder or constrain us also. This is true from early infancy onwards.*
>
> A **Identify** the possible implications for educators of this quotation, especially to what extent children need interaction with other people, and with whom.
>
> B **Consider** to what extent children learn by imitation, or by modelling the habits of others.
>
> C Try to **articulate** why hearing, telling and reading stories are especially important for young children's learning.

Comment

In Piaget's words, (cited in Papert, 1999), *children have real understanding only of that which they invent themselves and each time that we try to teach them something too quickly we keep them from re-inventing it themselves.* Adults too often see their task as one of delivery rather than interaction; as we saw with the story of Jessica and the volcanoes.

Vygotsky wrote: *Every function in the child's cultural development appears twice: first on the social level and later on the individual level; first between people and then inside the child* (cited in Daniels et al., 2007, page 309). His main concern was with cognitive functions and conceptual development, seeing these as reflecting and shaping our understanding of ourselves and what we experience and helping us to structure reality. Vygotsky's best-known idea is the zone of proximal development (ZPD) – the area 'just beyond' the learner's current level of understanding, between current abilities and possible independent action, with tasks pitched 'ahead' of the learner's current level of understanding, but not too far ahead. Vygotsky argued that conceptual development occurs primarily through interaction, especially with those with greater expertise and experience, through the use of tools, notably language (discussed in more detail in Chapter 8). However, these tools also include other means of symbolic expression, for instance play, art and ritual, to which young people gain access by participating in social activity. This informs the Reggio Emilia approach, mentioned at the start of Chapter 2. Education involves being incorporated into a culture by learning to use the tools of culture in increasingly sophisticated and appropriate ways. This is why an unfamiliar, or an alien, culture makes learning so difficult.

Young children, especially, learn kinaesthetically – through actions and manipulating materials – and visually more easily and effectively than through language; and will often respond to visual prompts more than spoken instruction. Seeing how to listen, to converse, to think, to act works much more powerfully than just being told how to do so. In Confucius' words, *I hear and I forget, I see and I believe, I do and I understand.* So, children adopt all sorts of learning (and other) habits from teachers and other adults. In the words of the playwright, James Baldwin (1961), *children never have been very good at listening to their elders but they have never failed to imitate them.* As Vygotsky demonstrated, we pick up habits such as thinking, remembering, noticing and talking from other people very easily. Trusted adults' actions, from being fascinated by prime numbers or wearing a bike helmet to wondering what will happen to a seed when it is planted or showing interest in a child's family, will all rub off to some extent on different children; which is why enthusiasm and curiosity are such underrated qualities in adults.

Key idea: **Narrative**

> **How do stories help children learn?**
>
> Stories are one of the most powerful and underrated tools to help children learn. But they are more than that. As Bruner (1996, page 147) suggests, we live in *a sea of stories* which paradoxically makes it hard to see why they are so powerful. Cupitt (1995, page ix) writes *[Stories] shape the process of life. It is through stories that our social selves, which are our real selves, are actually produced.* They help to explain and define ourselves in relation to others, forming a narrative which constantly changes. Bruner (1996, Chapter 6) argues that narratives provide coherence of meaning to otherwise disparate events, since they are (usually) about human agents with *desires, beliefs, knowledge, intentions, commitments.* In Anning's words (1991, page 37):
>
> > for children the function of narrative can be to enable them to move from the here and now of their immediate experiences to the more distanced ideas about what happened then and what might happen next. In other words, the narrative form is a potent resource to help children move to abstractions.

So, stories work in multiple, subtle, often unconscious ways, including:

- connecting with other people and cultures;
- posing questions to encourage investigation of inference and motivation;
- nurturing the imagination;
- prompting reflection;
- helping to provide a language through which to explore feelings and beliefs.

Each listener can respond in their own way. Let us think why. First, and most simply, stories are enjoyable and accessible, Second, good stories are open-ended. They allow for alternative possibilities and courses of action, though one feature of most stories is that they reach a conclusion, where whatever questions the story has raised are resolved. As Erricker (1998, page 109) writes, *real stories by virtue of being lived are necessarily unfinished and beg questions rather than provide answers...They involve a continual remembering of the story itself*. Third, stories suggest and resonate, rather than preach, at least when told well, because they bear repeated retelling by both teller and listener. Fourth, they link us to other cultures and generations and help to provide examples of what to do (or otherwise). Stories are basic to understanding history, religion and literature, rather like a framework for linking otherwise disjointed factual knowledge. History can be seen as a collection of narratives about the past and geography about the world. And central to most religious traditions have been the stories of faith, from those told about Abraham and Muhammed to those used by Jesus and the Buddha. Fifth, stories help us, in a safe space, to understand experience, both our own and other people's, and to integrate the two. We recognise ourselves in other people and other people in ourselves. For instance, a story like *The Gruffalo* helps a young child realise not only that her fears can be overcome, but that she can participate in this, in a way that is exciting and amusing; and the Greek myths are not just about heroes and gods long ago, but about universal themes of love and jealousy, honour and deception, courage and betrayal. Finally, stories help children to understand events, and themselves, as part of a continuity, of something bigger than themselves. It is worth pondering Macintyre's words (1999, page 216): *deprive children of their stories and you leave them unscripted, anxious stutterers in their actions as in their words*. In other words, understanding who one is, and where one fits in, depends on the story that one tells about oneself – whether in words or through other means.

Perhaps the most obvious use of stories, whether told or read, is to model aspects of both oracy and literacy in a way that is accessible, unthreatening and enjoyable. So, children learn how to create a story by seeing and hearing the various elements of structure and style. There is less chance of failure, since children are less pressured to commit themselves to a definite response, as one must when writing or drawing. So, when telling or reading stories, recognise the different ways in which they work, discuss and reflect on the questions they raise but leave space for the children to interpret them in their own way.

Key idea: **The whole child**

Where does personal, or spiritual, moral, social and cultural, development, fit in?

The 1988 Act, and subsequent legislation, all contain two main strands related to the aims of education. The Education Act 2002 requires that the curriculum for a maintained school or nursery *must be balanced and broadly based and:*

/continued

Key idea: **The whole child** – continued

- *promote the spiritual, moral, cultural, mental and physical development of pupils at the school and of society;*
- *prepare pupils at the school for the opportunities, responsibilities and experiences of later life.*

This reflects the dual role of education as the development of different facets of individuals, within the broader social context, and of preparation for later life: what the eighteenth-century philosopher Kant called the need to strengthen mental faculties and develop the character. Although the Education Act uses the term 'mental', I use 'cognitive' to refer to intellectual development, partly because 'mental' has unfortunate connotations, but mainly because 'the mind' – from which the term 'mental' comes – includes all these different aspects.

Prior to the 1988 Education Act, the term 'the whole child' was in common use. Although vague, it tried to capture that learning was not just about cognitive and physical development. Yet, despite their prominence in legislation, spiritual, moral, social and cultural development (SMSC) are rarely much emphasised in policy. For example, Rose (DCSF, 2009, page 27) dismisses the idea in a sentence, preferring the more general term 'personal development'. The Cambridge Review concentrates mainly on cognitive development, reflecting a suspicion of ideas such as 'character'. Ofsted inspections rarely mention SMSC in their key findings or points for schools to develop.

You may not think that this matters. After all, children have lessons in personal, social, health and citizenship education and many programmes such as SEAL (Social and Emotional Aspects of Learning) address this. However, I shall argue that personal development is too vague a term to 'get at' the different facets of the development of character and identity and that this must be addressed throughout school life, not just in separate lessons. SMSC and cognitive development are like interwoven strands of a rope. If these become separated, one result may be young people, whether academically successful or not, with little idea how to make relationships or to make sense of their own lives; and another, too many children with low levels of attainment, and the resulting low expectations (both their own and those of other people). Using Lovat and Toomey's (2009) metaphor, the two facets are like a double helix which rely on each other. When SMSC is overlooked, the danger is that success tends to be judged without reference to the whole range of children's learning and the broader aims of education are no longer up for discussion.

Critical thinking exercise 4: the development of the whole child

A **Articulate** (and **discuss**) the experiences and qualities you associate with each of:

- physical
- spiritual;
- moral;
- cultural development.

B **Identify** why policies and inspection rarely give prominence to SMSC, in practice.

C **Consider** what sorts of experience enhance children's spiritual, moral and cultural development.

Comment

Physical is perhaps the most 'natural' form of development. As children get older, they almost always grow bigger, stronger and better co-ordinated. How they do so will depend on their genes, their inherited characteristics, their early nurture and many other factors. However, this depends also on the environment in which they are brought up. For example, a healthy diet will, usually, result in stronger teeth and better muscle tone; and a poor one in greater proneness to disease or obesity. Disease or emotional abuse are likely to affect physical development. So, although physical development occurs naturally to a large extent, it is affected by what happens and takes place unevenly, with spurts of growth and times of consolidation. As we shall see, there are similarities, and differences, in respect to other types of development.

In Eaude (2008), I discuss SMSC in detail. The next four paragraphs summarise key aspects of this, leaving, for now, social development. The types of experience which people associate with SMSC are broad ranging, especially spiritual and cultural development. This indicates how disputed and hard to grasp these areas are, but also how they involve fundamental questions that anyone faces, such as the following.

Spiritual who am I? where do I fit in? why am I here?	Moral how should I act? what sort of person do I want to become?
Social how should I interact with other people?	Cultural where do I belong? what is my identity?

Spiritual development is often associated with those aspects of religion other than belief and doctrine. For some, this link with organised religion remains central, but increasingly spirituality is seen as separate from religious affiliation. It was associated especially in

---

discussion documents in the 1990s (e.g. NCC, 1993; SCAA, 1996) and by teachers of young children with 'awe and wonder' experiences. Although this reflects the element of search and questioning, spiritual development does not just involve an individualistic, 'interior' search but is bound up with relationships and values. Hay with Nye (1998) emphasise what they call 'relational consciousness', broken into the four types of awareness:

- of self;
- of others;
- of the environment;
- of (for some people) a transcendent other (or God).

This indicates an emerging sense of identity, with young children who are often focused on their own needs coming to recognise both their independence and interdependence and learning, over time, how they fit into a 'bigger picture'. Two intriguing aspects about spiritual development are that it deals with many aspects which are hard (for anyone) to understand; and that, in some respects, young children have many qualities – such as a capacity of joy, or for wonder – which are lost or suppressed in adulthood.

Moral development is usually associated with telling the difference 'between right and wrong'. This approach is usually known as 'duty ethics', which tends to be framed in terms of what one should not do, and with rules externally imposed by adults and society. As West-Burnham and Huws-Jones, (2007, page 38) suggest, *morality that is based on obedience, compliance and the threat of sanction will always be fragile because it is based on external, negative compulsion*. An alternative approach, known as 'virtue ethics', concentrates on what sort of person one wishes to become, and the positive virtues or attributes involved, to help children both to think about and practise these, based on their own, and their family and culture's expectations and hopes and the example set by other people. As discussed further in Chapter 6, virtue ethics emphasises positive qualities such as respect and co-operation, and helps develop intrinsic motivation.

In Eagleton's (2000, page 131) words, *culture is not only what we live by. It is, also, in great measure, what we live for. Affection, relationship, memory, kinship, place, community, emotional fulfilment, intellectual enjoyment, a sense of ultimate meaning.* Cultural development may relate to three different meanings of culture, namely:

- as identity, coming from the tending of natural growth, as in agriculture or horticulture, and one's roots, helping children understand the groups to which they belong, and their associated beliefs and practices, and similarities and differences of those in other groups;
- in the sense of art, music and literature, introducing children to a broadening and enriching range of experience;
- as the environment in which we live, understand and interpret our experiences as in 'classroom culture' or 'Western culture'.

So, cultural, like spiritual, development covers a very broad canvas and it is hard to pin down what this involves or how one can judge success. However, although related to fundamental aspects of life, these are rarely dealt with explicitly in policy. Possible reasons are that these are seen as processes which are:

- not really the main role of schools, which is related to cognitive learning;
- less linear than cognitive ones and harder to assess;
- too vague, uncertain or dangerous for educators to know how to try to develop them, and not susceptible to separate programmes.

The need to link different facets of learning and experience in and out of school, especially for young children, is the basis of my belief that educators should not just concentrate on cognition; and the second and third points emphasise why building up expertise to inform professional judgement is so important. Supporting children's spiritual, moral and cultural development involves helping them in trying to understand what is mysterious, appropriate and different from ourselves, through relationships, exploration and reflection. As we shall see, this requires attention to the whole environment for learning, relying more on aspects which are 'caught' than 'taught' (directly).

Conclusion

This chapter has presented learning as a creative process where meaning is constructed and new ideas are integrated into existing patterns of understanding, from birth onwards. This requires the active support of, and interaction with, other people rather than simply occurring naturally.

The critical thinking exercises will have helped you:

- ⊙ **consider** the roots of learning from early infancy, seeing that, from the start, we are active and reciprocal learners;
- ⊙ **compare** theories on the extent to which development takes place through stages, emphasising different modes of representation and how children draw on these depending on the context and task;
- ⊙ **identify** the importance of interaction, especially through language, and modelling;
- ⊙ **explore**, briefly, different aspects of the development of the 'whole child'.

In Chapter 4, we examine some fundamental assumptions about knowledge and intelligence to question further what schools should focus upon, and how.

Further Reading

Donaldson, M (1982) *Children's Minds.* Glasgow: Fontana
A classic book on the psychology of children's learning.
Eaude, T (2008) *Children's Spiritual, Moral, Social and Cultural Development –
Primary and Early Years.* Exeter: Learning Matters
A more detailed exploration of SMSC and the practical implications than is
possible here.
Gerhardt, S (2004) *Why Love Matters: How affection shapes a baby's brain.* Hove:
Routledge
A clearly written book about the importance of care and nurture in the
development of the brain.

4

Understanding knowledge and intelligence

Chapter Focus

The critical thinking exercises in this chapter focus on:

⊙ **challenging** some fundamental assumptions about concepts such as knowledge, intelligence and ability;

⊙ **considering** what sorts of knowledge and intelligence are most valued in schools and in society;

⊙ **illustrating** how one's understanding of these affect one's pedagogy;

⊙ **discussing** 'deep learning' and the importance of both conscious and unconscious processes.

The key ideas discussed are: **knowledge, intelligence, ability, emotional intelligence, habituation, metacognition**

This chapter is particularly relevant to QTS Standards: **10**, **18**, **25 b**, **26 b**, **29** and to Knowledge and Understanding and Application (*Education Studies*) and Subject knowledge and Subject skills (*Early Childhood Studies*)

Introduction

This chapter looks first at different types of knowledge, considering debates related to 'gifted and talented' and then 'emotional intelligence', followed by a discussion of different processes involved in learning. This provides the basis for the later argument that supporting the attributes of successful learners is central to effective pedagogy; and that emphasising short-term performance in a limited range of subject areas often impedes this.

CASE STUDY

I recently had a kitchen added to my house. The builder, a man close to retirement, did not commit much to paper. At his first visit, he assessed the task rapidly, asking a few questions. He undertook the planning and the skilled work himself, delegating much of the digging and removal of earth to his assistant. Of course, there were unforeseen obstacles requiring a change of plan.

/continued

CASE STUDY – continued

He negotiated with me, the architect and those in charge of building regulations. When I had to decide, for instance on tiles, he set out the options, guiding me when I was about to make unwise choices. He persuaded the architect about the benefits of a better insulating material than the one recommended. He was careful to make no more mess than necessary, keeping me informed about how I would be affected – and even finishing the work on time.

This story about a man who had, I guess, left school as soon as possible and with few qualifications raises questions about the nature of intelligence and knowledge and our attitudes towards them. For example, he would probably not have been seen as intelligent in the way this term is usually used; and the sort of knowledge he demonstrated is not what is most valued in terms of social prestige or status. But he showed what in Ancient Greece was called *phronesis*, or 'practical wisdom'. So, let us bear the builder in mind as we explore how intelligence and ability has been, and is still, understood.

Key idea: **Knowledge**

What sorts of knowledge do young children need to learn?

You may think this a strange question, because the National Curriculum sets out what children need to know – a set of facts to develop skills and understanding in the different subject areas. Surely, young children just need to know 'the basics' – facts such as dates and places and how to read, write and do maths? However, this introduces a distinction between propositional knowledge, or factual information – 'knowledge that' – and procedural knowledge – 'knowledge how'. Later, we consider experiential and emotional knowledge – 'knowledge of' oneself and other people.

Critical thinking exercise 1: what is knowledge?

Alexander (2010, page 199) argues that one aim of primary education should be to *help children recognise that knowledge is not only transmitted but also negotiated and re-created; and that each of us in the end makes our own sense out of the meeting of knowledge both personal and collective.*

A Thinking of at least two different activities, **analyse** to what extent the distinction between propositional and procedural knowledge is valid.

/continued

> **Critical thinking exercise 1** – continued
>
> B **Consider** whether the knowledge regarded as most important in schools and in life is factual or procedural; and why.
>
> C **Discuss** the possible implications for children of how some types of knowledge are valued in schools more than others.

Comment

We tend to think of, and present, propositional knowledge as 'fact' which is not open to question or interpretation, and procedural knowledge as fluid, because procedures depend on individual circumstance and context. However, while there is a body of 'factual' knowledge to be learned, from the answer to 6 times 9 to the name of the river flowing through London, this is rarely useful until connected to a real-life problem. Learning involves selecting and interpreting factual knowledge, to make sense of it or use to answer a question. What one knows can always be elaborated. This is most obvious when a young child is searching for number patterns or trying to blend separate sounds and syllables into words. But it is true also of a research scientist refining his or her understanding of how chemical compounds interact or a geographer examining patterns of settlement or migration.

In many ways, too sharp a distinction between propositional and procedural knowledge is unhelpful. My builder could not have mixed the concrete properly without propositional knowledge of how much sand, cement and water to use. And it would be little help to know what bricks were best if he did not know how to lay them correctly. A child learning to read requires factual knowledge as well as the skills to apply this (and much more besides); and doing a handstand is a skill which involves, and is enhanced by, some factual, theoretical knowledge. However, an emphasis on content and on tests tends to privilege propositional over procedural knowledge.

Too great an emphasis on propositional knowledge tends to encourage:

- children to see knowledge as something 'out there' to be gathered and hoarded;
- educators, especially teachers working with large groups, to adopt a transmission style, where the adult speaks, usually, or demonstrates and the child listens or watches, passively.

Too great emphasis on procedural knowledge tends to encourage:

- children to try to apply skills without there being a realistic chance of success;
- educators to leave children to explore, and experiment, without the tools or support necessary to enhance their conceptual understanding.

The TLRP (2006) principles emphasise learners building on their prior experience and the need for *activities, cultures and structures of intellectual, social and emotional support.* Factual information, on its own, is of little use till applied. Skills are rarely useful unless based on propositional knowledge. So 'skills' and 'content' need to be mutually supportive. We all need our learning to have a secure base, but to be able to move progressively away from it and to cope with new challenges and uncertainty. In Salmon's (1995, page 22) words, *learning is not a matter of acquiring 'nuggets of truth', a treasure-house of human certainties. In learning, so far from achieving final answers, we find instead new questions, the need to try things further.*

The TLRP principles affirm that effective pedagogy *engages with valued forms of knowledge,* going on to mention big ideas, skills and processes, modes of discourse, ways of thinking and practising, and attitudes and relationships. Think back to my builder and which aspects of his knowledge were most valuable. Yet, society values intellectual and analytical reasoning over practical activity, in terms of status and salary; and schools give a higher priority to literacy and numeracy than design or practical skills, both in the time allocated and in what counts for success.

Children soon learn that some types of knowledge and ways of learning matter, in school, more than others. For example, the prior experience which some children bring, of reading books or visiting museums, is usually valued more than those whose experience is of going fishing with their dad or playing football in the park. And Anning (cited in Willan et al., 2007, page 138) writes that children:

 start understanding imagery and learn to express ideas in graphical form in their pre-school years. Yet, as soon as they get to school, the primary means of communication gets narrowed down to writing and listening. These are the only skills that are valued, and drawing quickly becomes marginalised.

How some types of knowledge are privileged over others has considerable consequences in how children are engaged and motivated, discussed further in Chapter 6. Think for instance of the six-year-old who, apparently, could not add simple numbers, but was perfectly capable of measuring the correct amounts of feed for her pigeons and calculating when their cages needed cleaning or eggs would incubate. A great deal of learning – often that which most motivates children – takes place outside school. One Monday, two ten-year-old girls said to me that they had won a medal for disco dancing over the weekend. They were quite good at PE, but I had no idea that they spent much of their leisure time on this. When they agreed to show the class, we all saw that it was fantastic – athletic, graceful, energetic, co-operative; an example of the TLRP's principle of adults recognising the significance of informal learning. A more sobering example relates to a quiet, rather unassuming boy, in the school where I was head. He behaved well, but did not stand out as gifted or talented in any particular way. About seven years later, he had signed as a professional footballer and was transferred subsequently to play in the Premier League; an example of how children may have abilities, and passions, of which we know little until we start to look.

Much of my builder's knowledge came through practical, rather than, book learning. The focus of the curriculum, or the sorts of abilities which adults praise, give a message, however explicit or subtle, about which types of learning – and too often people – are most valued. Worryingly, adults often associate a wider range of experience with greater intelligence and as Resnick (1999, page 39) argues, *students who, over an extended period of time are treated as if they are intelligent, actually become more so. If they are taught demanding content and find connections…they learn more and learn more quickly. They [come to] think of themselves as learners. They are [better] able to bounce back in the face of short-term failures.* So, educators' views of what sorts of knowledge matter most is linked to their perceptions of intelligence and potential; and adult expectations exert a powerful influence on children's view of themselves and what they aspire to.

Key ideas: **Intelligence and ability**

What are your assumptions about intelligence and ability?

We all – educators, parents, children – have theories about intelligence and ability. Talking about children being 'bright', 'slow learners' or 'Level 2' is based on often-implicit assumptions. For example, intelligence may be seen as:

- inherent and fixed or emergent and malleable (changeable);
- measurable so as to predict future achievement accurately or fluid and not open to useful or equitable measurement;
- relating only to particular areas of learning, or transferable between these.

Many people link intelligence primarily with IQ tests based on linguistic and mathematical ability. These were devised in the first half of the twentieth century and used to select those regarded as suitable for particular types of education, including grammar schools and setting by ability. This is based on the assumption that such tests can predict individuals' potential with a good degree of accuracy, with intelligence seen as inherent, measurable and mostly unchanging. A concern with the validity of this and in particular the consequences of a fixed view of intelligence led researchers more recently to see intelligence as more fluid and changeable, covering a wider range of abilities and less open to accurate measurement (as an indicator of potential). The debate about the idea of 'gifted and talented' helps to illustrate these.

Critical thinking exercise 2: how do you understand the term 'gifted and talented'?

You may be expected to identify children who are gifted and talented. Often, this is assumed to be relatively straightforward, both practically and morally. So, although definitions are contested, those scoring highest on tests of reading and

/continued

Critical thinking exercise 2 – continued

maths are often identified as 'gifted'. 'Talented' is often seen to refer to those with special aptitude, skill or potential in the expressive arts (music and art) or in sport. Those who are gifted or talented are often offered a different range of activities and challenges, either within the class or with extracurricular activities; and may also be encouraged to attend other activities outside school time, often with those from other schools.

A **Identify** the assumptions of this approach and see if you wish to **challenge** any.

B **Consider** the possible advantages and disadvantages of identifying those who are gifted and talented.

C **Articulate** to what extent you see intelligence as fixed or malleable.

Comment

'Gifted and talented' has been understood in three main ways (or paradigms) (see Eyre, 2009), namely:

- the unique;
- the cohort;
- the human capital (often called the 'English model').

In brief, the first considers giftedness as a quality of a few, very special individuals. The second seeks to identify, and make a different type of provision for, a particular group deemed more gifted than the rest of the cohort, usually in one area of learning. The third is more concerned with providing opportunities for all to develop their gifts and talents, across a broad spectrum.

The unique paradigm is less relevant in this context because it refers to provision for an individual rather than a large group. The cohort paradigm is based on giftedness being identifiable, often through psychometric tests, with relatively accurate prediction of future success. The emphasis is usually, with older students, on mathematics, science and to a lesser extent linguistic skills. As such, it tends to see intelligence as inherent and domain-specific and to assume that special provision is necessary. While a strong argument can be made for provision to be adapted depending on children's interests and aptitudes, criticisms of this approach include:

- the difficulty of knowing whether the cohort selected is the 'right one';
- potential dangers of labelling some children as more gifted than their peers;
- whether additional provision is suitable only for that cohort, or a similar approach would benefit all (or most) children.

Lohman and Korb (2006) argue against the commonly held view that a child considered gifted at six would still be considered so at 16, giving examples of talented adults who were unexceptional as children and of children identified as gifted but not fulfilling what was expected. Moreover, there has been growing concern that children from affluent and white families are significantly more likely than others to be chosen as gifted than those from poorer or ethnic minority backgrounds. This raises questions about both the efficacy and the equity of identifying children as gifted to make separate provision for them, the more so the younger the children are. Although primary schools are often encouraged to identify gifted and talented children, most educators are cautious about this until children are at least seven years old. While some children may find it demoralising to be identified in one school as gifted or talented, but told otherwise in a different context, most of those selected for additional provision benefit. This may be unsurprising, but possibly more so is that most children benefit from the approaches which enhance the learning of gifted children. These include challenge and high expectations, with Eyre (2010, pages 398–399) suggesting a combination of breadth, depth and pace (though, in my view, one must be careful about too much pace).

The English model (see Eyre, 2010) tends to be based on a broader and more fluid view of giftedness, taking more account of less 'academic' domains such as the arts, sport or chess, and of attitudes and attributes such as task commitment, motivation and resilience. Its emphasis is less on current attainment and more on providing a wide range of opportunities to help all children discover and build on their gifts and talents. As such, it focuses more on improving ordinary teaching than on additional provision. Among the criticisms of this approach are that:

- in suggesting that most children have gifts and talents, little or no specific provision may be made for those who have extraordinary ability or potential, especially in one particular area of learning;
- without a high level of teacher expertise, such children's abilities will remain undeveloped and their interest and motivation may diminish.

What do these views indicate about ability, potential and intelligence?

The cohort paradigm and the English model vary not only in the practical implications but in the questions asked, and assumptions made, about children and intelligence and ability. For example, are gifted and talented children a breed apart or do all, or most, children have attributes of giftedness to be discovered and nurtured? Is giftedness largely an inherent and fixed quality or more like one learned and developed through the opportunities available and accessed?

Dweck (1999) describes two main views of intelligence, that it is:
- largely inherent and unchanging;
- to a greater extent learned, and multifaceted.

She calls the former the fixed, and the latter the growth, mindset of intelligence. Simon (see Chitty, 2010, page 257) referred to the 'educability' of all children, and Hart et al. (2004) make a similar distinction in encouraging us to think of children's 'transformability' rather than 'ability'. Chapter 3 alluded to the debate about genetic factors and temperament and what is learned. However, given the dynamic interaction of nature and nurture, inherited aspects can be enhanced by providing the best learning environment, though identifying what this involves will always be a matter of debate and depend on often-conflicting aims.

Many school policies and mission statements refer to children fulfilling their potential, or some similar phrase. Yet, we all have the potential to do what is wrong or undesirable as well as what is worthwhile or fulfilling. Therefore, even such an apparently simple idea prompts one to ask what sorts of potential we wish to realise, bringing us back to the aims of education. While it is absurd to suggest that anyone can achieve anything they want, we can all achieve more, in some respects, than we recognise, given the right support. Unless educators reflect, at least to some extent, the growth mindset of intelligence, their expectations will be set too low. As we shall see, low expectations are all too often self-fulfilling, which matters especially for those children whose cultural or family background is one of low aspiration.

Gardner (1993) suggests thinking of different types of intelligence, originally proposing:

- linguistic;
- logical-mathematical;
- musical;
- bodily-kinaesthetic;
- spatial;
- interpersonal;
- intrapersonal.

This approach is often referred to as 'multiple intelligences'. While one can argue about the exact number of intelligences, the idea of multiple intelligences prompts us to think about learners and learning differently, to rethink what intelligence consists of and what qualities we value, challenging the view that this is primarily about linguistic and mathematical ability. So far, we have looked mainly at knowledge 'that' and 'how'. However, my builder did not just build, but assessed and questioned, delegated and advised. He demonstrated technical skill and expertise, but these were in domains which included the mathematical, bodily-kinaesthetic and spatial. In particular, he showed intrapersonal qualities, such as perseverance and resourcefulness, and interpersonal ones, such as awareness of other people's feelings and negotiation. These are associated with another sort of intelligence, 'emotional intelligence'. This is more like knowledge 'of' – of ourselves, of other people and of the world around. Such knowledge matters especially for young children because they are still at an early stage of understanding themselves and other people.

Key idea: **Emotional intelligence**

What does emotional intelligence involve?

The terms 'emotional intelligence' (EI) and 'emotional literacy', associated especially with Goleman (1996), have gained considerable credence in recent years, notably in schools through the SEAL (Social and Emotional Aspects of Learning) programme and materials. As Claxton (2005, page 6) indicates, *the strong appeal of concepts like 'Emotional Intelligence' reflects a shift in social attitudes generally, as well as in education,* moving away from the previously held idea that abstract and rational thought was the epitome of intelligence. The recent focus on bullying, self-esteem, anger management and personal, social and health education (PSHE) as a separate subject are all manifestations of a greater emphasis on the affective, rather than cognitive, aspects of learning.

Critical thinking exercise 3: emotional intelligence

[The SEAL materials] will be used by schools…who know that the factors holding back learning in their setting include children's difficulties in understanding and managing their feelings, working co-operatively in groups, motivating themselves and demonstrating resilience in the face of setbacks.

(DfES, 2005a, page 1)

A **Articulate** what you understand by emotional intelligence and what you would add to the list above.

B **Illustrate** how you as an educator would help to build up EI with:
- four- and five-year-olds
- ten- and eleven-year-olds

Give examples of the types of activities and responses which help to do this.

C **Consider** whether there are any dangers in focusing on emotional intelligence directly.

Comment

As Claxton (2005, pages 8–9) indicates, Goleman initially presented EI as *comprising knowing one's emotions, managing one's emotions, motivating oneself, recognising emotions in others and handling relationships skilfully,* but with the concept later expanded to include (amongst many other things) self-confidence, initiative, optimism, leadership. In other words, just about everything *except the traditional educational concerns of literacy, numeracy, analytical thinking and knowledge about the world.* While some see 'emotional literacy' as different (and more robust), there seems little to distinguish this from EI. So, although exactly what is meant by EI is often vague, it is assumed to be a good thing, valuing qualities to do with regulation of emotion, social interaction and relationships.

One distinction, often overlooked, is between ends and means – what one wants to achieve and how to do so. It would be hard to argue against the value of people – adults or children – becoming more able to:

- understand their own and other people's emotions;
- regulate their own responses;
- form appropriate relationships.

Most people probably think that feeling good about oneself and being positive are worthwhile ends. However, how best to achieve these – and whether this is best done by direct teaching – is more contestable.

Young children seem to feel emotion more intensely than adults and find it harder to regulate their emotions and responses. They express joy and anxiety, pleasure and anger with less inhibition. So, a young child may become absorbed in an enjoyable activity in a way which adults rarely achieve, or have a very short attention span in the face of frustration. Dowling (2010, pages 36–9) emphasises that the first six or seven years are critical for the development of social skills. She discusses how children's ability to understand their own emotions and interpret other people's responses and emotional state varies, develops only gradually and depends heavily on familiarity and relationships. How we express our emotions is learned both through cultural norms and more explicit expectations. For example, children from certain cultures learn to show as little emotional response as possible; and what may be interpreted as being inquisitive in one context may be seen as being cheeky in another.

How best can emotional intelligence be nurtured?

Among activities commonly used to teach EI are:

- circle time in which children are expected to listen, and respond to, other people in particular ways and articulate how they feel;
- explicit lessons on social, emotional and behavioural skills;
- training in mediation and conflict-resolution skills;
- techniques such as calming and stilling.

The SEAL and other materials offer advice especially on the first two of these.

Many of these activities, done well, are helpful, For example, specific training in mediation and conflict resolution may help to empower children, especially in Key Stage 2. Children become calmer when they have the chance to be still, and experience silence, though my own preference is more on providing opportunities for this than adopting a specific set of techniques. Emotions, and how they affect behaviour, can be explored, though a variety of approaches such as using puppets and playing games works best, especially with young children, in part because these work in indirect, 'unpreachy' ways.

However, this section offers some cautionary words about how activities to promote EI are done and making them age-appropriate. For example, circle time may help young children to take turns, but does not encourage interaction or dialogue if a child has to wait for several others to speak before responding. Activities associated with EI tend to entail repeated praise and reaffirmation by the adult, both to encourage 'appropriate behaviour' and build self-esteem. While circle time may help children to regulate their emotions, expecting them always to be 'positive' or indeed happy when they are not can result in the suppression of emotion. So children may learn that anger and jealousy, for example, which are both involuntary and, in many contexts, appropriate are negative, rather than how to process such emotions and act appropriately.

While such approaches may provide simple strategies which many children find helpful, especially at first, more complex situations and emotions require more nuanced strategies. What will help a ten-year-old may differ from what a seven- or a four-year old needs, though the principles may be similar. This involves children not just following a formula which they have been taught, but exercising judgement about which parts of which strategies to adopt. When such programmes are taught well, this exercise of judgement is encouraged from the start.

Explicit teaching of specific skills related to EI works best when related to the children's own concerns, rather than following a set script. They become very skilled at 'talking the talk', but not necessarily adopting the strategies they have been taught. Sometimes, this is because a lack of experience of what is appropriate or an inability to regulate their emotions in that context. However, I recall an incident one afternoon when a group of mostly well-behaved nine-year-olds had been out that morning to demonstrate their interpersonal skills and strategies to a group of teachers. I happened to see one girl, when provoked, checking (unsuccessfully) that she was unobserved and quite viciously kicking the other child's ankle. When challenged, she looked daggers at me, clearly thinking that her actions, if not seen, bore no relationship to what she had, no doubt eloquently, said that morning.

Ecclestone and Hayes (2009) provide a wider-ranging critique of methods of teaching EI, arguing that an emphasis on feelings rather than knowledge creates a belief – usually unconsciously – that everyone is vulnerable and needs support. They write (page 145): *in primary schools, the development of emotional literacy and the 'skills' associated with emotional well-being begins children's preoccupation with themselves, introduces the idea that life makes us vulnerable and offer prescriptive rituals, scripts and appropriate ways of behaving emotionally.* They see this as discouraging children from engaging with the complexity and ambiguity of emotional responses and how these are affected by the child's specific circumstances and learning to cope with difficulty. As we shall see, much of our most profound learning occurs indirectly, in the case of EI through lived experience and relationships; and, in terms of school, through activities such as drama and literature, and situations such as group work and dialogue.

So, children need to recognise their own emotions, regulate their responses and understand other people's emotional state, both to develop their ability to behave appropriately according to the situation and to enable other sorts of learning. However, an uncritical use of some activities runs the risk of promoting particular types of response, of being simplistic especially for older children in primary schools and of creating a sense of vulnerability.

Key ideas: **Habituation and metacognition**

What does deep learning entail?

Perkins (cited in Gallagher, 2009, pages 123–124) distinguishes between three sorts of intelligence:

- neural – speed and precision of information processing;
- experiential – through extended experience, more like expertise;
- reflective – through metacognition and self-regulation.

The first of these reflects the value of instant recall of propositional knowledge through activities such as mental mathematics. This is useful as a tool, though not enough in itself. I recall Steven as a six-year-old who had a remarkable ability to 'do sums' in his head including hundreds, tens and units – accurately and instantly. I encouraged him to say how he did this, but he could (or at least would) not. With more complex problem-solving, he was lost. Experiential intelligence relates more to the application of skills and problem-solving, requiring resourcefulness and creativity, attributes demonstrated by my builder. In exploring what is meant by deep learning, this section considers both reflective intelligence and less deliberate and conscious processes.

Critical thinking exercise 4: metacognition and higher-order thinking

Metacognition is a general term which refers to a second-order form of thinking; thinking about learning. It includes a variety of self-awareness processes to help plan, process, monitor, orchestrate, and control one's own learning… using particular strategies which hinge on self-questioning… to get the purpose of learning clear, searching for connections and conflicts with what is already known and judging whether understanding of the material is sufficient for the task.

(Gipps and MacGilchrist, 1999, page 48)

/continued

Critical thinking exercise 4 – continued

A **Consider** the benefits and disadvantages of rote learning, encouraging immediate responses.

B **Identify** what the quotation above might mean in practice for:

- a ten-year-old tennis player trying to improve her serve;
- a group of seven-year-olds making a pendulum;
- a four-year-old looking at a picture book with a nursery nurse.

C **Discuss** to what extent learning processes are always conscious and deliberate.

Comment

Rote learning can help provide immediate responses and embed habits. This is useful in many respects, but too much reliance on these stunts creativity and independence. It is tempting to imagine that repetition is necessarily a good way of developing expertise. Studies of high-performing athletes or musicians suggest that thousands of repetitions are required to make good habits 'second nature'. In the old saying, practice makes perfect. However, this is not so, if one practises the wrong thing. For example, practising forming letters or holding the pencil incorrectly tends to embed a bad habit. It is all too easy for children – or adults – to become habituated to a passive approach to learning through low-level activities; or to reliance on rewards to provide motivation. In contrast, deep learning involves developing good, not mindless, habits.

Often when trying to perform a complex skill such as playing tennis, it helps to remind oneself of good habits to remember and bad ones to avoid. This enables a more considered approach, less open to excitement or frustration. So the ten-year-old may tell herself to keep her body well balanced when serving. One seven-year-old may say to others in the group that counting the number of swings in a minute helps know how fast a pendulum swings. And a four-year-old may point to, or say out loud, the changes in *The Very Hungry Caterpillar* while reading the book, or listening to it being read. All of these are, in different ways, types of metacognition, where learning is reflected on, with the processes involved articulated and so made more available to conscious choice. Metacognition is usually thought of in individual terms, where one reminds, or 'has a conversation with', oneself of strategies to adopt or errors to avoid. Yet, one key role that an adult can play is to provide the child with metacognitive 'prompts' to help him regulate his anxieties and remember alternative strategies; and one great benefit of group work is that children are not left to themselves to struggle alone with the challenges of learning.

Metacognition is an idea closely associated, and often interchangeable, with those such as 'higher-order thinking skills' and 'learning about learning.' The idea of higher-order thinking skills is associated with Bloom (1956), who emphasised that learning involves three domains: cognitive (knowledge), affective (attitude) and psychomotor (skills), a distinction still evident in the QTS Standards. Bloom broke 'thinking skills' into six areas – knowledge acquisition, comprehension, application, analysis, synthesis and evaluation. The last three, especially, are often referred to as higher-order thinking skills. Passey (no date, page 7) explains the difference between cognitive and metacognitive strategies as shown in Table 3.

Table 3

	Cognitive (what to do/undertake a task)	Metacognitive (how to approach a task, possible processes and strategies)
Knowledge acquisition	Can read a text to find specific details	Knows ways for finding which texts might contain specific details
Comprehension	Can answer questions about a document	Knows how to pick out key features and how to identify what is not known
Application	Can use information/techniques in variety of situations	Knows which techniques to use to recall information/skills to use
Analysis	Can ask questions about information and compare and contrast with existing knowledge	Knows which techniques to use when questions are asked of data
Synthesis	Can assemble information from various sources and create a coherent outcome	Knows a range of techniques to create coherent outcomes when various sources of information are used
Evaluation	Can make decisions about information/ideas using specific criteria	Knows which techniques enable evaluation to be reasonable and reliable

Higher-order thinking and metacognition require tasks and activities which are cognitively demanding, rather than constant repetition of low-level tasks – although, of course, there is a place for reinforcement of good habits. For example, children who are finding it difficult to read benefit from discussing character and plot as well as decoding text. Developing greater conceptual awareness in mathematics is more likely when children explore alternative strategies and solve, and to set their own, problems than doing more sums or the same operations with larger numbers. Children learning English as an additional language need to hear (with appropriate support) English used in the more sophisticated ways that native speakers use it, involving different nuances of speech and inference – and so gradually learn to use English confidently in such ways.

Although surface learning and low-level tasks are easier for both the child and the adult, most children benefit from developing metacognitive strategies, so that they know about, and are in more control of, their own learning, though they may need support to do so. You may think that very young children, or some of those with special educational needs, will find metacognition difficult or impossible. Very young children are caught up in their immediate experience and find self-regulation difficult. And (some) children with special needs may find higher-order thinking hard. However, pedagogy is a gradual, long-term process intended to develop expertise and a wider repertoire of skills and approaches. And this can start from an early age, for example by encouraging very young children to think about other people's feelings and ideas and praising them when they do; or by asking why Cinderella's sisters were so unkind to her or how we can tell where, and why, a shadow forms.

The TLRP suggests that *learning processes… do not fundamentally change as children become adults.* A similar view is set out in the Cambridge Primary Review (summary, page 13) *babies and young children learn, think and reason in all the same ways as adults – what they lack is the experience to make sense of what they find.* I'm not so sure because, although many processes are similar, one of Vygotsky's key ideas was that one's conceptual structure – the tools for thought – is what enables higher-order thinking. Metacognition involves learners taking (at least some) control of how they learn and deliberately and consciously adapting their approach. As Sternberg (2004, page 609) writes, *intelligent children know their own strengths and weaknesses and find ways to capitalise on their strengths and either to compensate for or correct their weaknesses.* While metacognition is one vital element in tackling complex problems successfully, learning involves intuition and imagination, including processes which are often unintended and unconscious.

Is all learning conscious?

Donaldson (1992, page 20) writes *some kinds of knowledge are in the light of full awareness. Others are in the shadows, on the edge of the bright circle. Still others are in the darkness beyond.* Claxton (1997, page 2) calls 'conscious, deliberate, purposeful' learning 'd-mode thinking' (where 'd' stands for deliberation). This involves trying consciously to use existing knowledge to solve a problem already defined as a problem; for example, sounding out a word phonetically or deciding which instruments to use in playing a tune. He contrasts this with instantaneous, 'instinctive' reactions and with another mental register that is *less purposeful and clear-cut, more playful, leisurely or dreamy.* Deep learning does not just involve conscious effort, important though this is. Instantaneous reactions happen too fast for conscious thought, including instinctive ones such as the anxiety prompted by chemical releases in the event of danger and learned responses such as those of an expert reader or musician. As adults, we rely (too) heavily on d-mode and assume, often implicitly, but mistakenly, that this is the best, or indeed, the only approach for young children.

Claxton (1997) describes 'slow ways of knowing' in which the brain discovers patterns and develops responses, often without conscious thought, involving intuition and imagination as well as cognition. Conscious thought will often help (and sometimes hinder) this process, by introducing an element of deliberation, as happens in self-regulation and metacognition. Examples include where an idea from a picture or a story is allowed to resonate, rather than being subjected to immediate scrutiny, enabling connections and associations to be made. Often, deep learning occurs when we do not immediately know the answer to a particular question so that less deliberate ways of understanding and representing experience are used. Enactive and iconic representation and response seem at times to be able bypass conscious processes, as when a child learns to use a saw by imitation or to appreciate an artist's intentions. Too much effort, or interference, may block the search for meaning. For the unconscious to be allowed to work requires space and time with the conscious not too busy, calling for opportunities for thought, reflection and silence, as well input, immediate response and words. So, an appropriate environment for learning must involve opportunities for both.

Conclusion

This chapter has explored the complexity of apparently simple terms like intelligence and ability. The critical thinking exercises will have helped you to:

- ◉ **compare** different types of knowledge and which are most valued in society and schools;
- ◉ **consider** intelligence as fluid and multifaceted, based on a 'growth mindset', and not just related to linguistic and mathematical reasoning;
- ◉ **explore** what emotional intelligence means and how best to develop it;
- ◉ **identify** what deep learning entails and how to enable this.

In Chapter 5, we explore the attributes of successful learners and some of the barriers which make this difficult for many children.

Further Reading

Claxton, G (1997) *Hare Brain, Tortoise Mind – Why intelligence increases when you think less.* London: Fourth Estate
An accessible book which challenges the view that learning is all about pace, challenge and conscious intention.

Claxton, G (2005) *An Intelligent Look at Emotional Intelligence.* London: Association of Teachers and Lecturers
A pamphlet which summarises the dangers of an over-simple view of EI in an accessible and constructive way.

Donaldson, M (1992) *Human Minds – An exploration.* London: Allen Lane
A deceptively simple but profound discussion of the complexity of the human mind.

Eyre, D (2010) Gifted and Talented. pages 388–401 of Arthur, J and Cremin, T (eds) *Learning to Teach in the Primary School* (2nd edition). Abingdon: Routledge
A straightforward discussion of identification of, and provision for, gifted and talented children, including practical strategies.

Gardner, H (1993) *Frames of Mind: The Theory of Multiple Intelligences.* London, Fontana
A book which will make you think quite differently about intelligence.

Identifying the attributes of, and barriers to, successful learning

---

Chapter Focus

The critical thinking exercises in this chapter focus on:

- **identifying** the attributes of successful learners;
- **discussing** self-concept and why this affects how children learn;
- **considering** the factors which affect how children are motivated and engage with learning;
- **analysing** why the 'hidden curriculum' matters so much.

The key ideas discussed are: **creativity, resilience, self-concept, cultural capital, the hidden curriculum**

This chapter is particularly relevant to QTS Standards: **1**, **2**, **8**, **10**, **18**, **26 b**, **29** and to Knowledge and Understanding and reflection (*Education Studies*) and Subject knowledge and Subject skills (*Early Childhood Studies*)

Introduction

This chapter discusses first, the attributes, or qualities, associated with successful learners; and then self-concept to understand why children's responses to the same experience vary so much. The third critical thinking exercise explores how the factors in children's background affect how they engage with school learning; and the fourth the often hidden assumptions of schools. This provides the basis of Chapters 6, 7 and 8, which discuss learning environments, the activities and experience which provide breadth and balance and how adults can best support successful learning; and the later chapters' argument that educators must exercise professional judgement, since no 'one-size-fits-all' approach is appropriate for every individual or class.

CASE STUDY

Anwar's father came in to complain that his eight-year-old son who was not yet a confident speaker of English kept opening and shutting the fridge door and talking to himself. Anwar had said that his teacher had told him to. Somewhat

/continued

CASE STUDY continued

puzzled, I promised to investigate. It turned out that the teacher had talked about pushing and pulling, words the meaning of which Anwar was unsure about. So when he went home, he practised his pushing and pulling and talked himself through the process as he did so. He was determined to succeed at this unusual, self-initiated type of homework.

Anwar demonstrated some attributes of a good learner. To identify these, try to recall how you learned a specific physical skill (such as handwriting or riding a bicycle) that you found difficult when you were young, thinking about how you felt and what helped.

This exercise is more difficult than it seems – and far harder when applied to a more complex set of skills such as learning a new language or conducting a scientific experiment. You may not know quite what is involved. However, there were probably elements of how you felt or did, such as:

• being motivated to learn this skill or activity;
• rehearsing, in a situation where experiment is possible and failure not too costly;
• practising, initially supported, and then more independently and in other contexts;
• consciously theorising how to do the activity.

Consider also what someone else did, such as:

• giving instructions, including words and gestures;
• demonstrating the skill;
• providing feedback, whether in the form of encouragement, or correction of errors.

Verbal instructions probably helped, though a demonstration may have been more useful. However, the value of this and of any feedback is likely to have depended on what this was like and whether it empowered you or not. Without motivation, or if you were fearful or overanxious, you probably would not have persisted. Depending on the complexity of the task, the chance to rehearse or practise without the pressure to perform, initially tentatively, then with greater confidence, reflects the need for emotional security and a gradual move towards independence, as Anwar's story indicates. Further practice, maybe with more support and feedback, was almost certainly needed to build confidence and embed the skill. Although conscious theorising, for instance in recalling particular sub-skills or reminding oneself of what to do, or to avoid, may have helped, expertise is achieved, mostly without conscious thought, so that recourse to such theorising becomes necessary only at times of uncertainty. So, learning involves many different processes, individual and social, physical and cognitive. The relative importance of these depends on the task, the context, the support available and, especially, what the learner brings. Learning is like a structure built up of interlocking pieces, where each element, ideally, supports others.

Key ideas: **Creativity and resilience**

What are the attributes of successful learners?

The government's remit to the Rose Review (DCSF, 2009, page 142) stated that the proposals *must provide all pupils with a broad and balanced entitlement to learning which encourages creativity and inspires in them a commitment to learning that will last a lifetime.* The Early Years Foundation Stage (EYFS) includes the sentence: *Every child is a competent learner from birth who can be resilient, capable, confident and self-assured.* It would seem strange not to wish to equip children with the tools to enable them to be lifelong learners and not to build on the attributes which children have from birth.

Dweck (1999, page 1) writes that *the hallmark of successful individuals is that they love learning, they seek challenges, they value effort and they persist in the face of obstacles.* She describes those who show these qualities as having a 'mastery-oriented' approach, associating this with a growth mindset of intelligence. She contrasts this with 'learned helplessness', which leads to children seeing obstacles as a threat, prompting self-doubt and withdrawal, rather than a natural part of learning. Personally, I dislike the term mastery-orientation and prefer 'attributes of successful learners' because this helps identify particular qualities and approaches to be encouraged.

Critical thinking exercise 1: the attributes of successful learners

A **Consider** whether, and in what sense, you think children can be creative or original. To do this, **imagine** one situation or activity where a child is being creative and one activity where a group is being creative. Think about the features of what distinguishes this from other sorts of activity.

B Try to **identify** and **illustrate** the attributes of successful learners. It may help to **consider** what you demonstrate (or otherwise) when faced with an unfamiliar task.

C **Articulate** how each of the four attributes identified in the EYFS – being resilient, capable, confident and self-assured – contribute to successful learning. For example, why is resilience important? And why does confidence matter?

Comment

All Our Futures, often called the Robinson Report, provides a helpful definition of creativity as *imaginative activity fashioned so as to produce outcomes that are both original and of value* (NACCCE, 1999, page 29). However, this, in my view, misses out one important aspect of most creative activity – that the exact outcome changes between the planning and the performance stages. A choreographer is initially uncertain quite how the dance will turn out. A website designer will experiment with the structure and the look of the site. Writers, starting out, are unsure what the final text will look like. Creativity involves imagining possible outcomes, without this being too definite at the outset.

To think in what sense young children can be original, consider Robinson's (NACCCE, 1999, page 30) distinction between *historic, relative* and *individual* originality. The first is confined to a few geniuses. Relative originality occurs when a child takes an approach or arrives at an outcome which is original compared with other children's. Individual originality relates to the child's previous work, so that a child trying out unfamiliar ways of applying paint or discovering a mathematical pattern new to him or herself can be seen as original. Relative and individual originality roughly correspond with what Craft (Craft et al., 2001, pages 45–62, and 2009) calls 'little c creativity', with 'big C' creativity reserved for historic originality. So young children can be creative in making a discovery original to themselves – but this requires an active and divergent approach, not just following someone else's ideas. To achieve a successful outcome requires knowledge and skills, but imagination and divergent thinking come first. This involves some risk and part of adults' role is to ensure that children can cope with the consequences of possible failure. Otherwise, they, especially those who lack resilience, will be discouraged from trying again.

Since each child constructs and creates the most important forms of knowledge anew, creativity and imagination are not optional extras, but central to how we learn and perceive ourselves. Eaude (2009a) discusses the close link between creativity and SMSC. Young children often show a much greater capacity for divergence than adults because they have fewer inhibitions and cross boundaries more easily. But they find it harder to converge on a successful outcome, because of inexperience or lack of specific skills. However, adults underestimate young children's scope for creativity and can develop it by providing activities and expecting outcomes that are challenging and interesting.

Claxton (2002), coining the term 'learnacy' to describe what is involved in 'learning-to-learn', highlights what he calls the 4Rs, which are:

- resilience;
- resourcefulness;
- reflectiveness;
- reciprocity.

Engagement is more likely when children enjoy what they are doing, especially when they have set their own challenges. However, learning usually involves challenge and difficulties, requiring determination and persistence. For example, planning how to run a stall at the school fete or putting together a presentation is not easy though it may be satisfying; and rehearsing the Christmas play or struggling to complete a model requires persistence but the finished product makes it worthwhile. So, resilience – being able to persist in the face of confusion, frustration and uncertainty – is one key attribute of successful learning.

Resourcefulness entails drawing on a wide range of strategies and sources of information, rather than relying on only a limited repertoire. So, imagining different approaches and solutions to a problem, trusting (but testing out) one's ideas and hunches and borrowing and adapting other people's are all attributes of a good learner. These require the confidence to take risks and make, but learn from, mistakes – a confidence dependent on how the learner feels, the nature of the activity and the context. For me, the prospect of singing in public immediately comes to mind. My identity-as-a-singer is fragile, disabling what I know consciously, that I must breathe deeply and not tighten up. Yet, even when my self-concept is strong, for instance teaching a familiar class in a subject where I am confident, this can be rapidly undermined by one child's response or an inspector watching.

Reflectiveness implies giving thought to how to approach a task, being aware of one's own capabilities and strengths, stepping back and adapting new strategies, and is closely associated with metacognition. This usually requires time and space in which to dwell on alternative possibilities, rather than an approach which is not too focused on the immediate or rapid results.

Chapter 3 suggested that reciprocity is essential in how very young children learn to understand themselves, how they and other people relate to each other, and to talk. Unless children recognise, and empathise with, other people's feelings and responses and learn to co-operate and compromise, they will be isolated from one of the most basic sources of learning – other people.

Claxton's list is by no means exclusive. In Eaude (2008, page 63), I list others, suggesting that many, including the 4Rs and sociability, are *protective*, while others such as curiosity or playfulness, imagination and creativity are *transformational*, with attributes such as thoughtfulness, insight and enthusiasm helping both to protect and to transform. These are the building blocks of successful learning.

The EYFS statement that every child from birth can be resilient, capable, confident and self-assured highlights attributes that very young children can demonstrate. In the right context, tiny children show great resilience and capability, for instance solving a (self-set) challenge, from the hugely demanding tasks of learning to walk and to talk to smaller ones like balancing on a narrow plank or using new words in telling a story. And they can be confident and self-assured, as when a bilingual child switches between languages, apparently without effort, depending on who they are talking to or when. Of course, children need (the right sort of) help and support. However, too often adults see young children as incapable and discourage them from building on their existing strengths.

Developing the attributes of successful learners requires practice and habituation. Claxton uses the metaphor of the 4Rs as being like muscles. They are strengthened by gentle but repeated stretching, rather than violent jerks. They may ache for a while after use, but soon recover, but they become slack or atrophy if not used regularly. No one becomes resilient or resourceful overnight. We learn to be resilient by overcoming challenges, to be resourceful by adopting different approaches, to be reflective by regularly slowing down, and stepping back, to be reciprocal by interacting with other people. One key aspect of the educator's role is constantly to reinforce the attributes of successful learners. Very often, as we shall see, this involves little, everyday actions, so that children become habituated, over time, to be:

- responsible, by taking responsibility;
- resilient, by overcoming challenges;
- creative, by practising originality;
- confident, by believing in themselves.

Key idea: **Self-concept**

How is self-concept developed?

Chapter 4 suggested that the search for identity is central to spiritual and cultural development. This is associated especially with adolescence, largely because it is most intense then and affects those involved and others adults, such as parents/carers and teachers, most obtrusively. However, in Chapter 3, we saw how, from the start, young children are active makers of meaning and develop internal working models. These remain important as children seek to answer questions such as 'who am I?' and 'where do I fit in?', and to feel safe, reflecting a common need for security and belonging.

Critical thinking exercise 2: multiple identities

Imagine that you are in each of four different situations: a disco, a family gathering, an unfamiliar place of worship and the room in your house where you feel most comfortable.

A **Identify** your feelings and what this tells us about your identity, especially whether it is always the same or varies.

B **Consider** how this is affected by external signs (or markers) of identity, such as a religious symbol or branded clothes.

C Try to **articulate** why identity, especially identity-as-a-learner, matters so much.

Comment

I imagine that your behaviour and feelings in the four situations above vary, for example behaving loudly at the disco and more formally at the family gathering, being unsure in the place of worship and with more confidence where you feel comfortable. We feel and act differently with our parents, at school or on the beach. The context helps to define how one should act; and, in an important sense, how we see ourselves. We each have multiple identities. These may be, for a five-year-old, as a girl, a sister, a daughter, a friend, a Hindu and as a confident speaker in one language but not another and as nervous about being bullied; or for a ten-year-old as a star sportsman, popular with his friends, but less confident in reading and writing or making new friendships.

All people's identities are affected by factors such as gender and ethnicity and where and how one is brought up. Our social, cultural and historical background helps to shape who we become. For some, such as those born into some religious traditions, their identity is defined closely by this. For most, especially in Western countries, a wider and less definite range of influences affect our identity, or identities, and how we see and understand ourselves. As Salmon (1995, page 63) indicates,

 identity … is forged out of interaction with others. Who we are is inextricably bound up with who we are known to be. Children bring to school very particular family identities, identities which facilitate some kinds of learning, but inhibit others. Social relationships with other young people, and participation in school culture, act to produce new dimensions in the sense of self, which frame the meaning of pupils' classroom conduct and closely govern what they may and may not do.

Learning involves from the very beginning making sense of a range of fragmentary, often conflicting, experiences. Therefore, our understanding of ourselves can be seen as a constant search for a coherent personal narrative, discussed in more detail in Eaude (2008, pages 59–61). The story we tell of ourselves both reflects who we are and shapes who we become. A useful way of understanding this is Kelly's idea of 'personal constructs', which is complex but explained accessibly in Salmon (1995). This suggests that how individuals interpret, or make sense, of their experiences depends on a complex web of constructs, each on a spectrum between two opposites. Simple examples are heavy/light, safe/threatening and brave/timid, with many of the most important ones developed before these can be verbalised. Any person or event is understood by 'where they are' in relation to the spectrum of many constructs.

Kelly (1991) believed that each individual's personality is made up of a unique set of constructs. These do not just enable one to describe the world, but to predict, often without conscious thought, what will happen. For example, calling a friend honest both refers to their previous, and predicts their future, actions – and so affects your relationship, and interaction, with them. Or regarding someone as threatening draws on previous occasions when you have felt threatened, or beliefs about who or what may be dangerous. While this is, in part, biological, as a means of defence against what appears to be dangerous, it is also, in part, learned, both from prior experience and one's own culture – whether of the family, the community or more widely.

In Salmon's (1995, page 20) words:

 our personal construct systems define the understanding we each live by. This means that learning is never the acquisition of a single, isolated piece of knowledge. Our ways of seeing things are inextricably intertwined. To alter one assumption means that others, too, are brought into question.

Therefore, any child (or adult) has a fluid identity, a sense of self, though cultural beliefs and prior experience help to shape how we approach, and respond to, new experience. Part of one's identity is one's identity-as-a-learner, or rather identities-as-a-learner. Certain ethnic groups, such as the Chinese, grow up within a culture where hard work is expected. Boys may find it hard to retain, or at least make public, an interest in reading if those in their peer group do not. Similar reasons affect why so many boys give up singing and why football remains so popular; or why girls are often keener on reading than boys and enjoy fashion.

Identity is often signalled by external markers, such as a cross, a headscarf or a uniform. These may indicate a sense of belonging and of pride, especially when associated with a religious tradition or an organisation, such as a football team or the Brownies. However, identity is heavily influenced by the culture of the peer group, especially during, and in the years just before, adolescence. The pressure to belong by wearing the 'right' clothes or liking the latest fashion in music is often very strong. Children's identity easily comes to depend on appearance and brand and so becomes fragile. Not having the newest trainers or mobile phone may seem unimportant to an adult; but can be the cause of misery or bullying for some children. As discussed in Chapter 2, many pressures usually associated with adolescence have increasingly impinged on younger children's identity, through the greater emphasis on consumerism and body image, especially with the pervasive messages of the media. Paradoxically, the search for individual identity often leads towards conformity.

Embarrassment, and the fear of public failure, is a major reason why children (and adults) are reluctant to take the risks which make success likely. One should not underestimate the influence of peer-group pressure, to conform, to belong, both within the classroom and beyond, with this becoming more powerful as children move through Key Stage 2. In Bruner's (1996, page 38) words, *school, more than we have realized, competes with myriad forms of 'anti-school' as a provider of agency, identity and self-esteem – no less at the middle-class suburban mall than on the ghetto streets.*

As Dweck (1999, page xi) writes, *people's beliefs about themselves ... can create different psychological worlds, leading them to think feel and act differently in identical situations.* Self-concept is a major factor in how intelligence is enhanced, knowledge internalised and development encouraged. Think about the implications for you as an educator. You cannot sensibly assume that children will feel or act the same as you or as each other - even if you think that they should or do so. Adults who work with young children have both to understand and work with children's emerging identities and recognise that adults help to shape these by their expectations and responses. Self-concept affects how children remain engaged and motivated. If a child perceives herself as stupid or inadequate, or as successful or resourceful, she is more likely to become so. This involves not just accepting who she is but imagining, and so helping to create, what she might become.

We tend to assume that success leads to greater determination to succeed. However, Dweck writes (1999, page 1) that rather than embolden and energise them, *success in itself does little to boost [students'] desire for challenge or their ability to cope with setbacks... and can have quite the opposite effect*, especially when it makes them afraid of failure. And the expectations of adults, whether parents, or teachers, or others, help to create, to reinforce, and sadly sometimes to undermine, this self-concept. For example, recently, an adult student in her thirties described to me being told at primary school that she was not capable of academic study and should set her sights lower – and how it had taken her twenty years to get over (at least in part) this belief.

Key idea: **Cultural capital**

What external factors affect children's engagement and motivation in school?

Most toddlers have developed many of the attributes of successful learners, at least in areas they know well and where they feel safe. For example, as they play, or listen to a story, they may be inquisitive, creative, resourceful and reflective. However, they are rarely resilient and their level of reciprocity depends on who they are with. They are easily distracted and tied up with their own concerns, except when engaged in interaction or conversation with a trusted adult. So, as educators, we are always working with already-started structures. Many children thrive, but others become disengaged from school learning, though not necessarily from all learning. By the end of primary school, some have not only failed to learn, they have learned to fail.

As Cummins (cited in Hart et al., 2004, page 26) states, *the ways in which identities are negotiated in these interactions (in the classroom) can be understood only in relation to patterns of historical and current power relations in broader society*. Remember that you are a successful learner (at least relatively); and what motivates and engages children may be different for those who are not. So, the challenge is to find what does motivate individuals and groups, not what should. And that requires from educators a leap of the imagination to understand the obstacles that children encounter and what helps to engage them, or otherwise.

> **Critical thinking exercise 3:** external factors affecting children's engagement and motivation
>
> Thomson and Hall (2008, page 89) write, *children come to school with virtual school bags of knowledge, experiences and dispositions. However, school only draws on the contents of some children's school bags, those whose resources match those required in the game of education.*
>
> A **Articulate** the factors – influences which affect children's progress – from their experience out of school which help or hinder them from engaging with learning at school.
>
> B **Identify** what may make it easier or harder for children at points of transition, especially from home to school, to settle in.
>
> C **Consider** to what extent children disengaged from school learning should adapt; and to what extent the educator or the curriculum should alter.

Comment

Each person's identity is shaped not only by what they inherit, but by experience. So, while being born as a girl, or as a Christian, as physically able or in poverty does not determine identity and self-concept, it affects it. While girls do not necessarily adopt interests or traits associated with femininity, the expectations of family, of the peer group and of society tend to encourage these. The beliefs and practices of the family or religious group may help to shape one's character and worldview, though these are not unchanging. A child with Down's syndrome may find school learning difficult, but a classroom attuned to her needs can make a huge difference. And living in poverty makes successful learning more difficult, though not impossible.

Children, inevitably, come to school with a range of beliefs and knowledge, experiences and expectations – both of themselves and of learning. Without this, life would be dull. However, some of these make success more or less likely, which is obvious, and school culture contributes to this, which may be less so. For instance, some arrive already with a wider experience of spoken English and of text. Some come from a background of less secure relationships and lower aspirations. So, it is not a 'level playing field'. It is tempting to think that a background of poverty or of domestic violence makes educational success impossible; or that a professional background or one of secure relationships makes it inevitable. This is not so, but factors such as how children have been treated and their experience of language make success or failure more likely. The EPPE study (Sylva et al., 2010, pages 60–67) indicates that the home learning environment is crucial to later success. However, EPPE argues that *what parents do is more important than what they are*, though the parents' own level of education affects how their actions fit with what schools will value. A child used to looking at books or having reasons explained is likely to find it easier to fit into school than one for whom books are unfamiliar or who is used to being shouted at.

While educators must understand the obstacles children face, these should not be excuses for low aspiration or for giving up. We all face obstacles and have to learn how to get over them; and be helped to do so. This matters especially when we feel unsure or unsafe. However, the home situation usually makes those around the child – parents/carers, siblings and friends – more or less able to offer appropriate support; especially when they lack what is called the necessary 'cultural capital'; that is, the sorts of knowledge to enable them to know what is expected.

Cultural capital relates to the familiarity, or otherwise, of an individual or group, with the environment. Much of this involves implicit rules. To understand this, it may help to think of situations where you feel 'at home' or uneasy. For me, as a middle-class man, some types of pub make me comfortable, others less so. You may feel at ease, or not, at a loud party, in a place of worship or a foreign country. This is largely about whether you 'fit in'. If you do, you have the necessary capital; if not, you don't. This may be compared with money, where coins which have value in one place do not in another; or with where someone not fluent in one language picks up only some of the messages when this is the language spoken. Brooker (2002, Chapter 2) provides an excellent discussion of how cultural (and other sorts of) capital operate in practice in a multicultural, Reception-age classroom.

Parents/carers who find reading or maths difficult are likely to find it harder to support their child's learning. However, educators should not devalue different cultural beliefs about learning to read or do maths which do not match school policy. For instance, Gregory and Williams' (2000) work with Bangladeshi-heritage children in Tower Hamlets shows how their reading is often supported by repeating the text after hearing a more experienced reader, often an older sibling. They argue that:

- being poor is not necessarily linked to poor literacy skills;
- early reading success does not depend on a particular approach to parenting;
- different approaches at home and at school do not result in difficulties in learning to read;
- no one method of teaching reading is correct for everyone.

One difficulty for educators is that those who lack cultural capital experience its impact much more than those who do. In Thomson and Hall's (2008, page 89) words:

 children who 'know' and can 'do' school are ... advantaged in the classroom right from the outset, while those who are not privileged in having the required ways of speaking, acting and knowing start at a disadvantage. Through the ... practices of pedagogy, the gap grows between these children and their peers who are born fortunate by virtue of their class, heritage or gender.

If children do not find their sense of identity reinforced by what happens school, they will often withdraw or search for it elsewhere. The (often implicit) rules and the sorts of knowledge which schools value mean that some children and parents do not 'fit in'. Their cultural capital lacks value in that context. Too often, children do not thrive at school because what builds their self-concept is found outside the school gates; just as the many who do succeed do so because they fit in with what is expected. Often, such rules and expectations are unconscious, but the consequences can be considerable. For instance, we saw in Chapter 4 how gifted and talented children were more likely to come from privileged backgrounds; and Gillborn and Mirza (2000, page 16) show how children of Afro-Caribbean heritage start as one of the higher-achieving ethnic groups but are overtaken by most others before the end of primary school. So, educators must constantly be aware of what they expect, work to keep aspirations high and think how best to engage and motivate children with differing interests and abilities. While important for all children, this is especially so for those whose aspirations, and their families', are low and who are most at risk of disengagement from school learning. So, educators need to know and understand children's social and cultural background, not simply treat them 'all the same'.

Key idea: **The hidden curriculum**

Why does the learning environment matter?

The previous sections have started to indicate why the learning environment matters so much. Learning is a social as well as an individual enterprise. Context matters for all children but especially for those who are less experienced learners, and those less able to cope with uncertainty. For children, this is because both adults and the peer group exert so great an influence, with children's own aspirations and self-concept strongly affected by the expectations of others. One reason why it is harder for children to learn, and teachers to teach, successfully, in a culture of low expectations is that these become self-fulfilling, not only in terms of results and behaviour, but less tangible matters such as attitudes and motivation. In a culture where school learning, and academic success, are not highly valued, it is hard to 'swim against the stream'. High but realistic expectations make these more likely to be met. More practically, the learning environment is one area over which teachers, especially, have considerable influence. However, any social environment such as a classroom is complicated and constantly changing; and, especially for young children, the emotional and cognitive, physical and mental, social and individual aspects are closely enmeshed.

The curriculum can be seen as having three elements – the formal, the informal, and the hidden. The formal curriculum is, broadly speaking, what is taught explicitly; and the informal what takes place outside the classroom, such as in lunchtimes, playtimes and 'extracurricular' activities. This last term shows how dominated our thinking often is by the formal curriculum. The hidden curriculum is more like the unspoken messages, beliefs and values embedded in the DNA of the school or class. It is referred to as 'hidden' because the most significant features are often least obvious.

Critical thinking exercise 4: the hidden curriculum

Imagine or, even better, draw a plan of the physical layout of a classroom you have observed. Note down what furniture there is and how it is organised. For example, are there activity areas for sand, water, construction, a book corner, a whiteboard, a computer? Are the chairs and tables in rows facing a board, or in a horseshoe shape, or around tables? Is there a teacher's desk? If so, where is it?

A **Consider** (and **discuss**) the assumptions (many implicit) about learning of how the classroom is arranged. And about teaching. For example, is this arranged for individual, group or whole-class work? What does this say about how the teacher expects to teach and children to respond?

B **Articulate** what expectations are created by the layout of the room. For instance, how much choice of activity or resources do the children have? Are they expected to move about or stay still?

C **Identify** what this tells us about the types of activities and responses being encouraged.

Take a long time on this if you can. If not, do it as a separate exercise. It is very revealing.

Comment

Jackson et al. (1993) report on a project where a group of researchers and teachers (of different age groups) worked together for two and a half years to explore what influenced children's moral development. They concluded that direct programmes are less influential than the unspoken messages, many of which teachers take for granted. For example, the physical environment indicates:

- what types of activity are valued, for instance in the range, quality and availability of equipment, or in how the outdoor environment is used, especially in Early Years settings;
- what sorts of response are expected, for instance in how the furniture is arranged for individual, group or whole-class work;
- what areas of work, and whose, are given most prominence, for instance by the written messages, how children's work is treated and the displays.

The main message of Jackson et al.'s book, called *The Moral Life of Schools*, is that education is intimately tied up with questions of what is deemed worthwhile, whether one likes it or not. So, the quality, availability and accessibility of high-quality books, or of paint, or of play equipment sends a message about the value given to each of these. Having children sit in rows, or on the floor, or in different groupings is not simply a matter of convenience, but indicates, and shapes, the type of learning and teaching expected. Where teachers stand, or sit, and how they store their own materials, or treat children's work is indicative, even when they do this unconsciously, of their assumptions and expectations about what matters.

Even very young children – and maybe them in particular – pick up such subtle, unspoken messages about learning, about what is expected and about themselves. Bruner (2006, vol 1, page 131) cites Barker's comment that *the best way to predict the behavior of a human being is to know where he is. In a post office, he behaves post office. At church he behaves church.* These unspoken messages prompt particular behaviours, as long as the rules are understood. For example, two parents whom I knew well were discussing when their oldest child was about to leave how he had been when he first started. His father recounted how they would quiz him unsuccessfully about what he had learned that day. With a chuckle, he recalled how the five-year-old, exasperated, had finally said to both of them *you don't understand, it's not that sort of school.* Ireson et al. (1999, page 217) write *generally, learners adapt to the learning situations in which they find themselves and maximize their potential for success.* However, 'success' is often defined by the environment. So a classroom where conformity is valued will tend to lead most children to conform; and a school which prioritises academic success over good learning habits will usually encourage children to attend more to results than to processes. And, while most Early Years settings recognise the importance of the outdoor environment, how children are encouraged to use this varies enormously.

So, there is more to teaching than technical competence. While all that happens in classrooms affects learning, the teacher – and other adults – model both how to think, to act and to be. Jackson et al. (1993, pages 286–287) comment that the teachers involved in their study did not use the term 'role model' much and suggest that this may be because it seems too 'heroic' a role. Rather than virtues like courage, wisdom and generosity, they spoke of 'humbler virtues' such as:

- showing respect for others;
- demonstrating what it means to be intellectually absorbed;
- paying close attention to what is being said;
- being a 'good sport';
- showing that it is OK to make mistakes and to be confused.

Environments are not neutral. They give messages about who, and what, are valued. Teachers who are welcoming or a learning mentor who is sympathetic are doing more than being pleasant or kind. They are helping children (and parents/carers) understand how to act and interact; one reason why valuing young children's cultural backgrounds and prior knowledge is so important. As an educator, you are creating, by your actions and your words, an environment which embodies your expectations and helps to shape the children's.

While the learning environment can help to include and motivate, it will inevitably impact on different individuals in varying ways. In particular, as we have seen, the sorts of experience and knowledge which are valued will affect how young children, especially, are motivated and engaged. So educators need to be aware both of individual circumstances and of prior experience and expectations in planning appropriate 'routes into learning'. In exploring this, we shall encounter a series of dilemmas such as how much to:

- understand and respect, yet challenge and extend, children's existing beliefs;
- expect conformity, yet encourage divergence;
- provide structure, yet offer opportunities.

Conclusion

This chapter has explored how experience and expectations in the years before children come to school and outside and in school shape how they approach learning, helping to show why children respond differently to similar experiences.

The critical thinking exercises will have helped you to:

- ◉ **articulate** the attributes of successful learners;
- ◉ **consider** why self-concept and adult expectations affect how children approach learning;
- ◉ **identify** factors which affect children's level of engagement, many of them rooted in cultural experiences and assumptions;
- ◉ **analyse** why the hidden curriculum and implicit aspects of a learning environment matter so much.

So, we turn, in Chapter 6, to consider the features of an inclusive learning environment which encourages motivation and engagement.

Further Reading

Brooker, L (2002) *Starting School: Young children learning cultures.* Buckingham: Open University Press
A thoughtful and accessible account of how children from different backgrounds manage the transition from home to school, with Chapter 2 especially good on cultural capital.

Claxton, G (2002) *Building Learning Power.* Bristol: TLO Ltd.
An easy-to-read discussion of the attributes of successful learners and how to encourage these.

/continued

Jackson, PW, Boostrom, RE and Hansen, DT (1993) *The Moral Life of Schools.* San Francisco: Jossey Bass
A fascinating description of how researchers and teachers worked together to decide on what teachers really valued in their practice.
Salmon, P (1995) *Psychology in the Classroom – Reconstructing teachers and learners.* London: Cassell
Although not specific to younger children, this is especially good on how identity as a learner is constructed.

6 Creating an inclusive learning environment

Chapter Focus

The critical thinking exercises in this chapter focus on:

⊙ **analysing** different aspects of the term 'inclusion';
⊙ **illustrating** the features of an inclusive learning environment, given how children's needs vary;
⊙ **considering** how children are motivated and engaged;
⊙ **articulating** the implications for educators.

The key ideas discussed are: **inclusion, hospitable space, motivation, discipline, choice, consistency**

This chapter is particularly relevant to QTS Standards: **1, 2, 10, 18, 19, 21 b, 25 a,b,c,d, 30, 31** and to Knowledge and Understanding (*Education Studies*) and Subject knowledge and Subject skills (*Early Childhood Studies*)

Introduction

Among the factors which Gipps (1994, page 35) highlights as marking out effective primary teaching are *a good positive atmosphere in the classroom, with plenty of encouragement and praise, high levels of expectation of all children and high levels of work-related talk and discussion,* continuing that children are capable of more than adults expect as long as they understand what is required and that there should be *an emphasis on language and challenge rather than quiet 'busy' work.* These ideas are explored in the next three chapters.

This chapter explores the features of inclusive environments for young children. We start by examining the background to the moves towards inclusion and the benefits and challenges of doing so, before thinking what a learning environment appropriate for a wide range of learners will 'look (and feel) like'. Unsurprisingly, this involves learners who are active, engaged and independent, working sometimes together, sometimes alone; and adults who steer and guide learning, 'going with the flow' rather than trying to force learning on unwilling recipients. This leads into a discussion of what motivates children and how adults can support children in regulating their behaviour and exercising choice, emphasising the need for structures which enable and allow rather than dominate and control.

CASE STUDY

My second teaching post involved moving from a suburban to a new-town school. Many activities which had worked well previously, such as creative dance and writing poetry, no longer did so. This was partly because these Year 5 and 6 children were not used to that way of working but it was more because they saw such activities as 'not for them'. For example, one boy disrupted dance lessons which he saw as 'for fairies'. Two others, who were very good at asking questions which amused the rest of the class but annoyed me, both underachieved significantly. Both were capable readers but read very little until I found *The Balaclava Boys*, books about boys similar to themselves which they really enjoyed. Others, unused to independent learning, found it hard at first but started to flourish, trying new approaches and activities, such as problem-solving or working with fabrics. Gradually, some children who had become disengaged from school learning became more motivated. However, others continued to find it hard to fit in to an approach which expected them to participate in activities they found unfamiliar or challenging.

This case study illustrates how an approach which worked well in one school was less appropriate in another. What motivates one class may not work for a parallel group in the same school. What helps to engage and include one child may lead to another feeling excluded. The reasons are complex, related to the self-concept of individuals, the group dynamics, the previous experience and expectations of the class, the nature of the curriculum, the activities and experiences presented and external expectations; but an educator has to work with all these factors in creating an inclusive learning environment.

Key idea: **Inclusion**

Can, and should, all children be included in mainstream classes?

One important strand of policy over the last 20 years has been the move towards 'inclusion', closely linked with the ideas of entitlement and equity. This has been associated with the closure of special schools, which were considered as, too often, leading to a culture of low expectations. Special schools for children with physical disabilities were often seen as promoting a culture of separation rather than integration, although many argue specialist provision helped to boost the self-concept of some groups. And less obvious forms of exclusion included many schools in socio-economically disadvantaged areas having low standards of achievement and an over-representation of certain ethnic or social groups in

/continued

Key idea: **Inclusion** – continued

special schools, such as the numbers of those of African-Caribbean heritage in schools for children with learning difficulties. One rationale of the move towards inclusion has been to ensure that all children have the opportunities to which they are entitled and to raise the expectations of adults and children alike. However, as we shall see, the situation is more complicated in practice.

Concern over the low attainment of children of African-Caribbean heritage and of some, but not all, ethnic minority groups, remains (see, for example, Gillborn and Mirza, 2000; Demie, 2001). While racism plays a part in this, this explanation is too simple, given the low levels of achievement and disengagement from learning of white working-class children, especially boys. Mayall (2010, page 66) argues that variations in children's achievement may be profoundly rooted in school's social attitudes, emphasising that schools have a pivotal role in providing a counter to the often-confusing world which young children inhabit, through what she calls the *moral order of the school*. In particular, educators provide both a protection for those who may otherwise be excluded and an example to those who may be inclined to exclude others.

Critical thinking exercise 1: the benefits and challenges of inclusion

Inclusion needs to be considered not only in terms of subjects and lessons but also in terms of where learners are taught, the pastoral support they receive, the relevance of what they are taught and how they are grouped. All these can be approached systematically by addressing differentiation, motivation and barriers to learning.

(QCDA, 1999)

A **Consider** to what extent all children should be educated in mainstream classrooms or if some may benefit from separate provision, for example in a special school or unit, and if so why.

B **Compare** the possible benefits of inclusion in a mainstream classroom, both for the child and for the rest of the class, of:

i) a four-year-old with a physical disability;
ii) a seven-year-old who has just arrived in England and not yet started to learn English;
iii) a ten-year-old with emotional and behavioural difficulties (EBD).

C **Articulate** the possible implications for educators of ensuring that all learners can access an 'entitlement curriculum' in the mainstream classroom.

Comment

In many poor countries, the main challenge of inclusion is to ensure that children are able to go to school at all. It is humbling to recognise that the millennium goal *to ensure that, by 2015, children everywhere, boys and girls alike, will be able to complete a full course of primary schooling* (see UN, no date) are far from being met; and unlikely to be so by 2015. The situation is very much worse for girls, for those with disabilities and those growing up in poverty. In this country, most of these inequities have been resolved, at least in terms of school places.

Many children with disabilities, especially physical ones, for whom provision in mainstream classes would previously have been regarded as impossible, are now included in such classes. This is valuable both for such children and their families and for other children learning to both understand and include children with different challenges to overcome and gifts to offer. A child in a wheelchair will require support to settle in, but can help other children recognise what those with mobility difficulties can do. Children with EBD may be the hardest group to integrate and include, because of the impact on the class. However, the 1994 Salamanca declaration (see UNESCO, 1994), a decisive moment in the move towards greater inclusion for those with special educational needs, asserts that all children have a right to be included.

It is easy to pretend that children are included when they are not. Inclusion does not just entail putting all children together in the same class or school. It relates to them receiving the education to which they are entitled. For example, consider where:

- a girl with visual hearing impairment does not receive adequate support;
- a boy in the early stages of learning English is grouped with those with learning difficulties and not offered enough cognitive challenge;
- children are constantly placed in situations where they cannot cope.

One may reasonably ask to what extent they are included. If 'Every Child Matters', how resources are deployed, how expertise is accessed and how children's aspirations and adult expectations are raised requires constant thinking through. For example:

- children who bully others and adults who do not address this exclude those who are bullied;
- adults have a responsibility to link with specialists and parents to ensure that provision is appropriate for the individual;
- how children are grouped can, subtly or otherwise, affect how they are included, or otherwise.

So, an inclusive pedagogy is one which enables all children to belong and to contribute.

Adult expectations are a vital element of inclusion, for example believing that the class like that in the case study, the group who disrupt lessons or the quiet child who seems not to engage can succeed (albeit in different ways), maintaining and fostering the 'growth mindset' of intelligence. But this is hard, because it often involves believing 'against the odds'.

As Ireson et al. (1999, page 216) write:

> *the problem is that high expectations … have to spring naturally from the belief and aspirations of the teacher and learner. They have to be genuine or they become counterproductive … Expectations are passed between teacher and learner in subtle, often undetected, ways … Underpinning teachers' attitudes to the capabilities of their students is their belief about intelligence … If … teachers believe that intelligence can be modified by experience, they will be more likely to pitch their expectations positively.*

However, educators have a particular responsibility to 'believe in' the child – and so to promote high aspirations – even when the evidence does not feel very compelling – one reason for looking for gifts and talents beyond the conventional boundaries of school knowledge.

The playwright David Hare, writes (2008, pages 69–70)

> *education has to be a mixture of haven and challenge. Reassurance of course. Stability. But also incentive. It's finding that balance. Finding it, keeping it there … You care for them. You offer them security. You give them an environment where they feel they can grow. But you also make bloody sure you challenge them. You make sure they realise learning is hard. Because if you only make the safe haven [and] if it's all clap-happy and 'everything the kids do is great' … then what are you creating? Emotional toffees … who then have to go back and face the real world.*

Key idea: **Hospitable space**

What does an inclusive learning environment for young children look and feel like?

The previous section indicated that inclusion is:

- more like a philosophy than a programme;
- less a matter of structures than of expectations.

Inclusion, or exclusion, take place in very subtle ways and what includes one child, or group, may exclude another. However, if equity is to be an aim of education, working to create an inclusive learning environment is essential. 'Real-world' pedagogy usually involves balancing varying approaches, depending on the aim, the activity and the child, to try to achieve, as far as possible, entitlement for all, while meeting the needs of individuals.

Critical thinking exercise 2: balancing varying needs

Kimes Myers (1997, page 63) writes about children needing space which is *hospitable – in which old and new experiences are accepted, dealt with and transcended.*

A **Imagine** what an inclusive learning environment might look like with a class/age group with young children. For example, would you expect them to be:

- moving around or sitting still;
- noisy or quiet;
- focused on the same, or different, activities?

B **Discuss** what a classroom which offers hospitable space might look like and what the possible benefits and dangers of this might be for:

- a five-year-old in the early stages of learning English who has just joined a new class;
- a seven-year-old who is attaining at a high level and especially enjoys working with her friends;
- a nine-year-old who is not doing well in school, in part because of his behaviour.

C **Consider** what contrasting elements – such as structure/freedom and challenge/nurture – are needed in an inclusive learning environment.

Comment

In answering the first of these questions, I expect (and hope) that your answer will have been something on the lines of 'It depends…'. When working in groups, for example conducting an experiment, children are likely to need to move, to discuss, to try out. At times, this will require movement and noise, at times reflection and quiet. One valid criticism of the developmental tradition was that having a large number of different activities going on simultaneously was enormously demanding for the teacher and often confusing for children who required explicit structure. However, too much whole-class teaching, especially where children are not active participants, restricts their opportunity for curiosity and creativity – and practising the attributes of successful learners. So, an inclusive learning environment, while usually calm and purposeful, will not always look or feel the same all the time.

Rapid progress tends to be associated with challenge and pace. One widely acknowledged improvement resulting from the Numeracy Strategy was the emphasis on children being able to manipulate numbers quickly – 'mental maths'. Frequently, the challenge of a time limit prompts us, children or adults, to achieve results. However, this does not mean that the learning environment should always be pacy. Real challenge usually results from having to solve a problem, rather than just to talk or think about it. A painting requires time to plan, to ponder, to adapt. A good story may need an outline plan, a first draft, correction, rewriting – none of them giving instant results. Problem-solving involves analysing, thinking out, and trying, alternative strategies, adopting new approaches. In particular, metacognition often involves stepping back from the immediate situation, reflecting on one's own learning and pondering about what to do next. However, having too much time can lead to children being bored or avoiding any definite outcome.

Children need to feel safe, but to be challenged. Striking this balance is one of the hardest aspects of creating an inclusive learning environment. Challenge is integral to learning, which most children – and adults – enjoy, as long as this is pitched at the right level. Too hard and one becomes dispirited and disengaged; too easy and one becomes complacent and bored. If the high-jump bar is impossibly high, we give up. If too low, we do not have to work at our technique. However, at times, we need to rest, take stock or reflect.

More experienced and confident learners can cope better with change. Those who are less confident need more security and reinforcement. An activity which one person finds a motivating challenge may be an insuperable obstacle for another, Yet, everyone feels worried at times, depending on the task or the situation, especially in domains where we are inexperienced or have a history of failure. So, any learner needs access to a haven – some more so, and more often. This may involve being involved in another activity or sitting somewhere different, working with an adult or simply having the chance to 'chill out'.

For children to learn to regulate their actions is vital, but this is harder for some than others, and at particular times. Being worried or anxious is demanding and tiring, often making it hard to concentrate. This will affect, especially, children who are hungry or worn out, who have significant responsibilities as a carer or who are being bullied, even if, for many of them, school may feel like a haven. For such children to thrive requires that they feel safe and nurtured and that their anxiety is contained. This does not entail adults accepting any behaviour, but rather recognising children's need for care and attention, as well as for boundaries and challenge, especially when they are young or anxious. However, many of those who most need nurture are those who are hardest to nurture, especially in a class situation. Such children benefit from the chance for sustained engagement and continuity of relationships. Yet the learning experience, for the most vulnerable learners, is too often fragmented and full of inconsistent relationships and responses – like their lives.

A five-year-old starting in a new class is likely to need reassurance and the opportunity to listen, to rehearse and to settle. A high-attaining seven-year-old may enjoy success and working with her friends, but benefit more from new types of challenge and working with others less familiar to her, so that she draws on new resources and learns to cope with uncertainty. The nine-year-old who is finding school, and especially behaviour, hard may need an approach which provides opportunities for different activities which draw on his strengths and interests and break learning into more manageable chunks, making expectations more explicit and success more immediate. So, any group will need different activities, experiences and expectations if all are to be included.

Previous chapters have suggested that effective pedagogy must recognise that successful learning involves elements which are:

cognitive		affective
propositional	and	procedural
collective		individual
conscious		unconscious

The crucial word here is 'and'. As discussed in Chapter 2, the 'standards' agenda tends to assume that those in the left-hand column are what enhances learning most, with the developmental tradition tending to emphasise those in the right-hand. If, as educators, we concentrate exclusively on only one side of this chart, we risk, at best, unbalancing and limiting children's learning and, at worst, disempowering and disengaging them as learners.

So, creating hospitable space involves searching for a balance between:

structure		freedom
challenge		haven
pace		space
competition	and	co-operation
risk		safety
conformity		creativity
independence		interdependence
application		enjoyment

However, an inclusive environment will always be designed with the well-being of both individuals and the whole group in mind, especially the children, but also yourself and other adults. So, there needs to be time to think, to plan, to talk, to experiment, to dream, to be still, to enjoy and to belong; and to experience learning more like an encyclopaedia than a manual, an album than a song, a journey than a sprint.

Key ideas: **Motivation and discipline**

What encourages motivation and discipline?

Probably, the main concern of those working with children, when they first start, especially class teachers, is how to manage behaviour. The two boys mentioned in the case study made life very difficult both for me and for other children. The class only gradually, and to some extent, developed the discipline to apply their skills in less familiar activities. Unless children are engaged and motivated and learn to regulate their actions, they are unlikely to achieve well; and may prevent others from learning. However, while behaviour management is often seen as separate from learning, *the quality of learning, teaching and behaviour*, as Steer wrote (DfES, 2005b, page 2) in his report on school behaviour and discipline, *are inseparable issues and the responsibility of all staff*. So, the relationships, the activities, the expectations, the ethos, the sorts of rewards and punishment used all contribute to good behaviour; and too insistent a focus on behaviour tends to mean that adults and children alike become concerned with that rather than learning.

A useful distinction is between the intrinsic – where the reason for one's actions comes from 'within' – and the extrinsic, where this is external. Discipline may be intrinsic, such as keeping to the speed limit or obeying the school rules because this is the right thing to do; or extrinsic, such as avoiding parking in the wrong place or running in the school corridors for fear of being caught and punished. Similarly, children may be motivated to play the piano, read a book or leave someone alone – or not – because of self-generated reasons or adult directives. The story of the girl who kicked someone because she thought she would not be seen exemplifies a lack of intrinsic motivation, 'knowing' what she should do, but ignoring this if she could get away with it. While motivation is rarely entirely intrinsic or extrinsic, educators should work towards developing intrinsic motivation, if children are to become independent learners. External structures are essential, but the challenge is for children to learn to discipline themselves, to internalise how to conduct themselves and so to become less dependent on such structure.

Critical thinking exercise 3: keeping children engaged

A **Discuss** what you understand by the term discipline and which sort of discipline is most valuable in building the attributes of successful learners.

/continued

Critical thinking exercise 3 – continued

B **Compare** what sorts of rewards and punishments are, or were, most effective in developing discipline and motivation for:

- you, preferably when you were younger;
- young children, by focusing on a class you know or have observed.

C **Consider** the relative benefits of extrinsic and intrinsic motivation in both the short term and the long term.

Comment

The origins of the term 'discipline' are associated with (external) control and punishment. In Chapter 3, I referred to two different conceptions of moral development, duty and virtue ethics. Duty ethics is based on an external code of what one should, and should not, do, usually based on training so that good behaviour becomes habitual. This may provide a child with a clear sense of what is expected, but tends to encourage conformity rather than intrinsic motivation. A virtue-ethics approach is based on the child developing a picture of what it is to be a good person, and adopting these attributes by thinking about, and practising, appropriate behaviour. This encourages intrinsic motivation but may not provide enough structure to ensure that other reasons for acting in a particular way become more compelling.

As the TLRP indicates, relationships are fundamental to effective pedagogy. Young children, especially, are usually very keen on adult approval for their actions. So, you, as an educator, are a major source of motivation. While this may be less obvious for children towards the end of the primary school, in part because of the growing importance of the approval of friends, most children wish to please adults, especially those whom they respect. Therefore:

- praise is almost always more effective than reprimand, though as we shall see some types of praise are more beneficial than others;
- reward and incentive work better than punishment, though the latter may be necessary;
- knowledge of, and respect for, children pays dividends, though this is not the main reason for developing these.

A different approach is to think about how activities encourage their own discipline. So, creating music or dance, working as a mathematician or a scientist, gardening or fishing, all have their own internal discipline, necessary for success. One well-known example is how boxing, or other physical activities, can help to develop discipline for many boys from very disadvantaged backgrounds. There is a close connection between particular activities and the self-discipline that these encourage, considered further in Chapter 8.

However, for this to happen, the child must be engaged and not over-dependent on external forms of discipline, although these may be necessary, especially at first. Of course, prohibition and reprimand are needed at times, as well as guidance and example.

Engagement depends on a match between the child's interests, the nature of the activity and the level of challenge. Young children are far more likely to be engaged when they see the point of what they are doing, not least because they are less used to abstract thinking. A five-year-old who can concentrate for hours on a computer game may not manage two minutes of being talked at; or to learn to send text messages before they can write fluently, in part because they see the point, in part because of the physical difficulties involved in writing. A nine-year-old who finds fractions hard may be capable of working these out when working on a problem she has generated herself or is keen to solve it. Too often what children are asked to do at school seems to them (and may be) pointless.

Unchallenging activities may lead either to contented passivity, such as when colouring a worksheet, or to misbehaviour, especially for those who become frustrated because they are not occupied. So, educators must steer a course between tasks which lack challenge and those which are too demanding. Both are likely to lead to disengagement, the former through boredom, the latter frustration. However, the disengagement is likely to be more serious and long-lasting when tasks which are too demanding become the norm and there is pressure for children to achieve what they cannot. Repeated failure undermines identity-as-a-learner and leads to disengagement. More worryingly, children may disengage from school learning if what they are expected to do seems pointless or unrelated to their lives outside school.

Ireson et al. (1999, pages 216–219) summarise many of the key factors which help to maintain motivation, emphasising teachers' beliefs and expectations. However, part of the difficulty of understanding children's motivation is that it is so individual. Collecting facts or doing quizzes motivates some children and turns others off. Goals and targets, discussed in Chapter 9, and time pressure may motivate or discourage. For example, many children enjoy the challenge of 'mental maths' as long as the pressure to perform successfully in public is not too intense. And one reason why children enjoy drawing is that it gives time to plan and to think without having to respond immediately. Similar considerations apply to the role of competition as a motivator. Competition 'against oneself' to improve on one's previous best may help some children, whereas others seem to need the inter-, rather than, intra-personal element of competition. Competition with others spurs some children to greater efforts while it may discourage or simply not interest others. The challenge for educators is often to ensure that what motivates one child or group does not discourage another.

More challengingly, the structure of schools is not neutral in terms of motivation. In Brantlinger's (2003, page 13) words:

 because [working-class and lower-income families] rarely benefit from it, the competitive school structure does not play the same motivating role for them as for middle class students. Class advantage may be invisible to those who benefit, but subordinates are acutely aware of barriers to opportunity.

An overemphasis on performance may exclude some children, however unwittingly. A lack of respect for what children value tends to lead to disengagement. For example, if a child is very expert in computer games or has a deep knowledge of his religious heritage, but these skills and this knowledge are not valued in school, children soon recognise this.

Many adults would accept intrinsic motivation as a long-term aim, but argue that very young children are not old or experienced enough to internalise motivation. So they use stickers and smiley faces; or for older children treats or even bribes; or for a class, some additional time to play or to choose their own activities. These can provide explicit symbols of adult approval, helping to make the link between this and the child's action. However, the danger is if the motivation for action comes to depend on this. Moreover, while stickers may motivate very young children, the appeal of this palls with older children. So, there may be a place for such an approach with children who need a very clear link between behaviour and consequence, especially individuals finding self-control difficult. But reliance on extrinsic reward and punishment discourages the intrinsic motivation essential to lifelong learning.

Key ideas: **Choice and consistency**

How can adults encourage children to be motivated and engaged?

Managing behaviour is often presented, for example in school behaviour policies, as involving clear boundaries, with children expected to think about the consequences of their choices and making appropriate choices and adults acting in a consistent way. Wragg (2004) emphasises rules and relationships in managing children's behaviour. Rules and boundaries provide a structure which helps to make clear what is acceptable and so to reduce possible choice and contain anxiety. However, rules must be applied both fairly and consistently and with some flexibility. So, relationships are vital in adults knowing how to adapt to changing circumstances.

Critical thinking exercise 4: choice and consistency

I was watching the teacher leading circle time with a group of 12 four-year-olds. One girl kept calling out, a practice which the teacher discouraged not by telling-off, but by ignoring her and praising other children who were behaving as expected. Because I was doing research, I counted the number of times this happened, within a short period of time – 17! She didn't raise her voice, but was quick to praise when the little girl 'got the message' and did as expected.

Recently, I was teaching a class of seven- and eight-year-olds. I asked one boy to come and sit down – what seemed (to me) a perfectly reasonable request. He refused and walked off to the other side of the room, laughing nervously. I repeated the request, fairly calmly, and he refused, several times. Eventually, to ensure that the class could continue, I involved the head teacher, in line with the school's behaviour policy.

A **Consider** your reactions to these two stories and to what extent the adult's behaviour was both consistent and appropriate.

B **Discuss** to what extent young children are able to make appropriate choices and what makes this easier or more difficult.

C **Identify** which aspects of the learning environment you can control to make it easier for children to regulate their behaviour.

Comment

I wonder how you respond to these incidents. I admired the teacher I was watching but doubt she was right to be so patient. I was disappointed with my response because it backed the boy into a corner; and made me feel inflexible. Yet, both teachers were consistent, following the school's agreed policy. So, while consistency may be a good starting point, there are times when one needs to be flexible. If we treat all children just the same, we are not responding to their needs. Yet if we treat the same behaviour differently, we run the risk of being unfair.

We have seen, mostly in Chapter 3:

* the importance of the search for predictability from infancy onwards;
* how anxiety can lead any of us either to become aggressive or to withdraw – fight-or-flight responses;
* how patterns of attachment, self-concept and prior experience may lead to children responding quite differently in similar situations.

This emphasises the importance of children learning to regulate their responses and of adults helping them, especially those who find this most difficult, to do so. But, while educators need to be consistent and predictable, this may, paradoxically, not always involve responding to the same action in the same way. Similar actions from different children may rightly prompt varying responses. So the consistency required is one of principle rather than that of an automaton. There may also be times when your expectations are different from usual or why you act differently from your usual approach – deliberately or not. In such situations, it is helpful, especially for children who depend on rules to regulate their behaviour, to let them know what to expect; and to explain and discuss the reasons when you behave differently. This is all part of modelling how to regulate one's behaviour – including (at times) saying that you wished you had acted differently – and of helping children to cope with the unexpected.

As they mature, children become more able to exercise conscious choice. An emphasis on choice, while appropriate for most children most of the time, overlooks the fact that some children, especially those with disorganised models of attachment, find it incredibly hard to make appropriate conscious choices in stressful situations. Especially when an individual's anxiety becomes overwhelming, these strategies may be disabled and earlier, deeper types of response etched in infancy become evident, recalling the discussion about models of attachment. This may lead to aggressive comments or behaviour, especially with older children, to withdrawal, or to inappropriate and puzzling responses, as with the boy described in the box above. This is not to say that children should be protected from stress or challenge. However, dealing with these may require containing the level of anxiety, for example by removing an individual child temporarily from a difficult situation rather than expecting behaviour of which he is incapable at that time; or altering the activity. Flare-ups are not only hard to deal with, but repeated failures on the child's part to access conscious ways of regulating his behaviour undermines resilience and tends to lead to a loss of self-esteem and to disengagement.

Making expectations explicit can be very helpful, though these are more effective when children understand why, rather than complying without thought. In one school I visited, a nine-year-old boy picked up my uncertainty about whether an approach based on explicit values had really been helpful. With great intensity, he said *you don't understand. Before this, I really didn't know how to behave and now I do.* Rules are more likely to be helpful, and kept to, if children have helped to devise them. This helps them to see why and to have a point of reference other than 'because adults say so'. Behaviour policies based on sanctions and warnings, such as yellow cards or names written on the board, may help to control behaviour in the short term; but are less likely to develop intrinsic motivation. Teachers who are too controlling end up with children who are used to, and dependent on, this.

A rarely discussed issue is how anxiety affects us as adults. For example, when under pressure or scrutiny, we may respond by being more cautious, controlling or confrontational. In the context of children's behaviour, this involves realising that the adult–child relationship is not a one-way process. Kimes Myers (1997, page 8), drawing on Erikson's work, writes *when we engage in relationship with young children the child within us also has a developing edge*, calling this 'cog-wheeling'. Recently, I was working with an unfamiliar class of ten-year-olds and had been warned how difficult one particular boy could be. So, I started briskly and authoritatively. However, when he called out in a cheeky way, I made the mistake of answering him and then of becoming involved in an interchange which led to my authority being undermined. This left the class uncertain who was in charge. Uncomfortable though it may be that some individuals and situations prompt strong emotional responses in ourselves which we find hard to explain and to deal with, one must recognise this to find ways of regulating one's own behaviour, as an adult.

One of the most important, but overlooked, aspects of the class teacher's role, and that of other adults, in helping children to conduct themselves appropriately, is to establish the ethos – the longer-term atmosphere – and alter the mood of the class, something more immediate. While an inclusive learning environment caters for the whole range of children and for all of their learning needs it is impossible, and not even desirable, that each individual 'does their own thing'. Alexander (2000, pages 380–384) emphasises routines, rules and rituals as central to how teachers manage to cope with complexity. Rules we have discussed, but the simple routines of greeting, of taking the register, of settling to work, of listening respectfully, of opening doors, of sending home are central to how an inclusive learning environment works. By habituation, such actions become normal, setting up expectations of relationship and of reciprocity, without undue conscious effort. Creating such routines without them becoming onerous or unchangeable is one of the (apparently effortless) qualities of an expert teacher. With an unfamiliar teacher, or towards the end of term, poor behaviour often ensues, because the routines which help contain uncertainty and anxiety are no longer in place. And the class in the case study found the activities and approaches I adopted unsettling, partly because this took them outside their comfort zone.

Many factors affect the mood: the time of the day, the weather, the activity, what has happened during lunchtime, the teacher's own emotional state, a particular incident. When a group is fully engaged, the mood can be more relaxed. When more unsettled, a tighter structure, a change of activity, or gathering the children together may be required. Skilled teachers are able both to sense the need for, and to manage, this, like adjusting the valve in a central heating system.

So, the challenge is to create, where possible with the children:

- structures which control without being too controlling;
- rules which are fair but flexible when necessary;
- relationships which are reciprocal and respectful;
- a learning environment which encourages the attributes of successful learners for children whose self-concepts and motivation vary enormously.

This requires knowledge of, and attunement to, the needs and dynamics of that particular group, recognising to what extent specific children, or the class, thrive on structure or freedom, challenge or nurture, competition or co-operation.

Conclusion

This chapter has considered the type of learning environment most likely to encourage motivation and engagement, emphasising that this relies on a combination of many factors and will vary between individuals, so that adults, especially teachers, need constantly to be sensitive to how this should be adjusted.

The critical thinking exercises will have helped you to:

- ⊙ **identify** the rationale of inclusion and challenges involved;
- ⊙ **discuss** different aspects to be balanced in creating an inclusive learning environment;
- ⊙ **compare** intrinsic and extrinsic motivation and the implications in terms of reward and punishment;
- ⊙ **consider** how to enable children to regulate their behaviour, providing both consistency and flexibility depending on the circumstances of the group and of individuals.

In Chapter 7, we look at the sorts of activity and experience which help to make an environment inclusive and enriching, emphasising breadth and balance.

Further Reading

Dweck, CS (1999) *Self Theories: Their role in motivation, personality and development.* Philadelphia: Psychology Press
A very clear summary of her research, showing why children react in different ways and explaining why 'common-sense' ideas about intelligence and motivation are too simple.

Ellis, S and Tod, J (2010) Providing for Inclusion. Pages 258–273 of Arthur, J and Cremin, T (eds) *Learning to Teach in the Primary School.* Abingdon: Routledge
A useful chapter outlining the history and current challenges of inclusion, especially in relation to special educational needs.

Wragg, EC (2004) The Two Rs – Rules and relationships. Pages 60–71 of Wragg, EC (ed) *The RoutledgeFalmer Reader in Teaching and Learning.* London: RoutledgeFalmer
While not specific to young children, this provides some useful examples of how rules and relationships affect how children respond.

7 Providing breadth and balance

Chapter Focus

The critical thinking exercises in this chapter focus on:

⊙ **challenging** whether the current focus on literacy and numeracy is appropriate;
⊙ **articulating** why opportunities for play matter so much, especially for young children;
⊙ **identifying** the benefits and disadvantages of first-hand experience;
⊙ **illustrating** how the expressive arts and the humanities contribute to the development of the 'whole child'.

The key ideas discussed are: **the basics, play, playfulness, first-hand experience, breadth, balance**

This chapter is particularly relevant to QTS Standards: **1**, **10**, **19**, **23**, **25 a,d**, **30** and to Application and Reflection (*Education Studies*) and Subject knowledge and Subject skills (*Early Childhood Studies*)

Introduction

Alexander (2010, page 307) writes that pedagogy *gives life to educational aims and values, lifts the curriculum from the printed page, mediates learning and knowing, engages, inspires and empowers learners – or sadly may fail to do so*. This entails finding a balance between different types of activity, experience and challenge. The *how* of learning matters more than the *what*, though these inevitably affect each other, with the National Curriculum and other policies and structures influencing pedagogy profoundly. As we shall discuss in Chapter 10, resources, materials and programmes are invaluable, especially where your own expertise is limited. This book does not recommend specific ones, partly because there are so many, but mainly because their value usually depends on how well they are used. The activities you choose must be tailored to the expectations, the curriculum and the policies and schemes of work of your school. So, you have to think through how best to use them in your own context.

In this chapter we first revisit the idea of 'the basics' to question whether the current focus on literacy and numeracy is appropriate, examining whether the curriculum, for young children especially, should be considered more in terms of activity and experience than content. You are encouraged to think through the types of activity, experience and interaction which enhance the attributes of successful learners. To some extent, this should be obvious. If we want children to become more resilient, activities must be challenging but not beyond them. If creativity matters, children must have opportunities to experiment, to think and act divergently and originally. To encourage reciprocity, resourcefulness and reflectiveness, educators must provide chances for dialogue and not 'spoonfeed' children. The other critical thinking exercises consider, first, play and playfulness, then direct experience and the role of the expressive arts and the humanities. All of these have a relatively low profile with the current emphasis on literacy and numeracy, although they help provide a broad foundation for young children's learning.

CASE STUDY

Two remarkable moments occurred when I was teaching history to a Year 5 and 6 class. In one, two very quiet girls were in a group acting out being evicted from their house because they had not paid their rent. Suddenly, there was a huge commotion where they were working. One was banging the table and shouting that she was not going to leave. The other groups went silent, amazed because she rarely raised her voice. After maybe thirty seconds, when the two girls shouted that they would not comply with the bailiff's demand, they stopped and looked around, surprised and amazed at their audacity. Something had touched them at a deep, emotional level, taking them beyond where they would have, under normal circumstances, dared to go.

At the end of the year, the topic on changes brought about by the Industrial Revolution had gone very successfully, I thought. A good TV series led to lots of drama, some vivid writing, drawing, models and so on. But the culmination came on a school trip when we went to Tenby Museum. Among the exhibits was a man-trap. Patrick looked at it and asked what it was. I explained that it was a trap to deter poachers of the sort we'd discussed during the year. *You mean,* he said incredulously, *that they were real.* He didn't look at any other item, I think, but sat for twenty minutes, utterly transfixed.

I wonder what you make of these stories. For me, the first illustrates the power of drama in helping children imagine themselves as somebody different, and to explore not only historical concepts but also their own feelings and identity; and in so doing to find a voice. The second indicates how children often regard school knowledge as completely separate from real life and that the engagement essential to successful learning often comes in unexpected and unplanned ways.

Key idea: **The 'basics'**

To what extent does an emphasis on 'the basics' promote an inclusive learning environment?
As the Rose Report (DCSF, 2009, Executive Summary paragraph 7) states:

the new curriculum must be underpinned by an understanding of the distinct but interlocking ways in which children learn and develop – physically, intellectually, emotionally, socially, culturally, morally and spiritually – between the ages of 5 and 11. Among other things, a well-planned, vibrant curriculum recognises that primary children relish learning independently and co-operatively; they love to be challenged and engaged in practical activities; they delight in the wealth of opportunities for understanding more about the world; and they readily empathise with others through working together and through experiences in the arts, literature, religious education and much else.

Alexander (2010, page 242) differentiates between Curriculum 1 (the basics) and Curriculum 2 (the rest), seeing this as an enduring but unhelpful distinction. The term 'basics' is commonly used to imply that the main role of primary schools is to teach a relatively narrow range of subjects and skills, almost always including reading, writing and working with numbers. At times, it may change a little, for instance with the inclusion of science as one of the core subjects in 1988, or the proposal, now dropped, to include ICT. The last 20 years has seen an unremitting emphasis, especially in primary schools, on 'the basics', particularly what can be tested, namely reading, writing and numeracy. Moreover, recent policy has moved towards introducing reading and writing at an increasingly early age, with children tested and expected to perform particular skills. This is based on the assumption that setting aside the majority of the timetable for direct teaching of literacy and numeracy, as subjects, and therefore giving less time to areas such as the expressive arts and humanities, is in children's best interests and the best way of ensuring that children become literate and numerate.

However, these assumptions are at least open to question. This section prompts you to think through this emphasis on 'the basics', both in the sense of whether this focuses on the correct elements of literacy and numeracy and whether it results in a loss of breadth and balance. This is not to say that literacy and numeracy are unimportant, but that their pre-eminence should not be taken for granted. What, for instance, would be the consequences of seeing play and drama or going on a residential visit, or becoming more confident or resilient, as part of 'the basics'?

Critical thinking exercise 1: curriculum – activity or knowledge?

The educator working with under fives must pay careful attention not just to the content of the child's learning, but also to the way in which that learning is offered to and experienced by the child, and the role of all those involved in the process. Children are affected by the context in which learning takes place, the people involved in it and the values and beliefs which are embedded in it.

(DES (the Rumbold Report), 1990, page 9)

The curriculum is to be thought of in terms of activity and experience rather than of knowledge to be acquired and facts to be stored.

(Hadow, 1931, section 113 para. 30)

A **Consider** why reading is regarded as basic when discussion is not. Is mathematics more basic than science? Or music? Or the humanities?

B **Identify** what sorts of activities and experiences may help young children to become literate and numerate, apart from literacy and numeracy.

C **Imagine** the possible implications for educators of the TLRP's call for *the conception of what is to be learned to be broadened beyond the notions of curricula and subjects associated with schools.*

Comment

The word 'curriculum' originally was based on the idea of running. The National Curriculum for children of five and older since the 1988 Act has been presented and understood largely in terms of subjects, with a strong emphasis on the core subjects, especially English and mathematics. This is more like a syllabus, a fairly static body of (mainly propositional) knowledge which children must acquire by a certain age. The curriculum for children under five has been structured rather differently, organised into areas of learning, rather than subjects. As the Rumbold Report suggests, young children's needs may be better served by a dynamic view of the curriculum, considering context, people and values and beliefs, rather than just content. And as the Hadow Report argued, the curriculum can be seen in terms of activities and experiences, a view which influenced the Plowden Report and many primary schools in the 1970s and 1980s.

Think what it means to be literate, especially in a society which increasingly relies on different forms of communication. Terms such as emotionally or culturally literate are in common use. Although such terms may be of doubtful value, they show that literacy is not just about decoding text, but making sense of different forms of communication. We saw in Chapter 3 the centrality of language in conceptual development. Both the Rose Review (DCSF, 2009) and the Cambridge Review (Alexander, 2010) emphasise oracy (speaking and listening) and Alexander (2000) indicates how, in Russian and French primary schools, pedagogy relies heavily on interactive dialogue (addressed further in Chapter 8). Oracy is more basic than reading and writing, since it not only provides the platform for these but enables interaction in a wide range of situations. Success in reading and writing is usually built on being a confident user of language – both as listener and speaker. However, success in school is usually defined mainly in terms of performance in reading and writing, because it is hard to measure progress in oracy, or at least to quantify this.

Few people question why numeracy is, with literacy, seen as the other 'pillar' of the basics. Personally, I wonder why 'doing sums' is given so much prominence, now that technological innovations such as calculators and spreadsheets have reduced the need for this. This is not to say that children should not be numerate but they should be exposed to a wider range of mathematics, with more problem-solving. More radically, it is unclear why mathematics should be seen as more basic than science, or the expressive arts, or humanities. If the answer is that mathematics is required as a foundation for future learning, this would seem no less true of the other aspects. This takes one back to what it means to be an educated person and the historic lack of priority given to 'Curriculum 2'. As the 1985 White Paper *Better Schools* (cited in Alexander, 2010, page 243) said:

> *the mistaken belief... that a concentration on basic skills is by itself enough to improve achievement in literacy and numeracy has left its mark; many children are still given too little opportunity in the practical, scientific and aesthetic areas... which increases not only their understanding in those areas but also their literacy and numeracy... overconcentration on the practice of basic skills in literacy and numeracy unrelated to a context in which they are needed means that those skills are insufficiently extended and applied.*

Moreover, Ofsted (2002, page 7), analysing factors in successful primary schools, emphasises that *the richness of the curriculum... and, in particular their achievement in the arts, contributed strongly to the development of pupils' imagination and the creative use of media and materials [with] the growth of pupils' self-confidence [helping] them to tackle more challenging work and develop a positive attitude towards school.* The report (pages 7–8) highlights the value of applying knowledge and skills learned in one subject to others, of first-hand experiences, including visits out of school, and of working with a range of adults and of extracurricular activities.

The debate on the best approach to early reading, especially on types of phonics, is too complicated to do justice to here. However, as the Cambridge Review (summary, page 16) reports, *in 14 of the 15 countries that scored higher than England in a major study of reading and literacy in 2006, children did not enter school until they were six or seven.* There are too many variables to draw definite conclusions on this, but it should make us wary of thinking that children starting school sooner will lead to improved standards of reading. Suggate's recent research (2010) suggests that children who start with formal literacy teaching at five do not achieve any better at age 11 than those who start at seven. He argues that 'ableness' does not imply readiness, and that *if you want a good harvest, you should plant the seed in the right season.* If children are introduced to formal activities too soon, they may become bored or discouraged, even if they learn to decode text or do sums correctly. To teach skills more easily learnt when children are older may deprive them of opportunities to develop their language skills and distract them from understanding the nuances of language. Moreover, the prominence given to literacy and numeracy gives a strong message about which forms of knowledge are most valued in school. The danger of this is to narrow the range of activities and experiences for all children, and to demotivate those children whose interests, and especially areas of successful learning, lie elsewhere. As Alexander (2010, pages 242–3) argues, this is not simply a question about a broad and balanced curriculum, but about success within 'the basics'.

It may seem obvious that children who are finding reading or writing difficult will benefit the more additional support they receive. Jackson et al. (1993) present the counterintuitive message that what the teacher intends to teach is not always what children learn and that direct instruction may not be the best way of promoting positive attitudes and values. If the most important messages about moral education come through indirect routes, this may be true of environmental awareness and of elements of reading or mathematics. Using puppets, drama or stories may be more effective than working with written text. Moreover, as we shall see in Chapter 8, too sharp a focus on details and skills rather than approaching an activity as a whole may be positively unhelpful.

You may still be convinced that young children must learn 'the basics'. I agree. However, this does not imply that they should spend most of their time on these. Building learning on narrow foundations may lead to later problems, even if the immediate results look impressive. Young children benefit from a breadth of activity and experience, enabling them to make connections between different areas of learning and experiences. This is essential to their well-being both in the here-and-now and to extend their repertoire of skills and attributes to underpin their later learning. Moreover, it helps create an inclusive learning environment, not just for high-achievers, but for all children, drawing on the varied interests and experiences they bring. To take the view that young children need only learn the 'basics' is to underestimate their abilities and may encourage a narrow view of learning and a sense that they are not competent learners.

Key ideas: **Play and playfulness**

Why does play matter?

In England, play is usually thought of as a type of activity which is the opposite of work and which children should grow out of. This is in contrast to those societies

/continued

Key idea: **Play and playfulness** – continued

with a stronger tradition of theory underpinning practice in the Early Years. The Scandinavian countries, for example, place a strong emphasis on play until children start formal schooling, usually around six years old. They believe that too early an introduction to formal 'work' at the expense of play risks leaving the children without secure foundations, emotionally, socially and intellectually.

Critical thinking exercise 2: exploring play and playfulness

A **Compare** the underlying assumptions about the two views of play set out above. Are there any of these which you would **challenge?**

B What is play? The best way to do this may be to **illustrate** what distinguishes play from other activities with examples.

C **Consider** the benefits which play offers and to what extent this is relevant through the primary years and beyond.

Comment

The English view of play described above contains (at least) three assumptions to be challenged, that play is:

- just an activity;
- only for children;
- not serious.

Play is both an activity and a process. One of a baby's most basic activities is to play, as a way of making sense of his or her relationship with the people, things and environment encountered. Indeed, biologists have long recognised that other mammals, such as dogs and monkeys, play and that social play helps them learn to understand the intention of other members of the species, with Bekoff (2001) suggesting that the interactive mechanisms involved provide a basis of co-operation and engagement.

While primarily associated with childhood, play remains important in many adults' lives, for example in sport, or music, or acting. However, such play is usually more structured and rule-bound than children's play; and (usually) linked to leisure, something peripheral, or in contrast, to the world of work, with 'real learning', we learn, taking place only when we 'work at it'.

These assumptions, inevitably, affect us. Think for example of how most primary schools separate work, structurally, from 'playtime'; and how many have a 'golden time' when children, having completed their (serious) 'work' have a chance to 'play'. Play is implicitly looked down on. For young children, play is work, until they are taught otherwise.

This begs the question of what play is. Finding a satisfactory definition is hard because the term covers so many types of activity and process. In McMahon's words (1992, page 1) play is *a spontaneous and active process in which thinking, feeling and doing can flourish since they are separated from the fear of failure or disastrous consequences.* One fundamental feature of play is that things and people can assume, or be given, different identities. So, a stick can become a magic wand, or a conductor's baton or a gun. A timid girl can become a princess or a dragon and a macho boy can dress as his grandma or a wolf. The child can operate with the meaning of something detached from what it appears to be, or is 'in reality'. Think about the words of the psychoanalyst, Winnicott (1980, page 63) *it is in playing and only in playing that the individual child or adult is able to be creative and to use the whole personality. It is only in being creative that the individual discovers the self.*

In play, the individual, however small or insignificant, can be in control and can experiment and explore, without having to take the consequences, especially the emotional ones, of failure. In other words, play provides hospitable space to take risks safely, both with things and emotions. For some, especially those who are feeling most anxious, it may be the only way of doing so. One vivid example occurred, when a Year 2 teacher was suddenly ill and I had, as head, to take over her class without any preparation. As the children finished the tasks set for them, I suggested that they take out different activities and play with them. One boy headed straight for a house with little figures of people. He had been involved in a horrific incident where two relatives had died and he had only just survived. In the intervening two months, he had barely spoken. Yet, as he moved the figures around, he could, on his own, start to process his experiences and emotions.

Tassoni and Hucker (2005, page 9) characterise five stages of play – solitary, spectator, parallel, partnership and co-operative – whereby individuals learn about, and practise, relationships with increasing levels of interaction and co-operation. In Siraj-Blatchford's words (1999, page 29), *Piaget argued that reciprocity in peer relations provides the foundations for perspective taking and for decentring. This suggests that collaborative play is exceptionally important for children.* Play offers an unforced way from individual to socialised activity.

Play also supports conceptual development and metacognition, since in Vygotsky's words (cited in Daniels et al., 2007, page 261) *action according to rules begins to be determined by ideas and not the objects themselves.* So, play helps to move towards more general and abstract thinking, but in a way where the child remains in control.

One dilemma is how much adults should intervene in children's play. Tassoni and Hucker (2005, pages 3–4) discuss the need for both free and structured play, which provides good opportunities to model ways of acting. However, there is a danger that when adults intervene to structure play, some of its essential features are lost, especially the child's control. There is no easy answer to this, but as a rule of thumb it seems best to intervene little and with suggestions rather than demands, ensuring that adults do not control the process. A good example is given by Siraj-Blatchford (1999, page 26):

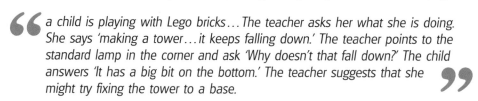

> a child is playing with Lego bricks... The teacher asks her what she is doing. She says 'making a tower...it keeps falling down.' The teacher points to the standard lamp in the corner and ask 'Why doesn't that fall down?' The child answers 'It has a big bit on the bottom.' The teacher suggests that she might try fixing the tower to a base.

Even when young children's need to play is (partly) recognised, playfulness is often overlooked, especially with older children. Inventors, artists and authors frequently attest that being playful, divergent, not over-focused on immediate results is essential in the creative process. Learning to talk involves being playful with the structures and meaning of words, such as recognising and repeating rhymes and finding unexpected similarities and variations. Writing a good story or article requires being prepared to try different ideas and words. Imagining and playing with alternative possibilities help when composing an original picture or a piece of music, even though these need a framework. The girls' response in the case study depended on them imagining, experimenting and overcoming their inhibitions. Playfulness can not only make learning more enjoyable but helps to steer it into new areas, building on the child's interests rather than just what adults prescribe or plan. Since it is a process, a way of working, playfulness can happen in any domain of learning, given the right environment, though it is easier is some than in others, as considered later in this chapter.

Key idea: **First-hand experience**

What are the benefits of first-hand experience?

Collins (cited in the Cambridge Primary Review summary, page 26) emphasises that children *need things you can touch, feel and taste*. This builds on the strong tradition among educators in the Early Years on first-hand experience, for instance with active exploration of materials and the outdoor environment, and the emphasis of the Plowden Report (HMSO, 1967) on direct, first-hand experience in primary schools. Yet, especially with the greater emphasis on instruction and the wider availability and use of technology, both at home and school, such experience is often limited, especially for children in Key Stages 1 and 2.

Critical thinking exercise 3: first-hand experience

A **Illustrate** with an example what you would think of first-hand experience, and one which you think is not, in the following domains:
- science;
- mathematics;
- music;
- religious education;
- one other subject area;
- one activity unrelated to school.

B **Consider** the benefits and disadvantages of first-hand experience.

C **Identify** which factors have led to a reduced emphasis on first-hand experience.

Comment

Examples are probably the best way of indicating what I mean by first-hand experience. These would include, in science, doing an experiment or making a model rather than reading a book about stars and, in mathematics, measuring the height of a group of children rather than completing a page of sums. It involves singing or composing or listening to music, and visiting a place of worship or taking part in a festival, rather than just learning about composers or religious beliefs; or observing an egg hatch, a plant grow or a pet die, rather than seeing a picture or being told about such events. Or discovering that sailors wore a gold earring to pay for their burial if drowned – as I did, as an adult, with a group of children, on a school trip – by seeing and talking with someone dressed in that way. In short, doing and experiencing directly, rather than relying on someone else's interpretation.

This is not to downplay the importance of knowledge being presented or interpreted in books, on film, or by an adult. These enable children to have a range of experiences way beyond the range of what is possible directly. And we have seen how language and other cultural tools are vital in developing a more secure conceptual understanding. However, especially for those less able, or used, to engage in abstract thought, first-hand experience, and the chance to represent experience in different ways, such as actions and drawing, help provide the foundation to support this.

A deep conceptual understanding requires practice and application, not simply instruction. The less the child's experience in any domain, the more important first-hand experience is to provide the foundation of learning. Once learners have a greater understanding of concepts, they can think more abstractly. But introducing symbolic representation too soon risks causing confusion. The danger for educators is to assume a conceptual understanding which individual children do not have. Many people have been put off mathematics because they never understood what fractions or algebra were all about. And too often scientific understanding is limited by an emphasis on facts rather than understanding, on the teacher's knowledge rather than the child's question. Do you recall Jessica's question about who made volcanoes at the start of Chapter 3?

A further benefit is that first-hand experience provides the opportunity to attend to detail and so to develop the learner's own aesthetic sense. To have observed and drawn the doorway of a Norman church or a daffodil can extend an individual's knowledge and appreciation of them in a way that is different, and deeper, than reading a description or seeing a picture. To have sung in a large choir, or been part of a team playing in a cup final, touches aspects of ourselves, in ways that are more intense than hearing about such events. One facet of spiritual development is how experiences of awe and wonder – the power of the sea or the beauty of a mathematical pattern – help children (and adults) to gain a sense of their own perspective. The value of such experiences cannot be judged in terms of measurable outcomes.

A less obvious benefit is that first-hand experience helps provide a (more) 'level playing field' in that all children, whatever their prior experience of language and culture, have access to the same stimulus. For example, reading or writing about a real or imaginary journey is likely to be easier for children with experiences both of journeys and books about them; whereas the experience of 'Forest School', in the Early Years, or making a working model, makes differences as a result of prior learning experiences less significant.

One major challenge facing educators is how to engage and motivate children in a culture where they are used to instant responses. It is tempting to think that first-hand experience motivates young children and encourages creativity. In my experience, often it does, especially when art and practical activities are involved. However, Chapter 5 suggested that children are motivated in very different ways. Activities which are unfamiliar and challenging may be seen as threatening. Computer games are motivating because they create a safe but exciting world. So, first-hand experience, as such, may not engage children if this leads to anxiety, especially by being subjected to the judgement of, and comparison with, other people.

Despite the importance of direct, first-hand experience, many of the activities and experiences involved tend to be slower than those mediated by the teacher and the results harder to measure. This helps explain why the current emphasis in schools on pace and on results downplays first-hand experience, especially with older children. For children to understand at a deep level, especially where their age or inexperience makes abstract thought difficult, they require a balance of first-hand and mediated experience. The developmental tradition tended to underestimate the need for adult mediation; and that of the standards agenda to overestimate it.

Opportunities for direct experience exist in any subject area, though these are easier and more obvious in some, such as the expressive arts, as discussed in the next section.

Key ideas: **Breadth and balance**

What do children learn from the expressive arts and humanities?

Above, we encountered the distinction between Curriculum 1 and Curriculum 2, and how a succession of reports have emphasised the importance of a broad and balanced curriculum. Excellence and Enjoyment states (DfES, 2003, page 9) that *in outstanding primary schools, there is no sense of a tension between high standards and exciting learning.* However, the Cambridge Primary Review is adamant that external pressures, notably those associated with testing and inspection, lead to a narrowing of the curriculum. And Williams (2003, page 114) suggests why, in writing: *too often, the institution as a whole is pushing tense, driven messages, messages of anxiety about filling up empty spaces and never wasting time. This can mean that the arts and music and drama, even sport, are pushed to the edges except as further forms of competition.* Therefore, external pressures to perform make it harder to provide breadth and balance, but developing the attributes of successful learners and promoting children's well-being entails doing so.

Critical thinking exercise 4: the role of the expressive arts and the humanities

Ofsted (2010, page 4), in a report which evaluates and illustrates how 44 schools in all phases used creative approaches to learning, suggest that almost all:

were making effective use of creative approaches to learning. Most of the teachers felt confident in encouraging pupils to make connections across traditional boundaries, speculate constructively, maintain an open mind while exploring a wide range of options, and reflect critically on ideas and outcomes. This had a perceptible and positive impact on pupils' personal development, and on their preparation for life beyond school.

A **Discuss** and **imagine** what a child can gain from:

- dressing up in the home corner;
- painting a picture;
- listening to a steel band.

Is this different at 4 or 5 years old and at 9 or 10?

B **Consider** what skills or outcomes you would want young children to gain from learning:

- history, geography and religious education;
- music, art and physical education.

C **Articulate** in what ways these areas of learning contribute to the development of the 'whole child'.

Comment

Young children usually enjoy and are engaged by art, music, drama and physical activity, However, these are not peripheral, fun, 'Friday-afternoon', activities to be undertaken when the serious business of learning has taken place; but central to young children's learning.

Chapter 3 considered how very young children rely initially on enactive representation, 'acting their way into thinking', with this remaining important, even when other ways of representation are available. So, for example, dressing up and pretending to be someone or somewhere else is not just an enjoyable activity in the Nursery. It encourages imagination and helps children to explore themselves and others and the emotions and relationships involved. Drama remains one main route into self-understanding, whatever one's age. Maybe, it is just that adults need an excuse to dress up. To take another example of enactive representation, making a working model is the best way of understanding electricity or gravity, not least because learning from success and failure provides a good route into abstract generalisation. There is no test so severe as that of experience.

We saw that iconic follows enactive representation in developmental terms, though it is not to be discarded when symbolic forms of representation become available. Painting a scene in the park or drawing a skull or a machine is not just an activity to fill time. It is for a young child an alternative, usually more accessible, way of making meaning than describing it in words; and for older children and adults a way of deepening and enriching understanding, at a level different from that available through language. While language, especially, and other forms of symbolic representation provide a very powerful way of dealing with abstract ideas, other forms of representation offer different routes into understanding. Remember, how when we struggle with abstract thought, we will often use models or drawings to represent our thoughts. These may be alternatives, or mutually reinforcing, and are especially important when any one of us is at the limits of our understanding.

Listening to a steel band may be enjoyable and extend children's awareness of how sounds are made in unfamiliar ways. For many children, it may provide a route into greater awareness and discussion of different cultural traditions. For some, it may give recognition to their own cultural traditions. For a few, it may prompt a lifelong interest in a particular genre of music whether as listener or player. We never quite know the impact of such experiences, especially at unconscious levels. However, educators are too often concerned that children will not 'understand' activities such as art and music, poetry and dance. Yet this is to misunderstand how such experiences, or the arts themselves, 'work'. In Salmon's words, (1995, pages 57–8):

 non-verbal materials, the use of images…are perhaps particularly fertile in eliciting responses from highly personal, deeply intuitive levels of understanding. Trying too soon to find words for something felt but not yet known can often drive it into inaccessibility. Only after it has been anchored within a visual form can efforts to give it clear verbal formulation be valuable.

Understanding is not just about being able to put thoughts into words. A group of eight-and nine-year-olds saw in Picasso's picture *Guernica* meanings that I hadn't. Often, children will understand a poem at one level, even if they have not understood all the nuances, or in the way that an adult would. A child's response may be simpler, but not necessarily less profound, than an adult's. However, knowledge of oneself is a personal journey, rather than a competition against others.

The foundation subjects include two main areas, the expressive arts and the humanities, though young children's learning should not be confined by subject boundaries. Therefore, while it may be useful to approach planning in terms of subject-specific content or skills, working with children involves enabling them to establish connections across these boundaries. For example, literacy may be best learned, and applied, through historical research or describing a science experiment; and numeracy by designing a garden or comparing the results of football teams.

The expressive arts are usually seen as including art, music and physical activity such as dance. The developmental tradition regards these as central to young children's learning. Donaldson (1992, page 43) suggests that the visual arts and crafts, whether for adults or children, *belong to a large extent in point mode*. In other words, they nurture or encourage a more immediate type of response, an absorption, recapturing something of young children's way of understanding. To make or to enjoy a picture or a piece of music is to construct something new or to access one's own, and other people's, creativity. To hear a beautiful poem or story, or to write one, is to tap into, and join, a tradition of how cultures and other people have expressed their feelings and beliefs. To go to the theatre, be part of a choir or to play a new sport may help to extend the horizons of one's world. Many Early Years educators, especially, have retained a belief in the importance of the expressive arts, as with the Reggio Emilia approach. The greater emphasis on symbolic representation, notably reading and writing, and even more so the focus on literacy and numeracy, makes this harder with older children, though it is no less important.

The humanities are usually seen as including history, geography and religious education (RE). History is related to time, geography to place and RE to belief. However, literature is also part of the humanities. These are central to the developmental tradition, though criticism of how they were taught through topic work in English schools in the 1970s and 1980s reflects that this often lacked rigour. As discussed further in Chapter 8, history and geography does not just involve learning the dates of kings and queens and the names of rivers and cities; and RE provides a chance to understand (at least something) about oneself and the world through the lens of faith and different faiths. Therefore, talking with a very old person or exploring ancient buildings, mapping out one's locality or interpreting a landscape, handling a holy book or visiting a church or a mosque are not just interesting experiences. They can provide a window into other times and places and worldviews.

In thinking why the expressive arts and humanities matter, one must therefore consider what these can offer when taught well, when too often they have not been, whether through lack of expertise, rigour or time. In particular, they provide the chance for experiences which help children both to understand themselves and their own immediate environment and to reach beyond it. The case study indicates how, temporarily, the girls could become peasants facing homelessness and Patrick understand something about the cruel punishments in the eighteenth century. I think of the expressive arts as helping children to express themselves in creative and original ways and the humanities as making us more humane. So, however necessary the skills associated with the core subjects, those involved in the foundation subjects both support these and help to develop different aspects of children's lives and open up new opportunities. To deny children these is to limit their lives within narrow confines, to know only part of their own story, to limit the boundaries of their well-being.

Conclusion

This chapter has explored the idea of the curriculum for young children, especially, being seen in terms of activity and experience rather than subject content. We have considered some types of activity and experience necessary to provide secure foundations for young children's learning, recognising that this list is by no means exclusive. The critical thinking exercises will have helped you:

- **challenge** what the 'basics' means to see why breadth and balance matter;
- **consider** the importance of play and playfulness, seeing these both as activities and as an approach associated with creativity;
- **explore** what is meant by direct or first-hand experience and why young children need this;
- **identify** the role of the expressive arts and the humanities in young children's learning.

In Chapter 8, the focus turns more specifically to how adults can support children as successful learners.

Further reading

Ball, C (1994) *Start Right: The importance of early learning.* London: Royal Society for the encouragement of Arts, Manufacture and Commerce
A report which summarises accessibly the link between research, policy and practice in the Early Years.

NACCCE (National Advisory Committee on Creative and Cultural Education) (1999) *All Our Futures: Creativity, culture and education.* London: DfEE
A clear and thoughtful report, with particularly good chapters (pages 27–53) on creative and cultural education.

Supporting successful learning

Introduction

In Chapter 1, various approaches to pedagogy were introduced, distinguishing between didactic and exploratory approaches, since as Alexander (2010, page 305) writes, *different kinds of learning demand different kinds of teaching – declarative and procedural knowledge require direct teaching, while conceptual and metacognitive knowledge require co-construction and dialogue.* This chapter extends the discussion of the last two chapters, focusing more on the role of adults. We start by looking at the idea of 'scaffolding' and then feedback, to see that both are more complex than may appear at first sight. We then discuss interactive talk and dialogue and finally to what extent adults can help different types of expertise with young children. Underlying this is a view that there are many 'routes into' learning and that therefore educators must draw on a wide repertoire.

CASE STUDY

Susie and Gemma were both in Year 2. Susie started as a non-reader, needing constant support and repetition to remember how to decode even the simplest words. A rather solitary girl, she enjoyed staying in for a few minutes at lunchtime to read to herself or just to look at books. Gemma, in contrast, was a

---

CASE STUDY continued

keen reader who needed little direct teaching but loved the opportunity to read to herself and would often stay with Susie to take on the role of 'teacher'. So, while I tidied or prepared, they would sit and read together. By the end of the year, Susie had become a far more independent reader, though she probably never became a fluent one. So, both girls benefited, in terms of self-concept as well as performance, by becoming engaged, at different levels, in the community of readers.

This story reminds us that there is no one route into reading, or any other type of learning. In their different ways, both girls were motivated, one by the sheer joy of reading, the other by an unexpected determination and their relationship with each other and me. Gemma needed little support and Susie probably benefited more from Gemma's patient prompting than my direct instruction. As we shall see, the best forms of scaffolding and feedback come in many varieties and sometimes from unlikely sources, though adults have distinctive roles, especially in helping establish ways of working and thinking together.

Key idea: **Scaffolding**

How can adults best support young children's learning?

In Bruner's (1996, page 120) words:

> There are stages of development that constrain how fast and how far a child can leap ahead in abstraction…The child's mind does not move to higher levels of abstraction like the tide coming in. Development depends also…upon the child's grasp of the context or situation in which he or she has to reason. A good intuitive, practical grasp of a domain at one stage of development leads to better, earlier and deeper thinking in the next stage when the child meets challenging new problems in that domain. As a teacher, you do not wait for readiness to happen; you foster or 'scaffold' it by deepening the child's powers at the stage where you find him or her now.

Scaffolding is a well-known aspect of pedagogy. Tharp and Gallimore (cited in Bliss et al., 1996, page 41) suggest that scaffolding's *three major mechanisms…are modelling, contingency management and feedback.* We have discussed modelling to some extent and will come to it further in relation to dialogue, but it draws on the learner's need to see and experience how a task is successfully approached and practise this with guidance and supervision. We shall discuss feedback, showing that it is subtler and less

---

talk-related than one may think, requiring the ability to respond to events (that is contingency management), for instance by rewarding or correcting the learner's responses. And we shall explore in Chapter 9 to what extent, and how, these processes can be planned for.

Critical thinking exercise 1: scaffolding

Discovery provides a large problem space; expository teaching a more delimited one. Each has its risks. Too large a problem space and a child may never hit on a solution; define it too narrowly a student may simply memorize a solution (Olson, 2001, page 113).

Although the scaffolding process has been shown…to underpin teaching in a reading intervention, we are less confident that it is useful in understanding ordinary classroom teaching (Hobsbaum et al., 1996, page 32).

A **Consider** what you understand by the term scaffolding in the light of these two quotations.

B **Identify** what to do, and to avoid, in scaffolding a young child's learning.

C **Articulate** what adults need to know in order to 'scaffold' learning successfully.

Comment

Scaffolding involves providing support for someone less knowledgeable or experienced from someone with more knowledge and experience. Langer and Applebee (cited in Daniels et al., 2007, page 319) highlight the key features:

- ownership – of the activity to be learned;
- appropriateness – to the student's current knowledge;
- structure – embodying a 'natural' sequence of thought and action;
- collaboration – between teacher and student;
- internalisation – via gradual withdrawal of the scaffolding and transfer of control.

'Ownership' implies that, for scaffolding to be successful, the learner must be engaged with the task. So, scaffolding a child who is uninterested in a book, or a problem, is less likely to work than when motivation is strong. Appropriateness to current understanding is vital. Remember the zone of proximal development (ZPD) – the area 'just beyond' the learner's current level of understanding. Too simple a task is unlikely to lead to conceptual development. One which is too hard will make it impossible, at least in the way intended. The need for a natural sequence of thought and action and for collaboration emphasises that scaffolding needs to follow the less experienced person's own thought processes, rather than these being imposed by the more experienced one; and that scaffolding requires working together. Since the purpose of scaffolding is internalisation and independence of thought, it must be planned with a view to being gradually withdrawn, with the level of support required varying, depending on how independently the learner is able to work. Buildings which are more intricate or complicated may require different types of support during construction, but any architect or builder must plan for such support to be temporary rather than a permanent feature.

Bliss et al. (1996, page 39) cite Greenfield's view that *scaffolding... does not involve simplifying the task... Instead, it holds the task constant while simplifying the learner's role through the graduated intervention of the teacher.* For instance, children in the early stages of learning English as an additional language do not need language structures to be oversimplified, but for the level of cognitive challenge and linguistic richness to be maintained but with additional support, for example by:

● providing visual prompts and activities;
● allowing listening and rehearsal rather than insisting too soon on public performance;
● modelling language well, for example by saying half-sentences to complete and then reinforcing this by repetition, perhaps in a more elaborated or more conventional form.

Hobsbaum et al. (1996, page 28), discussing one-to-one interventions in writing, identify three phases of scaffolding where the adult:

● monitors very closely and intervenes a great deal;
● acts as a prompt or 'memory amplifier'; and finally
● is essentially reactive, with the child acting more independently having internalised prompts and being able to monitor her own work.

This supports children in regulating their own learning, without encouraging too much dependence.

This approach relies on accurate assessment of the learner's current state of knowledge. This is much easier when working with an individual or small group than with a class, both because there are so many children to assess and since large groups will almost always have a wider range of current understanding. This explains why assessment, as discussed in Chapter 9, is such a vital part of educators', and especially class teachers', repertoires.

It is especially helpful for children to learn to provide feedback to themselves, to recognise what they need to do to improve, as discussed in relation to metacognition. While this is usually associated with the learner's internal processes, one should not overlook the role of the adult in developing this. As indicated, instruction is not the best route to conceptual development. However, Tharp and Gallimore (see Bliss et al., 1996, page 41) point out that *the non-instructing teacher may be denying the learner the most valuable residue of the teaching interaction: that heard, regulating voice, a gradually internalised voice, that then becomes the pupil's self-regulating 'still small' instructor.* In other words, simple reminders can help children take increasing control of their own learning, whether in holding the pencil correctly or remembering which strategies to use when decoding words.

One important aspect of scaffolding is to enable children to think, to plan, to formulate time for a response. Often, this involves waiting. I recall I was playing a counting game with a very quiet girl in the early stages of learning English in a Reception class. This involved throwing a die and moving two little animals each along the board. We took turns, with her counting to herself and saying nothing out loud, and me talking through what I was doing. After two or three minutes, three animals were one move away from the finish, with the last trailing some way back. She turned and whispered, almost inaudibly, *Look, the snail's crying.* An immediate intervention would have prevented her from expressing her thoughts, resulting in too hasty (and inaccurate) a judgement about her competence in English. On another occasion, I was working with Year 4 children seeing how to change the swing of a pendulum. Going over to a group of boys apparently off task, and stopping to listen, indicated that they were thinking creatively about different ways of altering the pendulum, but without actually using the one they had made. Too soon or direct an intervention by an adult may stop children from formulating their own understanding.

While scaffolding is usually considered in cognitive terms, emotional scaffolding is necessary, especially for very young children and those who are anxious. It is vital that all children learn to regulate their emotions so that they are in control of their actions: what one might call, to invent a new word, 'metaemotion'. However, this is much harder for some children, and for all children whenever they are overwhelmed by anxiety. In such situations, adults may need to provide clearer boundaries and less choice, but always looking ultimately to make such emotional scaffolding unnecessary, so that children learn to regulate their own actions.

Key idea: **Feedback**

What sort of feedback enhances the attributes of successful learners?

Feedback, a term used in biology, is part of a process which enables a system to respond to new experience, to reinforce or to prompt change. As Black (1999, page 121) states, *teaching must start by exploring existing ideas and encouraging expression and defence of them in argument, for unless the learners' thinking is made explicit, to themselves as well as to their teachers, they cannot be fully aware of the need for conceptual modification.* Though this may overstate the role of conscious learning, providing feedback helps to reinforce or otherwise what children have done and to provide guidance on what to do next. However, feedback comes in many forms and, as educators, we cannot avoid giving feedback, so we need to understand and develop those types which enhance the attributes of successful learning.

Critical thinking exercise 2: feedback

Where parents give a child plenty of positive feedback for their efforts rather than results, and do not punish them for mistakes or lapses in behaviour that they cannot yet control, children will have a positive view of what they can achieve and realise that well-directed effort works.

(Alexander, 2010, page 82)

A **Articulate** as many types of feedback as you can and **compare** their purposes; for example, spoken or written, marks or 'smiley faces'.

B **Identify** what sorts of feedback are especially valuable in enhancing young children's learning.

C **Imagine** how educators can encourage young children to provide feedback to themselves.

Comment

Feedback must start from the child's own experience and actions. Given the importance of reciprocity, how feedback is both given and understood helps to set expectations and promote appropriate responses. Feedback may come either from the learner him or herself, from other children or from an adult. It may involve:

- formal aspects, such as grades, marks and comments, whether spoken or written;
- informal aspects, including body language such as smiles or hand gestures which express approval or discouragement, many of which may be unconscious.

Alexander's comment in the box above, although related to parents, emphasises the value of positive feedback. This is a good starting point, especially working with young children in group situations. It never ceases to amaze me how young children will respond to an adult who points out those who are doing what is expected, rather than those who are not. And encouragement is far more likely to ensure engagement than continually pointing out what is wrong.

Success is built on a high level of self-esteem – a belief that one can succeed. While a low level of self-esteem leads easily to disengagement, *self-esteem is much more potent when it is 'won through striving whole-heartedly for worthwhile ends, rather than derived from praise, especially praise that may be only loosely related to actual achievement'*, as Dweck (summarised in Claxton, 2005, page 17) argues. So good feedback does not consist simply in constant praise, regardless of how hard a child has tried. As discussed in relation to emotional intelligence, this can easily lead to children not recognising the importance of hard work and persistence.

Dweck highlights the importance of praising behaviours rather than ability. She challenges (1999, pages 1–2) the belief that (what she calls) mastery-oriented qualities:

- are more likely to be displayed by children with high ability;
- are directly fostered by success in school;
- depend on children's confidence in their intelligence;

Dweck argues that high levels of performance often makes children concerned about failure, writing (1999, page 2) *far from instilling confidence…praise (for smartness) can lead students to fear failure, avoid risks, doubt themselves when they fail, and cope poorly with setbacks,* unless they maintain a growth mindset of intelligence. While this may be surprising, Dweck makes a convincing case for praising children for (what I call) the attributes of successful learners rather than for intelligence or for successful completion of easy tasks.

Feedback, whether a score or a comment, may spur some children on or discourage others. Research (see Black and Wiliam, 1998, page 23) has demonstrated that children (and we) take more notice of grades or scores than of written comments intended to guide future actions, and that the giving of grades can undermine the positive help given by task comments. So, feedback needs to involve advice as well as affirmation, reassurance as well as challenge, but above all to maintain the child's motivation to continue. This is more likely when an adult starts from what the children are doing and saying, or their ideas and interests, and then giving immediate feedback, especially for young children, than providing comments unrelated to the child's current thoughts or actions.

Brooker (2002) explores why the transition from home or a pre-school setting to school is hard for many children. The expectations, of listening, of responding, of moving are very different. Yet adults often expect young children to understand and know this automatically. It is harder for those who because of cultural reasons are used to forms of feedback, reward or punishment different from those used in school. Moreover, Dowling (2010, page 90) indicates that young children learn to recognise the meaning behind other people's actions only gradually, starting with those whom they know well – one reason why familiarity and predictability matters especially in the Early Years. So, even when you believe that you are giving positive and formative feedback to young children, they may not always receive it as such.

While we tend to focus on formal, conscious aspects of feedback, many of the most important messages are given and received at an unconscious level. For example, beliefs about ability and potential are transmitted not only by words, but by small actions, by whose contributions are valued most, by how children are grouped. Whatever you say, your actions matter more. Children will take more notice of the example that you set; and be more adventurous or playful if adults encourage these qualities in what they say and do. They are more likely to be resilient or thoughtful with adults who model these attributes. And to prompt appropriate risk-taking, you need not only to encourage it verbally, but to take risks yourself. So, one central message is to 'walk the talk'.

Although feedback from adults is the most obvious type, children can often provide valuable feedback to each other, especially where the right atmosphere has been created. Of course, children can be hurtful or bully, but they can also be very supportive, for instance when a child overcomes his or her difficulties; or when a group achieves success. One great benefit of group work is that children are able to discuss and think together and to discuss with each other. Other children will often understand more accurately, or at least differently, difficulties that a child may have – and the child most able to connect and support may often be another child who is not a high performer. I am convinced that Susie, in the case study, learned to read because she drew on her own resources, in a relaxed situation, rather than having to listen to the insistent sound of an adult voice. So, sometimes the best sort of support is to let a child, or group, work out answers for themselves, as I did to some extent with Gemma and Susie.

While it is usually helpful for feedback to be specific about what to do next, adults must be careful not always to break tasks into tiny bits. Gregory Bateson, a biologist, described two different ways of trying to improve his shooting: *when shooting a rifle at a stationary target, it is best to keep correcting each separate act. However, when aiming at a flying bird, this does not work well, since a complex series of actions need to interact. Instead, one needs improved 'calibration' where, through practice, all of these actions come together in a whole single action* (1988, page 49). He continues: *as a boy, I spent terrible hours from the age of nine to eighteen trying to learn to play the violin and so far as music was concerned I learned precisely the wrong things. By continually trying to correct the individual note, I prevented myself from learning that music resides in the larger sequence.*

To try to understand this, when learning to drive I focused too much on the road and overcorrected until I was able to relax and to recognise that expertise entailed seeing the bigger picture, not responding to every tiny movement. I also recall, though I can hardly bear to do so, another boy's first completed piece of woodwork being thrown away just as he completed it. My own effort only just escaped the same fate. They were very poor pieces of carpentry, but not for lack of trying. In my case, it was probably the result of trying too hard. Too frequently, as adults, we inhibit children's learning by breaking tasks into tiny parts; and we should never rubbish genuine effort.

In thinking how this may relate to young children, it may be a good strategy at times when learning to read to decode by breaking words into parts; but at others it helps to get the flow of meaning for instance by reading on and returning to an unfamiliar word to understand the meaning in context. Writing a story requires narrative flow at least as much as the formal structure and conventions of story. And learning to throw a ball, or paint a picture, or understand how a map works is often inhibited by breaking activities into tiny steps rather than attempting the exercise and, in Bateson's terms, improving calibration through practice. So, appropriate feedback may include correcting specific errors and encouraging an activity or skill to be repeated in a similar or slightly changed context. Which is most appropriate at any point depends on judgement, based on knowledge of the child at least as much as subject knowledge.

Key idea: **Dialogue**

> **How can adults encourage high quality dialogue?**
>
> Alexander (2010, page 199) sets out as one of the aims of the Cambridge Primary Review, *to advance a pedagogy in which dialogue is central: between self and others, between personal and collective knowledge, between present and past, between different ways of making sense.* As Vygotsky showed, language is the key (though not the only) symbolic tool in developing conceptual understanding, requiring interaction. Bruner writes (1996, page 93): *it is not just sheer language acquisition that makes [learning possible]. Rather it is the give and take of talk that makes collaboration possible. For the agentive mind is not only active in nature, it seeks out dialogue and discourse with other active minds.* Reciprocal talk, both among children and between children and adults, is one of the key tools of pedagogy. As the EPPE project concludes (Sylva et al., 2010), sustained shared thinking is not only possible with very young children but a feature of effective Early Years settings.

Tizard and Hughes (1984) is one of many studies indicating that both the quality and quantity of young children's talk are much greater at home than in a more formal setting. Drury (2007) makes a similar point in relation to three- and four-year-old Punjabi-speaking girls. This section explores why it is so important, but so hard, in school to encourage the type of dialogue which enhances learning and how one can do so.

> **Critical thinking exercise 3:** encouraging high-quality talk and dialogue
>
> *Questioning…has a key role in pedagogy…however…in the classroom setting [it] is not straightforward and…its success is partly dependent on the quality of the teacher-pupil relationship* (Gipps and MacGilchrist, 1999, page 57). They go on (citing Rogoff) to highlight that:
>
> - where teachers' questions are usually restricted to lower order skills, those about understanding or application may be seen as unfair;
> - individual children may respond differently on the basis of expectations about the sorts of response which are acceptable or expected.
>
> /continued

> **Critical thinking exercise 3** – continued
>
> A Bearing this statement in mind, **consider** what sorts of questions (by adults) encourage or discourage the sort of talk which helps to enhance children's learning.
>
> B **Articulate** in the light of your experience (and what you have read) what adults can do (or not do) to encourage high-quality talk.
>
> C **Identify** how dialogue can be encouraged in the classroom, especially where children are unused to this.

Comment

Asking questions is one of the key ways in which children learn. This is neatly captured in the rhyme:

> *I have six honest working men*
> *Who taught me all I knew.*
> *Their names are what and where and when*
> *and how and why and who.*

I have always liked the story of the parent who said to his children at the end of each day not *what have you learned?* but *have you asked a good question today?* When we stop asking questions, our learning strategies are dramatically reduced. Similarly, asking questions (especially to prompt further questions) is a key tool in an educator's repertoire.

One simple distinction is between open and closed questions. Closed questions have a correct answer, usually which the person asking knows and related to factual knowledge, such as 'who is the Prime Minister?' or 'when was the outbreak of the Second World War?' Open questions, in contrast, imply some uncertainty and invite responses which are more tentative or prompt further questions, such as 'what do you suppose the hardest decision might be for the Prime Minister?' or 'can you think why the Second World War broke out when it did?'

A second distinction is made by Myhill et al. (2006, page 71), who suggest four good types of question, namely:

- factual;
- speculative;
- process;
- procedural (to explore whether children know what to do).

Factual and procedural questions are of course necessary and useful, but speculative and process questions invite a response where children can clarify and make explicit their understanding and make links. For instance, *I wonder who can tell me why a feather drops slowly to the ground when you let it go* invites children to think for themselves and articulate their existing understanding; and *could you explain how you worked out that 63 and 72 comes to 135?* encourages a child to make evident to others their cognitive (and metacognitive) processes.

A third distinction, made in Bliss et al. (1996), is between questions which assess and those which assist. The former are needed to know what a child understands (and so to plan appropriate activities), such as the question about the feather, while the latter can help a child or group to articulate, and so to explore further, their understanding.

Open questions which invite children to speculate and hypothesise are one of the best ways for adults to enhance learning, but the evidence suggests that adults dominate the interactions and that they find it hard to use questioning effectively. For example, Black (1999, page 127) writes:

 Stiggins et al. found that two thirds of questions [used in classroom dialogue] were tests of recall only and less than 20 per cent required deductive or inferential reasoning. This often happens because teachers want a quick response to questions addressed to a whole class – silence of more than a few seconds is regarded as embarrassing...So students have no time to think, whilst in order to maintain the dialogue the questions are simplified until they reach the level at which they can be answered without time for thought.

One reason is too great an emphasis on the right answer, rather than seeing mistakes or speculations as a way of learning. A succession of correct answers is pleasing, but actually does little to enhance learning. A second reason is that adults often see themselves as the repository of knowledge, where they know the answer, and for the child to replicate this demonstrates that learning has taken place. Even when this is not so, children may adopt a passive or cautious approach to learning, trying to discover the answer the adult wants before actually committing themselves to it. This may be because of a wish to be 'right' either to please the adult or to avoid the scorn of other children. Unconsciously, adults often reinforce this by only asking follow-up questions when the answer is wrong. Gipps (1994, pages 30–31) provides a useful summary of the ORACLE project's conclusion that teachers' and children's responses tend to be mutually reinforcing, leading to too much emphasis on surface learning and too little on genuine interactive dialogue.

Alexander (2010, page 306) suggests that exploiting the full potential of talk requires 'dialogic' teaching which is:

- collective – where learning tasks are approached together;
- reciprocal – where adults and children listen actively to each other;
- supportive – where children can articulate ideas freely without embarrassment;
- cumulative – where adults and children build on and link each others' ideas;
- purposeful – where dialogue is steered by adults with specific goals in mind.

Dialogue does not happen naturally in the classroom, especially in a climate emphasising outcomes rather than processes. It needs to be planned for, with children learning the conventions such as active listening, turn-taking or how to challenge someone else's view. This takes time, because children often have learned that their voice doesn't really count. So, educators need consciously and explicitly to establish an environment to enable this. This involves developing habits such as:

- children being encouraged to:
  - ask questions, especially when they are unsure;
  - talk and interact rather than just listen;
  - listen and respond respectfully but, where need be, challenge and make mistakes;

- adults being prepared to:
  - raise questions, especially those which invite exploration and speculation and which challenge, to develop metacognition;
  - model how to ask questions;
  - talk less and listen more;
  - allow space for thinking and for uncertainty;
  - support children brave enough to articulate their thoughts, especially those who are reticent about doing so.

These are not easy for either adults or children. Children often expect that this is how interaction in school 'works'. But, it helps to introduce routines gradually and practise until both you and the children become used to particular ways of working. So, for example, waiting – both you and the children – before taking answers to a question gives time for thinking, which is especially useful for reticent children or those who are unsure. In a class discussion, it helps to pair children to discuss a question before taking answers – a strategy which involves children more and encourages discussion in a safe environment rather than having to risk being wrong in front of the whole class. And (occasionally) repeating a question, or saying 'are you sure?' when the answer given is correct, though often unsettling, encourages children to think again and be assertive.

One important consideration is group size. Dialogue with a whole class can be especially useful to share ideas, for instance following group or individual work, but it is often difficult to enable interactive questioning. For example, although circle time has many benefits, its structure often inhibits genuine dialogue where people can interrupt and challenge. Discussion in small groups is hard to manage when teaching a whole class but is likely to encourage greater participation. To encourage sustained shared thinking, one needs to establish a learning community, where children become used to such ways of interacting.

Key idea: **Learning community**

Can, and should, young children be encouraged to act and think like experts?
The second of the TLRP's principles states that *pedagogy should engage learners with the big ideas, key skills and processes, modes of discourse, ways of thinking and practising.* Reed (2001, page 122) argues that *even the youngest children should be exposed to a broad and ambitious curriculum in the hope of identifying one or more areas at which each child excels or is motivated to learn.* This section considers to what extent there are specific ways of working in different domains of learning and it is possible, and advisable, to encourage this in young children; and explores the idea of a learning community – elaborating more on the type of learning environment which enables young children to develop the attributes of successful learning.

Critical thinking exercise 4: encouraging the development of different skills

In Bruner's words (1963, page 33), *we teach a subject not to produce little libraries…but rather to get a student to think mathematically…to consider matters as a historian does…*

Let us look at the three areas of learning:

- mathematics and science;
- history and geography;
- philosophy.

A **Articulate** to which extent these depend on propositional (factual) knowledge and the procedures and skills associated with each, thinking which generic (i.e. applicable to all learning) and which are specific to a particular domain (e.g. as a scientist or a geographer).

B **Consider** the implications of your answers for young children and in terms of your own subject knowledge.

C **Identify** the features of what a learning community might be like when working with young children.

Comment
The areas of learning in the box above were chosen because they are usually seen rather differently:

- mathematics and science, as hierarchical with definite answers;

- history and geography, as broad and open to different interpretations;
- philosophy, as a largely abstract discipline.

The expertise of a mathematician is usually seen as involving the accumulation of factual knowledge, where one can only progress to more complicated ideas when one understands simpler ones. A historian or a philosopher seeks to select, understand and interpret information and ideas in particular ways, analysing motivation, or meaning. Philosophy is often seen as too abstract a subject for young children. While such views are oversimple, they prompt one to ask to what extent young children can work in such ways, although obviously at a level appropriate to their current understanding.

Black and Harrison (2004, page 5) suggest that the essential ingredients for good science teaching are:

- challenging activities that promote thinking and discussion;
- rich questions;
- strategies to support all learners in revealing their ideas;
- opportunity for peer discussion about ideas;
- group or whole-class discussions which encourage open dialogue.

These types of approach relate to activity, to metacognition and in particular to collective learning rather than being specifically about science. Interestingly, despite the emphasis on factual knowledge in the training of a doctor or an engineer, much of the learning takes place alongside and under the supervision of someone with greater experience and expertise. This emphasises that propositional and procedural knowledge should be mutually supportive rather than learned or taught separately.

Thinking and working as a mathematician or a scientist involves making hypotheses, testing out ideas, looking for patterns and interpreting results. These are not very different from those of a historian, geographer or philosopher in seeking to understand cultures and ideas, both one's own and those of other people, separate in time and place. So, while any subject area has specific propositional knowledge, procedures and skills, there is more commonality than is often assumed. While it may be argued that an exceptional talent, for instance in sport or music, should be trained to achieve mastery in that domain, this risks an overemphasis on that area of learning at the expense of overall breadth and balance; and 'hot-housing' would rarely be seen as appropriate for very young children, though as always this depends on what the educator or parent wishes to achieve.

All domains of learning require propositional knowledge, for example about units of measurement or forces, significant events or geographical features. This is less obviously so in terms of philosophy, but even there arguments need to be based on evidence and examples. As we have seen, young children find abstract thought difficult, though this is easier when related to their own context and interests. With children of primary school age, it is probably best to use examples which children choose, on topics such as 'should one eat meat?' or 'is it ever right to break the law?' which help children to explore dilemmas and questions of value. Programmes such as Philosophy for Children

(P4C) provide specific guidance, based on separate sessions. However, an approach which helps children to speak and listen thoughtfully and to understand the acceptability of holding different views respectfully is appropriate in most areas of learning. In particular, such an approach enables and encourages children to question and express their views within a structure where uncertainty is allowable and even encouraged.

Watkins (2005, page 43) describes learning communities as aiming *to advance collective knowledge and in that way support the growth of individual knowledge.* One essential feature of a learning community is that all involved are learners. As educators, we create, often unintentionally, a belief that knowledge resides largely with the teacher and that young children's learning depends on accessing this. This tends to emphasise propositional knowledge and surface learning and to encourage 'learned helplessness' on the part of the child and 'spoonfeeding' on that of the adult. I like the story of the high-achieving girl who said that she does her best thinking 'on the playground'. When asked whether her teacher was not good, she replied *Oh no! She's very good, she does all the thinking for us.* The difficulty is that such spoonfeeding may work in terms of performance, for instance in memorising and recalling content, but *it works at the expense of something British schools have always been good at: turning out young people able to be inventive, creative, independent-minded, even awkward* (Hubbard, 2002). So teachers need to be seen – by both themselves or children – as always learning, not always knowing.

Hiebert et al. (1999, pages 160–1) write: *in reflective inquiry classrooms, students must take responsibility for sharing the results of their inquiries and for explaining and justifying their methods ... [and] ... to recognise that learning means learning from others, taking advantage of others' ideas and the results of their investigations. This requires students to listen.* While this is true, it is often difficult for young children unless they have had a lot of experience of working collaboratively. Moreover, the final sentence begs the question of 'listening to whom?' – the answer to which in a learning community must be 'each other' as well as the teacher.

Mayall (2010, pages 67–8) suggests that learning communities which are collaborative and within which children are valued and value each other lead to children being happier and academic results improving. This reflects the social nature of learning and the importance of respect both as a prerequisite for learning and to engage those who are uncertain or unfamiliar with what is expected.

One should be under no illusion that a learning community can be created overnight. A transmission mode of teaching is easier to manage. However, enabling this is part of the complex repertoire associated with experienced and effective teachers – and one that can gradually be built up by those newer to teaching.

Conclusion

In this chapter, we have looked at how adults can support children's learning both directly and through more subtle approaches, though with more emphasis on spoken language. The critical thinking exercises will have helped you to:

- ◎ **analyse** the idea of 'scaffolding' and different ways of supporting young children's learning;
- ◎ **compare** varying types and roles of feedback;
- ◎ **identify** the types of questions and response which enhance dialogue;
- ◎ **consider** to what extent young children should, and can, be introduced to how experts think and act in different domains of learning.

In Chapter 9, we discuss the link between assessment, planning and pedagogy.

Further reading

Alexander, R (2008) Talking, teaching, learning. Pages 92–120 of *Essays on Pedagogy*. Abingdon, Routledge
A very interesting chapter on the role of talk in pedagogy, with a useful discussion of different types of teaching, drawing on comparisons with Russian and French classrooms.

Bliss, J, Askew, M and Macrae S (1996) Effective Teaching and Learning: Scaffolding revisited. *Oxford Review of Education*, 22 (1): pages 37–61
An academic article with a detailed analysis of scaffolding in the primary classroom and some good examples about the practical implications.

Myhill, D, Jones, S, and Hopper, R (2006) *Talking, Listening, Learning – Effective talk in the primary classroom*. Maidenhead: Open University Press
A simply written and practical guide to the complexities of encouraging high-quality talk.

---

9 Assessing and planning for learning

The critical thinking exercises in this chapter focus on:

- ⊙ **identifying** different types and purposes of assessment;
- ⊙ **using** data intelligently and the implications for setting goals and targets;
- ⊙ **exploring** the advantages and difficulties of assessment for learning and different ways of grouping children;
- ⊙ **discussing** how to maintain a balance between personalised learning, scope for creativity and planned outcomes.

The key ideas discussed are: **assessment for learning, goals, targets, differentiation, grouping, personalisation**

This chapter is particularly relevant to QTS Standards: **8**, **10**, **11**, **12**, **13**, **19**, **21b**, **22**, **25c,d**, **26a,b**, **29** and to Knowledge and Understanding and Application (*Education Studies*) and Subject knowledge and Subject skills (*Early Childhood Studies*)

Introduction

This chapter considers the link between assessment, planning and pedagogy. These need to inform each other, with planning sufficiently flexible to respond to how the children's responses reflect their current knowledge, and with assessment inbuilt into planning, so that you can be clear about objectives and decide to what extent they have been met. As the TLRP states, *the interventions of teachers or trainers are most effective when planned in response to how learners are learning.* So, this chapter encourages you to take a broad view of:

- assessment, as discovering the child's current understanding, done both in the moment and more reflectively;
- planning, as working out the framework for the types of activities and experiences, skills and interactions to enhance children's learning, rather than deciding every detail in advance.

We start by considering the types and purposes of assessment, and how to use data intelligently, moving on to look at assessment for learning, personalisation and differentiation. Finally, we think about the link between assessment, planning and pedagogy, emphasising principles and judgement rather than any particular planning format.

To illustrate how assessment can inform planning, but leave space for professional judgement, consider this incident.

> ### CASE STUDY
>
> Jack, a six-year-old who had been assessed as on the autistic spectrum, was in my second class. His previous teacher described him (rightly) as thinking and working incredibly fast and easily upset. His spoken language, though somewhat deliberate, indicated a wide range of vocabulary. I was uncertain what to expect. For the first two weeks, he was the first to finish his written work and thrust it into my hand, before dashing off to the next task. I was convinced that Jack was capable of writing more than the sentence he had given me, but nervous about how to handle this. In the third week, I asked him to read his writing out to me, which he did. I said to him that it was a really good start to a story, but perhaps he could go and finish it. He looked at me uncertainly before going off, quite willingly, to write several sentences. That moment seemed to unleash a flow of written work of much greater quantity and quality over the following weeks.

Reflecting on this, my hunch at the time was that previous teachers' expectations of him were too low, emphasising protection rather than challenge; and that he was capable of greater quality and quantity in his writing. A formal assessment or test might have indicated this, but knowing what to do differently required me to assess his likely response, relying largely on intuition. My response had to be planned, but its implementation relied on waiting for what seemed to be the right moment.

Key ideas: **Goals and targets**

> ### How can data best be used to enhance learning?
>
> As the TLRP suggests, *assessment has various purposes and mechanisms ... with the goal of achieving maximum validity both in terms of learning outcomes and learning processes. It should help to advance learning as well as determine whether learning has occurred.* Assessment involves looking back at what has been learned and forward to how learning can be enhanced.

One common distinction is that between summative and formative assessment. We shall discuss the latter, which links what children have done with what they should do next, later in this chapter. Summative assessment is largely related to outcomes and so usually comes at the end of a teaching programme, though it can, and should, inform future planning and teaching. It frequently involves gathering quantitative data in the form of marks or grades, or giving these. The formality of these may range from a spelling test to national tests at the end of Key Stage 2. Historically, tests have been used to decide, for children, their next school and, for teachers, their level of pay. Increasingly, they have been used to predict future levels and to set targets both for teachers and for children, and establish whether these have been met. This has been used increasingly with younger children in the belief that the pressure to perform well in such tests will enhance performance and long-term success.

Teachers, schools and local authorities are increasingly expected to gather and interpret data. A huge amount of data is available on individual children and to compare different groups. Most of this is based on summative, level-based testing, in the subjects deemed to be most important, and other easily measured aspects such as attendance, behaviour and exclusions. Inspectors rely heavily on such data in making their judgements. While such data can be valuable, they are only part of the evidence available and must be used intelligently.

Critical thinking exercise 1: using data intelligently

A **Consider** the limitations of quantitative data from summative assessment; and how these data can be used most usefully.

B **Articulate** which sorts of goals and targets are most likely to be most useful for a particular class, or age group, which you know well; and why.

C **Discuss** to what extent an emphasis on goals and targets may skew your priorities.

Comment

Assessment, of whatever type, must be based on evidence, such as observations, evaluation of work, tests and other adults' (or the child's own) judgements. I was trying to combine these when asking Jack to write more. It is easy to set one's expectations too low, especially if the background of the children is made an excuse for accepting low levels of aspiration and potential. So, assessment is best done using the insights of a range of adults who know the child. This should involve, at some points, parents and, for some children, external support staff, such as those with specific expertise where a child has special educational needs or speaks English as an additional language. Tests are more valid when assessing propositional rather than procedural knowledge, since they deal with what can be measured. And much of our most important learning cannot be measured. Moreover, evidence is never value-free or culture-free and always needs to be interpreted. Sternberg (2007) illustrates ways in which cultural assumptions affect how children approach tasks designed to assess their abilities. For example, they may not understand what to do or what is expected or be worried, especially when asked to do something unfamiliar. Do you remember the story of the little girl with the snail game? Many children have a range of abilities and a depth of understanding and sensitivity that may not be immediately apparent.

The texts or examples chosen for summative assessment may involve ideas which are unfamiliar to some children, for example where those who have never been to the seaside have to describe it or a problem in mathematics involves shopping for items they do not know. Less formal assessments may be inaccurate as a result of adult expectations or conventions which the child does not understand, for instance where a child who is used to believing that one should never show one's lack of knowledge keeps silent. This emphasises the importance of:

- being aware, and taking account of, the child's background and prior learning;
- assessing a wide range of ability and responses to different situations, looking for both strengths and weaknesses;
- assessing over time, rather than with one-off tests, especially with young children and those still in the early stages of learning English.

An unintelligent use of data involves accepting the results of assessments as supplying definitive answers, rather than seeing these as raising further questions. Using data intelligently involves not only looking at the performance of individuals or groups, but asking why and what should be done differently. For example, tracking individual children's progress may reveal children who are struggling, but have been overlooked (often those who are quiet and unobtrusive), or those who are doing especially well. Looking at patterns of achievement may suggest the need for the following.

- Teaching directly a specific skill, such as a particular approach in maths, a pattern in spelling or mixing paint.
- Changing how children are grouped, such as using mixed-ability grouping or not relying only on performance scores if children are divided into sets.
- Providing additional support for individuals or a group, for instance as one school I visited where an analysis of data in science indicated that a group of Year 5 bilinguals were doing less well than expected. Further inquiry revealed that they did not understand some of the more 'technical' language. A short programme based on this helped to raise their understanding of scientific concepts, and their attainment, quite rapidly.

Analysed well and discussed honestly, data can help to challenge and raise teacher expectations, inform teaching and learning and identify priorities for teaching and professional development. However, summative assessment may be inaccurate in predicting future performance and not reflect the whole range of children's abilities. It is important to be wary of test scores, especially with very young children and with children where the assessment mechanisms may not be valid. The younger the child, the less reliable test scores are. This matters a great deal, especially when such assessments are used to group children, as we shall see.

Goals and targets are a feature of most classrooms, whether set for an individual and for a group or a class. Currently, teachers are often required to identify 'challenging' targets, based on what results a child has achieved and predicting what they can achieve in the future. Often children, even before they start school, are given a range of targets, including those which are academic, behavioural and personal. One assumption is that goals and targets will encourage children and adults to focus on what they need to improve upon, motivate them and so help to raise performance. Another is that children's development and performance will be (broadly) regular over time. However, as we have seen, what motivates children is complicated and progress often uneven and hard to predict. For instance, being expected to reach a certain level may discourage some, though it may motivate others, and young bilinguals may make progress which is slow initially and then more rapid than their peers once they have become more fluent in English.

Donaldson (1992, page 7) argues that setting goals for ourselves, often very diverse ones, is central to how we learn. As she states (page 257), *children enjoy solving problems, but, as Bruner puts it, 'they are not often either predisposed to, or skilled in, problem-finding'*. In the short term, externally set goals may seem to motivate many children, especially those who succeed, but these easily lead to children focusing only on what is being tested and avoiding lateral thinking and more divergent and metacognitive approaches. Dweck (1999) distinguishes between what she calls performance goals, based on attainment, and learning goals, based on what I have called the attributes of successful learning. She writes (pages 151–2) that both sorts of goal are *entirely natural, desirable and necessary… The problem with performance goals arises when proving ability becomes so important to students that it drives out learning goals.* She argues (page 2) that many children who perform well and appear to be most confident *do not want their intelligence too stringently tested, and their high confidence is too quickly shaken when they are confronted with difficulty* and that successful children who believe in fixed intelligence are most worried about failure and most likely to question their ability when they hit obstacles.

In contrast, those who see ability as malleable and have a mastery-oriented response to obstacles recognise that *this simply means that their present skills and knowledge need to be augmented, not that a permanent deficiency has been revealed,* (Dweck, 1999, page 152), making it more likely that such children, whatever their ability, will invest the effort necessary to succeed. While therefore performance goals can be useful, this must not be at the expense of goals based on learning attributes. Expecting children to show attributes such as resilience or creativity helps them to value and develop these. While it may be harder to assess to what extent such goals have been met, discussing with children to what extent they have demonstrated these may help them understand what these entail in that particular context. The discussion of what has led to, and what should result in, success, helps to make specific expectations clear and gradually to enable children to internalise these, rather than be dependent on extrinsic praise or reward.

So, we face the problem that most children benefit from having goals, especially ones that they have set themselves, but are often put off by externally set goals and may not be very good at setting goals appropriate to school learning. Some are discouraged by challenging targets, others are spurred to greater effort. So, educators need to be cautious about how these are used, especially when the targets are public. For instance, a common practice is to set group targets, based, for instance, on what *must, should* and *could* be learned. It seems useful to make explicit what everyone should aim to achieve, what a majority can expect to do and what a few may hope to. However, this often leads to children being grouped (explicitly or otherwise) as those who can only achieve the 'must' (lowest) level, while the 'brightest' are expected to reach the 'could' (highest); a selection by ability, even if unintentionally, which even very young children pick up quickly, with the danger of setting up self-fulfilling expectations.

The House of Commons Report on the National Curriculum (2009, especially pages 41–46) highlights that high-stakes summative assessment tends to skew the curriculum and encourage learning to the test and 'shallow learning'. We have seen that an emphasis on a narrow range of outcomes makes most children and adults focus on those areas. How mistakes are understood and processed can motivate or create fear of failure and low self-concept. The repeated emphasis on performance may discourage and disempower those who are hardest to engage. However, there is a broader, ethical issue. Assessment data are often used to focus resources, especially additional time, on children just below the border line, that is likely to reach a set level in an assessment. While this may help these children to reach that level, it means less support for other children, whether those easily able to reach the set level, or those judged to have no chance of doing so. As ever, such decisions are not value-free.

Key idea: **Assessment for learning**

Assessment, whether summative or formative, is like a diagnosis. Its value depends on how its results are understood and used. As Nutbrown (2001, page 70) writes, *effective assessment is dynamic, not static, and can identify for the educator what the learner's next steps might be.* A test may highlight a concept or a skill which an individual or group do not seem to understand, on which the teacher can provide further guidance. An observation may provide greater insight into why a child is acting in a particular way, to inform the adult's response. So, any means of assessment, like any diagnosis, is of value only in so far as it is used. It must enhance, not inhibit, active learning.

Formative assessment is a process which seeks to enable children to know what to do next to enhance their learning. It is often associated with Assessment for Learning (AfL), a useful idea, but one which in practice is used in a variety of ways. So, let us consider what these terms mean.

Critical thinking exercise 2: Assessment for Learning

Black and Wiliam (1998, pages 7–8) , recognising that formative assessment does not have a tightly defined and widely accepted meaning, suggest that it encompasses: *all those activities undertaken by teachers and/or by their students, which provide information to be used as feedback to modify the teaching and learning activities in which they are engaged.* However, among key features highlighted are:

- involving pupils in their learning to decide on next steps and identify who or what can help;
- sharing criteria about what is to be learned and what success would 'look like';
- giving children timely feedback about the quality of their work and how they can make it better.

A **Discuss** the potential benefits of encouraging children to assess their own level of understanding and how this can work in practice with young children.

B **Consider** why making learning objectives explicit can be useful and any possible disadvantages.

C **Identify** what may make Assessment for Learning difficult for the teacher.

Comment

Involving children in their learning and deciding on next steps can help them be active participants in, and steering, their own learning. Children setting and solving their own problems, although often difficult when outcomes are closely defined, can help to sustain engagement and motivation. Learning to evaluate their own, and each other's, work helps encourage reflection and metacognition. Such actions benefit all concerned, as long as children get used to identifying strengths as well as areas for improvement – a skill which requires modelling by adults and a good deal of practice because negatives are easier to spot than positives. For example, it takes a high level of expertise to know what a fluent reader or a good violinist does well and could do to improve – whereas almost anyone can identify what a poor one does.

One way in which AfL is used is 'traffic lights', where each child is encouraged to decide whether s/he has understood the ideas involved well, or quite well, or is confused. This has the dual benefit of encouraging children to think about their own learning, a fairly simple example of metacognition, and of enabling adults to know who needs additional help. However, the success of this depends on children being able to decide reasonably accurately and prepared to admit to difficulties. The former comes with practice, and adults will often wish, and need, to check the child's assessment. The latter depends on the environment and expectations created, since some children may, for reasons of culture or self-esteem, wish to exaggerate their knowledge and to hide their shortcomings; and others conversely, for reasons of modesty, not to overstate their knowledge.

A more worrying idea is the categorisation of children as visual, auditory and kinaesthetic (VAK) learners. VAK can usefully help remind teachers to present material in a range of different ways and to encourage enactive and iconic, as well as symbolic, representation – doing, making and drawing, rather than just listening and speaking and writing. However, VAK has led in some schools to children being encouraged to identify themselves in one of these categories. The danger is that they may come to see themselves as able to learn only in one style, rather than trying to improve in areas they find more difficult. Learning does not involve just practising what (we think) we are good at, but taking on new challenges. As a simple analogy, surely one would not expect right-footed footballers not to practise kicking with their left foot; or those who are good at reading not to work at mathematics or art?

As the second TLRP principle states, *learners need to understand what constitutes quality, standards and expertise in different settings*. Too frequently, children know what they are doing, but not what they are meant to achieve, or how to 'get there'. Learning objectives are often made explicit at the start of each lesson, for example in the Early Years, *remember to share the toys with other people*, or in Key Stage 2 *use a wider range of adjectives to improve writing*. The advantages of this may seem obvious, that:

- children know what to do to improve and whether they have succeeded;
- teachers can assess what has been learned;
- head teachers, inspectors and parents can know whether the formal curriculum has been covered.

Making expectations explicit is often helpful, but the possible disadvantages more subtle. This may make children, especially those who feel less secure, focus only on these objectives, rather than think laterally or follow other avenues. So it may, in practice, encourage conformity rather than the divergence essential to creativity. Moreover, learning objectives tend to focus on content or skills, rather than attributes, emphasising only what can be measured and conscious learning. This can lead to learning being seen in tiny pieces, rather than as a whole, with the teacher over-controlling the process, and not valuing children's responses and the knowledge they bring from their wider experience beyond school. A discussion with children of what your learning objectives are midway through, or at the end of, a lesson can encourage metacognition, by making children think about what they are supposed to be, and are, learning, rather than accepting what the teacher says. This can both provide useful feedback to you about what is being learned and help to build an environment where children's voice is heard and acted upon.

As we shall see in Chapter 10, accurate and sensitive assessment is one fundamental feature of teacher expertise. Assessment for Learning is not easy, especially those elements which require in-the-moment decisions. Giving grades and marks is quicker, though less useful, than either spoken or written feedback. Spoken comments, soon after or during work, are harder to organise, though receiving feedback as soon as possible, whether from an adult or other children, is especially important for young children, given their shorter attention span. But perhaps the two most difficult aspects of AfL are:

- for adults to hand over an element of control to the child, especially when there is pressure on the adult to cover a great deal of curriculum content;
- for both adults and children to counteract deep-rooted habits about how adults and children should interact, with children adopting passive attitudes, and adults, often unconsciously, encouraging these rather than active curiosity.

Key ideas: **Differentiation and grouping**

How can one plan for differentiation?

One basic challenge for educators, especially class teachers, is how to respond to individual needs, but provide for all, being equitable but taking account of the range of individual needs and responses. The idea of differentiation became popular in English schools in the early 1990s and remains part of the 'approved' model of pedagogy. This usually involves grouping within the class, or setting, especially in the core subjects, on the basis of ability, though different approaches are discussed below.

Critical thinking exercise 3: differentiation

Fox (2005, page 77) outlines four types of differentiation (which I summarise as by):

- **task** – where children do different tasks appropriate to their learning needs;
- **outcome** – where children do the same (or similar) activity but the expected outcome varies;
- **support** – where children do the same (or similar) activity but some are given additional support, such as materials or adult help;
- **questioning** – where groups or individuals are set (or encouraged to set for themselves) different levels or types of challenge.

A **Articulate** the reasoning behind each of these types of differentiation and **illustrate** when each might be most useful.

B **Consider** the main challenges in differentiating for a class of children with a wide range of attainment.

C **Discuss** the situations and types of activity when you might, or might not, group children by ability, by friendship and by gender; and any advantages in doing so.

Comment

Differentiation is usually based on an assumption that the most important difference relates to ability. However, Ofsted (2003, page 5) points out that:

> while in the English classrooms [for six-year-olds] children's work was sometimes differentiated by perceived ability and task, differentiation in [Denmark and Finland] was largely by outcome only. The emphasis instead, especially in Denmark, was on inclusion, co-operation and bringing children along together.

Osborn et al. (2003) indicate how in France keeping the class together is seen as essential. As a result, every child does the same work, with different levels of independence and the less confident or able receiving more support, based on a belief in children taking responsibility for their own learning and progression.

Differentiation by task or by teaching/support often leads to ability grouping, often with three bands of ability. Differentiation by outcome or questioning/challenge tends to be based on those deemed most able being expected to do either more or more demanding work. Each may be useful, but as with all pedagogical approaches this depends on what you are aiming to achieve. None of these approaches to differentiation are unproblematic. So, differentiation by:

- task may be valuable where children have very different levels of skill, but risks lowering expectations of lower achieving children;
- outcome can encourage different approaches to the same material, but may not provide enough support to those who lack confidence;
- support helps some children who may find learning difficult, but may reinforce a sense of inadequacy;
- questioning has the potential to enable children to set their own challenges, but may provide insufficient structure.

In Eaude (2008, page 83), I suggest a further type of differentiation, by response, which recognises that young children's learning has to be based on interaction and reciprocity, if it is not to be over-controlled by adults.

One aspect of planning to be considered carefully is how children are grouped. Grouping in this context refers to:

- the size of the group;
- the criteria used to group children;
- the way in which groups work.

We have seen the importance of expectations, both those which adults have of the child and which children have of themselves – and how the former can, often subtly, affect the latter. How children are grouped often has important implications for how they are seen – and see themselves – as learners. So, children treated as if they are incapable or vulnerable act as if they are and become so; and those treated as no good at science become no good at science. Conversely, regarding children as capable and confident learners tends to encourage these attributes and emphasising strengths and abilities to engage and motivate children and raise their aspirations and achievements. While differentiation may help adults to match content to children's current levels of understanding, it runs the risk of establishing self-fulfilling prophecies regarding success. So, even where tasks need to be made simpler for specific groups, it is vital to encourage the attributes of successful learning and the ways of working associated with this, such as collaboration and metacognition.

Adult expectations are expressed, as we have seen, in both explicit and implicit ways. Even where teachers try to hide the reasons for their choice, children are very shrewd at recognising how groups are made up. For instance, even when a class of five-year-olds is split into Butterflies, Bees and so on, the children know very well who are the best readers or those who need most adult help. The impact of this is reinforced where performance is associated with status, for example when it is seen as desirable to be in a top (ability) group. While, therefore, it is necessary to group children for practical purposes, adults need to be careful how groups are made up, based on what they want to achieve both in that activity and more broadly. Moreover, while this section concentrates on how children are grouped formally, they also form more informal groups, for instance sitting with those who share common interests or actively excluding children whom they do not wish to sit next to. To avoid unintended consequences, educators need to be aware of such informal arrangements as well as the formal groupings they establish.

The most appropriate size of group will depend on what one wants to achieve; and to some extent on the age of the children. For example, a whole school may be right for an assembly or a concert. The whole class may be appropriate for listening to a story. Dialogue may work effectively with a whole class of ten-year-olds, perhaps breaking briefly into pairs to discuss initial ideas, whereas younger children may benefit from smaller groups. Solving problems in mathematics may work best with a mixture of individual thinking and sharing ideas both in small groups and then as a class. Instruction in a specific skill or conducting experiments may be most effective in small groups to enable adequate oversight or involvement of all concerned. I have often found that groups of three can help to involve all children and make it less likely that one person dominates a group, or another is uninvolved. So, there is no one formula or answer. It is a matter of judgement, which should form part of one's planning.

The criteria by which groups are selected is trickier and potentially more controversial. Three main criteria used are ability, friendship and gender. Grouping by ability is currently common, either through separate sets or within-class differentiation. This has the advantage of making it easier to cover content because there is less spread of ability, but tends to reinforce children's (and parents') views of children's level of ability. Grouping by friendship is popular with children, but can easily exclude those who have fewer friends. Children need both to 'bond' with those who are similar and 'bridge' with those who are different. For example, in collaborative tasks, or drama, children may discover more about other people working in mixed ability groups than only with their friends; and this may not only reveal latent abilities but help children recognise the value of different approaches. Grouping by gender is often initially unpopular with children, but can be useful to encourage children to work with others with whom they would not normally work. Grouping children is one area where the demands of equity makes it appropriate to be directive, even when children are not keen.

Grouping is not simply a matter of who children sit with, but of how they work. The ORACLE research (see Galton et al., 1980, e.g. pages 45–7) demonstrated that often children were seated in groups, but actually working on their own. Of course, this may be appropriate at times, but if one wants collaborative working or focused (as opposed to social) conversation, this needs to be explicitly planned for, by how the activity is set up and ways of working are explained and developed over time. Alexander (2000, page 408) suggests that *the dearth of material on collaborative group work reflects its rarity in practice* despite the *dawning realization of its considerable potential, when properly organized, simultaneously to advance pupil's cognitive and social learning.* To make groupwork collaborative requires clear expectations and guidance, sensitive intervention to ensure that the group is working together – and the chance for children to draw on each other's strengths and ideas without too much adult intervention.

Key idea: **Personalisation**

How does assessment link to planning and pedagogy?

Planning involves not only written plans, but thinking through how you are going to work with children to meet a wide range of aims and deal with the unexpected, given that classrooms are inherently unpredictable places, especially with young children. An old army saying states that *no plan of action ever survived first contact with the enemy,* though, ideally, pedagogy is more like a conversation than a battle. So, I am encouraging you to see assessment and planning broadly and intimately bound up with, rather than separate from, pedagogy.

The term 'personalisation' has only been in common use in the last few years as part of a government approach to public services based on greater consumer, in this case parental and student, choice. In 2004, David Miliband, then a government minister, said that personalised learning must take account of the *learning styles, motivations and needs* of individuals; and so is an attempt to avoid teaching unresponsive to children's needs. Like many other policies, it has been understood and implemented in different ways.

Critical thinking exercise 4: personalisation and planning

A **Discuss** what you understand personalisation to mean and its possible benefits and disadvantages.

B **Consider** what the implications for written plans might be of taking more account of 'children's voice' and of educators changing what they do in response to this and to unforeseen events.

C Given that often there may be more than one adult working with a class, **explore** the implications for the teacher, and other educators, of the need for planning to be both rigorous and flexible.

Comment

Leadbeater (2005, pages 4–5) argues that personalisation is *a way to mobilise children and families as contributors in their own education. The aim is to turn passive recipients into active contributors.* He goes on (page 6) that *many of the basic building blocks of traditional education: the school, the year group, the class, the lesson, the blackboard and the teacher standing in front of a class of thirty children have become obstacles to personalised learning,* saying that it is not for the faint of heart. However, we saw in Chapter 2 how little schools alter over time, despite considerable changes of policy.

Personalisation is associated with adapting teaching to children's needs and helping children extend their interests and remain motivated and actively engaged, in line with Every Child Matters. You may think, as I do, that good teachers have always done this; and that this is what I was doing when challenging Jack in the case study.

Personalisation has also been used to call for more use of individual programmes, often using information technology. This is appropriate for some children, in certain respects, such as those with learning difficulties, who may find ICT programmes very valuable in learning to read or to understand mathematics. However, there is a risk of personalisation coming to mean individualisation, encouraging solitary work, often based on a computer, whereas building up cognitive and emotional intelligences requires social interaction. Leadbeater writes (2005, page 7), *personalised learning is not cafeteria style learning: picking your own curriculum from a wider self-service menu.* Rather, he sees personalisation as based on greater collaboration between families and a wide range of adults in and out of school, though as he states (page 22), *collaboration can be held back by regulation, inspection and funding regimes that encourage schools to think of themselves as... stand alone units.*

Planning has come to be associated mainly with detailed written lesson plans, building on medium-term plans, usually worked out collaboratively between teachers. Yet, the importance of the learning environment makes the physical layout of a classroom an essential part of planning. For example, the availability of sand and water and access to an outdoor learning environment, and how and when they can be accessed, are key features of Early Years settings; and children being able to access the learning 'tools' they need – from books to paint, from rulers to the internet – affects how independent and active their learning will be. If children are to be involved in planning, at more than a token level, they need the chance not only to influence medium-term plans, but to steer the direction of learning in the classroom. If agency, creativity and reciprocity are to be encouraged, lesson plans need to provide some flexibility to enable children to pursue their interests and adults to respond to these.

This involves adults being in control but without being controlling, guiding children, but allowing scope to develop their own ideas and interests. For example, the teacher may set the framework, by deciding on the activity and providing sufficient structure, but not controlling the children's activities and responses at the 'micro' level. This requires the teacher – and to a lesser extent other educators – to exercise constant judgement in the moment, but this is difficult when they are expected to cover a lot of content and assessed largely on measurable outcomes. So, there is always a tension between planning in detail and being responsive to children, but planning often needs to involve knowing the direction of travel rather than every step of the way.

Early Years settings have, for many years, involved several adults working together – teachers, nursery nurses, teaching assistants and parents. Partnership with parents helps them to understand and support the school's approach, though this is easier with very young children and when parents feel comfortable in school. Increasingly, in the last 15 years, primary classes have seen far more adults in a range of roles working with children. How they have worked varies enormously, with many gaining a great deal of expertise, often working with children with special needs or developing skills in a particular subject area; and with others being asked to take large groups for which they have few qualifications. A reluctance is evident, at least in Key Stage 2, to have several adults working together in class, with children often taken out despite the risk that they will not experience the same curriculum on offer as other children. As so often, educators and schools continue to work in familiar ways: an approach which can be a protection against new fads or a missed opportunity.

Conclusion

This chapter has suggested that planning and assessment should be seen more broadly than deciding what you are going to do in a lesson and then testing what has been learned. Assessment, planning and pedagogy must inform each other, be flexible and responsive to the range of needs of different children and take account of the full range of children's learning, over time. The critical thinking exercises will have helped you:

- ⊙ **explore** how data can be used intelligently, especially in identifying 'next steps', and some dangers in the use of goals and targets;

- ⊙ **identify** aspects of Assessment for Learning and its potential benefits and shortcomings when used simplistically;
- ⊙ **articulate** the underlying rationale and implications of differentiation and personalisation;
- ⊙ **consider** how to plan in a way that is both focused on aims and objectives and responsive to events.

Underlying this discussion has been a belief that educators must be both aware of children's current level of understanding and attuned to their emotional needs and to have planned what you intend to do, recognising and actively creating possibilities, and to assess – by watching, exploring, interpreting and judging – which approach is most appropriate. You may be left wondering how on earth you can work in this way, which is the subject of Chapter 10.

Further Reading

Hart, S, Dixon, A, Drummond, MJ and McIntyre, D (2004) *Learning Without Limits*. Maidenhead: Open University Press
A critique of an emphasis on ability, especially in terms of grouping, with detailed examples of how different views affect teachers' pedagogy.

Nutbrown, C (2001) Watching and Learning: The tools of assessment. Pages 66–77 of Pugh, G (ed) *Contemporary Issues in the Early Years – Working collaboratively for children*. London: Paul Chapman Publishing
A thoughtful discussion of the practical challenges of assessment in Early Years settings.

Sternberg, RJ (2007) Culture, Instruction and Assessment. *Comparative Education*, 43 (1): 5–22
An article which explains in simple language how culture affects assessment.

10 Building up your expertise

Introduction

As the TLRP says, *effective pedagogy depends on the learning of all those who support the learning of others*; and in Gipps and Macgilchrist's words (1999, page 47) *teachers need to develop a much more sophisticated understanding about learning and the impact of their beliefs and attitudes about learning and learners can have on what – and how – they teach in the classroom.*

We have explored the complexity of pedagogy and you may well be thinking, *this is all very well, but how can I do this?* This chapter turns the lens away from children to help you think through developing your expertise. We will find many resonances with previous messages about children's learning.

As discussed in the Introduction, the skills highlighted in the Standards for Achieving QTS and QAA Benchmark Standards are remarkably similar. So, we consider, first, the qualities required in working with young children, then what expertise 'looks like' and the expertise distinctive of teachers. The third section discusses how expertise can be built up, seeing this as a gradual process of continuous professional development, and the fourth the longer-term implications. Let us start by observing an incident at the same time remarkable and yet within the normal flow of an Early Years class.

CASE STUDY

As a researcher, I observed Rebecca, a timid four-year-old, approaching, and apparently wishing to enter, the home corner dominated by some boys playing noisily. She hesitated and watched, for several seconds, before seeking the help of the Nursery nurse, who told her to go back and say that Mrs H had said that she (Rebecca) can play in the house. Rebecca went back and looked into the playhouse, for about forty-five seconds, apparently impassive. She then went closer, smiled, and looked back, presumably for reassurance, at Mrs H, who was watching. Rebecca returned and said that the boys were playing dinosaurs. The Nursery nurse said *Go and say Mrs H says you can play in there – and the house is for everyone.* Rebecca looked doubtful but returned with two other girls. They held hands, waited for two or three seconds and then went in together.

This illustrates one of hundreds of interactions and judgements in which adults working with young children are involved every day. While it occurred during a fairly normal day, I was privileged to watch the individual children closely in a way rarely available to busy professionals. However, they usually know a great deal about individual children's histories and the social dynamics of a class.

Try to articulate what you think is happening, what Rebecca's actions tell us of her prior experience and of her self-concept; and how Mrs H's actions and words reflected her knowledge of Rebecca and influenced the child's actions and beliefs about herself and her ability to cope.

My own interpretation – and any observer will see different aspects – is that a rather shy girl, probably with anxious models of attachment, despite wanting to play in the home corner, lacked the confidence to do so in the face of a rather intimidating group of boys. Unsure of herself, she sought adult help, but still felt too scared to enter. Eventually – and time how long 45 seconds feels when you are uncertain – she returned for more verbal and emotional reassurance, and gathered two allies before finally crossing that threshold.

The Nursery nurse could have left Rebecca to manage as best she could, or called out to the boys or accompanied her. Instead, she drew on her knowledge based on close observation of, and attunement to, Rebecca's needs. As a result, she encouraged Rebecca to draw on her own resources, including some ability to explore from her own 'secure base' to build up her own confidence. The adult not intervening too soon or overtly, but encouraging Rebecca to be more resilient, indicates a tacit knowledge of the individual child's feelings, what she could achieve and how best to support this. She appealed explicitly to the need for fairness. Her pedagogy was informed by her understanding of the specific child and the context, much of which she would probably have found it difficult to express.

Key idea: **Equity**

Which qualities matter most when working with young children?

Alexander (2010, page 408) writes *a clear and simple message which emerged [from the Cambridge Primary Review] was that teachers need to be qualified and knowledgeable but also caring. Children, in particular, had little doubt about the qualities they wanted teachers to possess and we summarise them…as equity, empathy and expertise.* Although the Review focused on the primary years, and this quotation refers only to teachers, it provides a good starting point for identifying the qualities, or attributes, needed when working with young children.

Critical thinking exercise 1: equity, empathy, expertise?

A **Consider** whether you agree with the Cambridge Review's emphasis on equity, empathy and expertise as the qualities most important for those working with young children. What else, if anything, would you add?

B **Articulate** (and **discuss**) what you understand by empathy when working with young children; and any possible difficulties in being empathetic.

C Choose one activity in which you are really expert (it doesn't matter which) and **identify:**

- what makes you an expert, compared to a novice;
- whether this is natural or learned and relies on knowledge, skills or attributes?

It is helpful to do this individually, then in a group, to **compare** notes and see any common features.

Comment

The emphasis on equity is unsurprising. Children are concerned with whether adults' actions are fair, from brothers' and sisters' constant concern about whether one has been favoured to the (justifiable) complaint when a whole group is punished for the actions of a few. Most definitions of professionalism include a commitment not to favour some clients over others. So, for example, low expectations of a particular child or group as a result of stereotyping is (rightly) seen as unprofessional, and, as we saw in Chapter 2, the Every Child Matters agenda has been widely welcomed. However, this commitment is often not manifested in practice. Think, for example, of how often a child who does not fit in is bullied; how schools tend to value the achievements of high-attaining children above others; or, more uncomfortably, how we (often unconsciously) pay more attention to one group or child than others. So, the commitment to equity is always a struggle to achieve in practice.

Key ideas: **Empathy and attunement**

The emphasis on empathy reflects the traditions of educating young children, and of English education, including the TLRP's call to give more prominence to learning relationships. Educational traditions in other countries such as Russia and France tend to concentrate more on cognition and less on emotion (see Alexander, 2000), as do those who teach older students. Yet, Ofsted (2009, page 2) write, about outstanding schools serving disadvantaged communities: *what comes across most strongly is the passion of all who work in them for improving the chances and well-being of individual children.* This reflects Moyles' view, discussed in Chapter 1, that passion is one essential aspect of professionalism in working with young children. While such passion may be for a subject, it usually entails, with young children, a broader conception of success for the development of the 'whole child'. Who you are, and how you interact, matters, not just what content you teach.

The empathy required to work with young children involves the attributes of emotional intelligence, such as:

- understanding one's own and other people's emotions;
- regulating one's own responses;
- forming appropriate relationships.

Think how the Nursery nurse helped Rebecca to overcome her worries. This entailed making challenge more manageable, not avoiding it, and required knowledge of the individual child, built up over time where possible, paying attention to her emotional and social as well as cognitive needs. Empathy, or what I have called attunement, may lead to a child who is very upset being given space when in a situation which is too demanding, or extra time or support when things are difficult at home. It is not just being 'soft' and may involve challenging children or telling them off, encouraging them to try harder or be more adventurous. However, it does entail taking an interest in them and being sensitive to their particular needs and circumstances.

Effective pedagogy, especially with young children, relies on attention to little, ordinary, everyday human actions and responses as well as lesson plans and schemes of work. Much of this involves the small interactions, the comment, the smile which show that you notice and care for individuals. Remember that they may be more concerned about their pet's illness or tonight's football match than about completing a row of sums. Very often, success depends on the quick, appropriate word or gesture which expert teachers manage so effortlessly. For example, as a head, I walked into the classroom of a very experienced teacher who was marking and discussing a child's work. As I waited, I saw Malcolm (who was often quite disruptive) just about to throw something at another child. I was about to intervene but was not quick enough. The teacher, without looking up, asked Malcolm, very quietly, to come and help her by handing out some worksheets – which he did, so that no incident or confrontation occurred. An expert teacher knows not only how to intervene, but when to do so (and when not). As Hart et al. (2005, page 263) suggest, *good practice is not just about what teachers do, but also what they do not do.* Especially with less confident children, it may often require waiting and holding oneself back, enabling and encouraging rather than interfering and insisting.

In many ways, young children experience and understand the world differently from adults. Those who work with them need to recognise this both intellectually and to try, to some extent, to see the world from the child's point of view. This does not mean acting as a child or trying to be an 'equal'. I made the mistake, as a young teacher, of wanting to be too friendly, only gradually recognising the importance of professional boundaries. However, it does entail trying to share enthusiasms and interests and to recognise frustrations and uncertainties. Excitement, enthusiasm and a love of learning are qualities which, though too easily forgotten, are necessary if pedagogy is to be more than technical competence; and tend to be contagious.

It would be hard, in my view, to argue that teachers, as a group, have a greater commitment to either equity or empathy than other educators. Being equitable and empathetic with individual children may be harder for class teachers than those who work with small groups. Indeed, teaching assistants often have more opportunity to listen and attend to children's needs. So, equity, empathy and passion are not specific to teachers. However, the entry requirements and the training required suggest that expertise is.

You will probably have found it hard to put your finger on the features of expertise, even when you are an expert. Much of the knowledge involved is tacit and the skills appear (to the outsider) to be effortless. Indeed, the greater the expertise, the more tacit it seems. Good readers do not look at every letter or even every word. They learn to concentrate only on what matters, and ignore the rest, though at times they may need to focus on detail. An expert sports player develops what is often called 'muscle memory'. A learner driver must concentrate on every move, while an expert seems able to bypass conscious thought. The novice spends a disproportionate amount of time and effort on what does not matter. In contrast, an expert assesses the situation quickly, selecting what is most relevant, recognising patterns and discarding what does not matter. For example, an expert chess player knows with little conscious thought which moves are obviously wrong; and an expert doctor, in diagnosing, rapidly identifies those symptoms likely to be significant (without forgetting the possibility that this may be wrong and that one may need to start again, if later evidence does not fit with these initial hunches). While one tends to assume that experts do the same as novices, but do it better, they seem to work in subtly different ways. They can decide, very quickly, which aspects matter most and select appropriate strategies.

Key idea: **Expertise**

What is distinctive about the expertise of teachers of young children?

The professional status of teachers, and the training involved, imply that they have a distinctive expertise. In secondary schools or further or higher education, the need for a high level of subject expertise tends to be taken for granted. What distinguishes a teacher of young children in Early Years or primary schools is more elusive, one reason why the struggle for professional status proved so difficult. Yet, traditions of pedagogy with young children, for example in mainland Europe and Scandinavia, are based on teachers having theoretical expertise, especially in child development.

Critical thinking exercise 2: the teacher's expertise

The RSA report (Ball, 1994, pages 58–59) claims that:

early years teachers require a breadth of knowledge, understanding and experience...not required of those with older children, citing the importance of:

- *'mastery of curriculum content as well as having sound knowledge of child development';*
- *being able to lead, and plan for, a team of other adults, both professionals and parents;*
- *being 'responsible for the assessment of children and for monitoring progress and ensuring continuity and progression between stages and establishments'.*

A Try to **identify** the expertise of a teacher, compared with other educators working with the same children, thinking initially about what is different about the role.

B **Articulate** what an expert teacher does which a new teacher finds difficult.

C Bearing in mind the emphasis in the QTS Standards on knowledge and understanding, skills and attributes, **consider** which of these are most important in the class teacher's role.

Comment

The value of any programme or resource always depends on how it is used. Take, for example, the interactive whiteboard. When used by an expert, it has the potential to be used interactively, encouraging high-quality talk, based on a range of stimuli (such as images, sounds and information) not available to a teacher. However, very often, it is used as little more than a glorified black- or whiteboard, focusing the attention of the whole class on one place; and so tending towards a transmission model of teaching. This is just one example of why educators need to understand learning and children, rather than adopt the latest technology or programme unthinkingly.

One fascination, and challenge, of being a teacher, especially with young children, is the variety of roles. This may include being, within a few minutes, a facilitator, a disciplinarian, a co-learner, a manager of other adults, a coach or a shoulder to cry on. Classrooms are such complex places that teachers and other educators have to choose what to do and what to avoid, both in planning and responding to events. This is usually more complex for teachers either because they are dealing with larger groups – and a wider range of responses – or because the subject knowledge required is more specific, such as how to teach phonics or to perform a cartwheel. Teachers must understand both the bigger picture of what they are trying to achieve and the processes available to enable this (and the hazards to avoid).

The QTS Standards and QAA Benchmarks indicate that knowledge and understanding, skills and attributes are all interlinked. In Chapter 1, we saw that one feature of professionalism is *mastery of a knowledge base requiring a long period of training*. The QTS Standards do not specify the attributes of an expert teacher. However, these would seem to mirror those to be encouraged in children. Some, such as resilience and reflectiveness, provide protection against difficulties, while others, such as resourcefulness and creativity, help to change adults from deliverers into creators, from transmitters to transformers. Educators require reciprocity to build the two-way relationships which young children need to thrive, both emotionally and cognitively. Reflectiveness is required if one is to remain a learner, avoiding the fate of the teacher who claimed to have 30 years' experience but was told that he had, in fact, one year's experience 30 times over. However, an expert teacher of young children is also:

- authoritative without being too controlling, with that authority usually stemming from qualities such as empathy and confidence at least as much as subject knowledge;
- flexible, with the ability to adapt appropriately in the light of changed circumstances, so that she is not too dependent on planning at the micro level;
- aware of her own strengths and weaknesses, so that she does not try to do, or to be, what she cannot.

The sorts of knowledge and understanding required of teachers, compared with other educators, depends on their role. Teaching requires both domain (subject) and craft knowledge, as discussed in Alexander (2010, pages 413–4), though 'knowledge of self' is also emphasised. This involves a combination of theoretical knowledge of the subject matter and how children learn and practical knowledge on how to relate to, motivate and challenge children. Craft knowledge, including that of how children learn and the types of activities and environments to enhance this, is easy to overlook, because it is so tacit and elusive. It is described (Alexander, 2010,. page 414) as having *a different sort of rigour, one that places more confidence in the judgement of teachers, their feel for the work, their love for students and learning...*, but hard to access and validate since it is *embedded in practice and not readily articulated.*

The skills required to teach young children are very wide-ranging, both technical ones related to assessment and behaviour management and relational ones such as working with a wide range of adults and of children whose responses are often unpredictable. Alexander (2010, page 416) argues that *exceptional teaching...lies beyond mere competence and adds a degree of artistry, flexibility and originality whose precise features it may be difficult to pin down as measurable indicators; but we certainly know it when we see it;* and (page 417) *expert teachers appear to act effortlessly, fluidly and instinctively, apparently without calculation, drawing on deep reserves of tacit knowledge rather than explicit rules and maxims.* An expert teacher in one location, subject area or age group may not be in another. The skills useful in teaching PE or music may be less so teaching mathematics or history; or with a Year 5 than Year 1 class, partly because young children's learning depends so much on relationships.

Less obviously, expert teachers do something subtly different. In Hart et al.'s (2005, page 263) words, this involves *select(ing) those practices that seem most likely to increase young people's capacity to learn, and reject(ing) anything that might limit or impede the achievement of the core purposes for everybody.* So, they constantly draw on a repertoire, a 'tool box' of different possible strategies, choosing what is appropriate to that situation. Expertise consists, in part, of having, and being able to draw on, a wider range of tools than a novice. This challenges two views implicit in the Standards for QTS, namely that expertise:

- will be demonstrated by the same person in all or most contexts;
- entails doing more of the same, but doing it better.

Alexander (2010, page 418) argues that teachers need *deep representations of subject matter,* going on that this makes the task of the generalist class teacher very hard, especially when teaching older children in Key Stage 2. Teaching music, for instance, requires specific expertise – both propositional and procedural – beyond that of most teachers. The same might be said of other areas such as art, technology, modern foreign languages or mathematics. However, while such deep representations may be desirable, there is a danger that a subject-based approach may not make the connections across subject boundaries and lose the overview of the whole child associated with class teaching. Given the need for breadth and balance, the ability to make connections between subjects, and to ask the questions and set up the activities which will enable children to do so, suggests that expertise across different domains is important when teaching young children. Moreover, an emphasis on subject knowledge expertise may overstate the teacher's role rather than the learner's in developing the attributes of successful learning, such as creativity or resourcefulness.

There is, therefore, a tension between the breadth of knowledge possible when one teacher is responsible for all (or most) areas of learning and the depth possible only for the subject specialist. Other professionals, such as speech and language therapists or educational psychologists and, to a lesser extent, subject leaders or co-ordinators will have more detailed and specific knowledge in their area of expertise. However, the class teacher's role remains pivotal, especially with younger children to ensure that the 'whole child' is considered, which is the basis of thoughtful assessment and responsive planning; like an architect with a vision of the whole building, taking account of the different processes and details involved, even though surveyors or bricklayers may be responsible for specific aspects.

Salmon (1995, page 37) cites Kelly's words, that:

 each of us lives by hearing the whisper of recurrent themes in the events which reverberate around us. If teachers are to reach the young people who sit within their classrooms, they need to listen for widely varied yet distinctive themes. The teaching role is one demanding many kinds of understanding beyond those of the subject itself.

This requires an ability to reflect in action, both to observe what is going on and to decide how to intervene, for instance by stopping a dangerous or disruptive activity, commenting to the whole class on particular difficulties or strengths or suggesting to an individual what to do next. Expert teachers draw on a repertoire of different types of skills in assessment, to understand children's learning and to respond appropriately and flexibly. They comply with what matters most, without necessarily being compliant on every detail of pedagogy. Expertise consists in being able to move beyond the formula, but maintaining an emphasis on what really matters.

Key idea: **Repertoire**

How can you build up expertise?

In Day's (1999, page 53) words, *An expert can be defined as one who works on the leading edge of his or her knowledge and skill. Thus an expert seeks progressively to complicate the model of the problem to be solved whereas an experienced non-expert seeks to reduce the problem to fit available methods.* However, Hart et al. (2004, page 264) suggest that *faced with the ever-increasing complexity of classroom teaching as public expectations of schooling have risen, teachers themselves have found it necessary to simplify that complexity.*

You wouldn't expect, as a newly qualified surgeon, to perform a major operation straight away, without support, would you? Or as a surveyor straight out of college to be put in charge of a project without supervision? Similarly, no teacher should expect, or be expected, to emerge as a fully fledged professional at the end of initial training. Berliner (cited in Alexander, 2010, pages 416–7) argues that teachers move through a spectrum from novice to advanced beginner, then competent, proficient and finally expert. To start off with, you will often feel like a novice, or a juggler trying to keep several balls in the air at once, with the prospect of building up expertise probably fairly daunting.

Critical thinking exercise 3: building expertise

In the Cambridge Primary Review's words (Alexander, 2010, page 511), teachers should *work towards a pedagogy of repertoire rather than recipe and of principle rather than prescription.*

A **Illustrate** what some of the 'tools' are in the repertoire of a teacher of young children; and **discuss** the principles on which they should rely.

B **Identify** the main opportunities for you to build up expertise in your role.

C **Articulate** what you think 'reflective practice' means and how and where this can happen.

Comment

The first question prompts you to reflect on the tools we have discussed – from the layout of the room to the choice of activities, the expectations given and the support and feedback offered, the ways in which children are expected to work and the people – educators, parents/carers and other children – who are involved. Inevitably, the repertoire of an inexperienced educator is more limited than that of an expert, but remember that all are 'working towards', rather than having ever arrived. And the principles to guide action are not only those discussed earlier in the chapter, but reflect the distinctive beliefs and qualities you bring to the task.

Building up expertise comes primarily, but not exclusively, through experience because teaching is a practical activity. Kolb's learning cycle consists of four stages, illustrated in Figure 1, see page 165.

This indicates how learning involves a combination of doing, reflecting, thinking and planning, with this being a gradual and cumulative process. Alexander (2010, page 416) quotes Berliner's view that *expertise is specific to a domain, and particular contexts in domains, and is developed over hundreds of thousands of hours.* While this length of time may be questionable, expertise certainly requires a great deal of practice so that one's actions become 'second nature'. Understanding how children learn, and how this applies to a particular class or individual, is an essential part of professional expertise, but theory is of limited use, if you cannot apply it. Without a theoretical underpinning, practice may rely on recycling old ideas. You certainly don't need to memorise all the theory in this book, very little of which I knew even after many years' teaching; but building up expertise requires constant thinking through of pedagogy.

Concrete experience
(doing/having an experience)

Active experimentation
(planning/trying out what you have learned)

Reflective observation
(reviewing/reflecting on the experience)

Abstract conceptualisation
(concluding/learning from the experience)

Figure 1 Kolb's learning cycle

Teaching by repertoire requires resourcefulness. Most teachers are (rightly) pragmatic, innovating, copying and adapting other people's ideas, or in Hargreaves' (1999, page 130) memorable phrase, 'tinkering'. So, just as a cook starts from a recipe, but looks to move beyond, and adapt it, when more confident, it is sensible to start by relying on other people's plans and programmes, both those in school and outside. But building up expertise involves looking to adapt these, or devising new approaches which suit your children's learning and your own approach. However, this needs to be done gradually, especially at first and when you are less confident. Build on your strengths, but do not overlook your weaknesses. When lacking in confidence, you may decide to be less ambitious and maintain a tighter structure. When less sure about content, you may be more wary of open questions in case you find yourself out of your depth. However, while it is often right to simplify, oversimplifying comes at a cost, tending to discourage the metacognition and open dialogue which leads to deep learning.

Alexander (2008, page 93) argues that *we have two deeply seated pedagogical habits to contend with: recitation and pseudo-enquiry*. The first involves children essentially expecting, and being expected, to repeat what the teacher says, the second (to avoid this) that they are asked to find out for themselves, though usually the teacher knows what answer she wants – and the child tries to work this out. These deep habits are hard to avoid, especially when learning is seen largely in terms of performance. But if children are to develop the attributes of successful learning, educators must work against such habits and be helped to do so.

Inevitably, much of what children experience at school will involve surface learning, with tasks to provide reinforcement and practice, with relatively low cognitive demands. This book prompts you to alter the balance gradually to promote more engagement and excitement, to encourage more imagination and initiative, to steer children's expectations and experiences beyond the ordinary and the mundane. So, look to see how programmes and plans can be adapted to encourage the types of activities and attributes discussed; and how you can hand over more control for their learning to children.

While expertise appears to be effortless, it is almost always based on practising what matters most over a long period of time. The Nursery nurse with Rebecca did not gain such sensitivity overnight. Expertise is gathered bit by bit, gradually adding to your tool box. Sometimes, we talk of a 'natural' implying that someone has an inherited ability. As discussed in relation to children, our genes, our inherited qualities and temperament make us more or less predisposed to particular aspects, but how these are developed, or not, depends on experience, upbringing and habituation. As the golfer Gary Player said when told he was lucky, *Yes and the more I practice, the luckier I seem to be.*

Key idea: **Reflectiveness**

One key way to build up expertise is through reflective practice. In Leeson's words (2007, page 173), *reflection is not just thinking about what you do.* She writes (2007, page 176), *reflection... requires hard systematic thinking (and soft, intuitive insight) leading to a plan of action based on a critical evaluation of all the available evidence.* She draws (pages 173, 175) on Ghaye and Ghaye's work to say that it involves *being professionally self-critical without being destructive and overly negative* and suggests these five stages:

- descriptive – giving an account of what happened;
- perceptive – linking the description and one's own feelings;
- receptive – allowing oneself to be open to different perspectives;
- interactive – creating links with future action;
- critical – questioning accepted practice creatively and constructively to develop new theories and ways of working.

This process is like Schön's reflection-on-action, taking time to think about what has happened. This is like being in the audience at a theatre, recalling that the word 'theory' originally comes from the Greek for a spectator, where you learn to look at yourself and your children from afar, like actors on a stage. However, reflective practice also involves reflection-in-action, involving judgements in response to immediate events, which is hard, because responses can be only partly planned in advance; especially so for the class teacher. So, reflection is not an activity separate from the classroom, but integral to professional life.

Key idea: **Continuing professional development**

What is the most valuable type of CPD?

If your GP did not keep up to date with recent research, you would rightly be appalled. Equally, you would not think much of a lawyer who was unaware of recent legislative changes. How teachers (and other educators) build up their expertise is a long, often paradoxical, process of continuous professional development, usually shortened to CPD. This is usually thought of as staff meetings, courses or INSET days, either during the school day or after school.

Such courses may be useful, especially for disseminating new information or ideas. However, CPD is too rarely continuous or professional. So, discussion at staff meetings is too often about arrangements rather than pedagogy; and day courses about specific programmes or new policies. Yet, as Carr and Kemmis (1989, page 91) suggest, *practices are changed by changing the ways in which they are understood.* And in Fullan's words (1991, page 343) *the ultimate aim of in-service training is less to implement a specific innovation or policy and more to create individual and organisational habits and structures that make continuous learning a valued and endemic part of the culture of schools and teaching.*

Critical thinking exercise 4: looking further ahead

The General Teaching Council (GTCE, 2007) suggest that effective CPD:

- has a clear focus on pupil learning;
- involves teachers in identifying their needs;
- is grounded in what is known about effective adult learning;

with the last of these including:

- sustained access to coaching and mentoring;
- a range of opportunities for observation and feedback as part of collaborative and collegial working practices;
- opportunities for teachers to change practice, carry out research and engage in reflective practice;
- modelling of preferred practice (e.g. active learning) both in classrooms and in adult learning situations;
- sustained, structured and cumulative opportunities for practising what has been learnt.

A **Identify** where there may be opportunities for such activities.

B **Articulate** the main challenges to these ways of building expertise and how you might overcome them.

C **Consider** what sort of educator you are, and would like to be and how you can build on the attributes and strengths you bring to your role.

Comment

That effective CPD should focus on pupil learning, involve teachers in identifying their own needs and be grounded in effective adult learning strategies may seem obvious. However, CPD is too often based on teachers being told what to do, often in short sessions which do not allow for discussion and cumulative learning. Learning is a social rather than an individual process and working with children not just a solitary activity

---

(though at times it may feel like it). Ideally, building up expertise is like an apprenticeship, where one is guided by someone with greater experience. However, those who work in schools have remarkably few opportunities for structured reflection with another professional. Social workers, for example, have regular supervision. To some extent, performance management and monitoring can fulfil this role, but these are often focused on meeting external requirements.

Naturally, heads and policy-makers have to work within limited budgets – and replacing teachers for courses is expensive – recognising that there may be a tension between meeting the needs of individual educators and those of the school. So, as well as the more formal opportunities on offer, look out for, and create, your own opportunities, for example to:

● watch others at work and talk with others, both in your own school and elsewhere;
● reflect with other colleagues, for example by taking opportunities to be coached and mentored and to coach and mentor others;
● seek support, where need be, from more experienced colleagues;
● work with those in other schools, whether through formal networks or for particular projects;
● engage with, and possibly in, research, and take part in more sustained professional development, such as further qualifications or action research.

Much of the most valuable CPD links knowledge from outside – other schools, those with expertise in a subject area or special needs or research – with the context of your own school, so that your specific concerns are related to wider considerations and experience. While such opportunities may be formal, much of the best CPD occurs informally, through planning and assessment, moderation meetings or simply talking with other colleagues.

One important decision is to choose, if you can, the school you work in. Just as the classroom environment affects how young children learn, working in a school whose principles and values you share and which uses the skills and attributes you bring makes professional life both easier and more fulfilling. In the longer term, greater expertise requires broadening one's experience. So, for instance, be prepared (and ask) to change:

● age group, so that you have experience of children of different ages;
● subject specialisms, so that you acquire breadth;
● school, so that you do not become too immersed in one's school culture and expectations.

Among the main challenges when you start in school are tiredness, isolation, lack of confidence and pressures external to the classroom. While working with young children can be a wonderfully enriching experience, it is incredibly tiring, in part because children are emotionally demanding, in part because life is so busy with the demands of planning and assessment, recording and marking. School life is often isolating, especially for class teachers, because they spend so much time with one group, and particularly when things are not going well. Probably the most common concern of those working with young children, especially class teachers in Key Stage 2, relates to managing behaviour. This often leads to a cycle of working even harder and becoming more tired – and often unwell. So, look after yourself, both physically and mentally; and do activities which nurture you, both for your own sake and the children's.

Other constraints which affect all educators may include large class sizes, a lack of resources, an emphasis on test results and targets, the pressure of inspection and monitoring. These operate both obviously and more subtly. For example, Hart et al. (2005, page 9) write: *the…emphasis on target-setting and value-added measures of achievement have made it increasingly difficult for teachers who reject the fixed view of measurable ability to hold on to their principles, since they are continually being required to act as if they subscribe to it.* So, teachers, especially, need resilience and resourcefulness not to be overwhelmed and to adopt oversimple solutions, because these are more measurable, safer and easier. This is especially so for those working in challenging circumstances where raising attainment, as measured by test scores, is very hard; and where the opportunity for breadth and balance of experience is most restricted for those children who, arguably, would benefit most from it.

However, remember that even when you cannot do everything you want, or believe to be right, there is much that you can do. Recognise your influence in the classroom and in the school because new staff often make up in enthusiasm and energy for what they may lack in experience. There is more scope for creativity within current constraints than is often thought, but work with what you can influence. Much of this lies in the detail of pedagogy. So:

- enjoy the children's company, interests and humour and learn with, and from, them;
- be playful and curious and encourage children to do likewise;
- learn to live with uncertainty and try to help children do so;
- keep asking yourself why a particular activity or intervention works or not;
- build relationships, with colleagues, parents/carers and, above all, children.

In Chapter 6, the importance of building a coherent narrative was discussed in relation to children's identity. This is just as true in forming your identity as a teacher. Knowing who you are, understanding your areas of expertise and the children you work with, recognising your strengths and limitations are all part of establishing yourself as someone confident and authoritative in the classroom.

Above all, try to focus on what really matters, prioritising the welfare and well-being of the children. An adult who helps to enhance lifelong learning is creating something very precious. But this requires a process of development which is both continuous and professional, constantly adding to your repertoire and exercising judgement on the basis of principle.

Conclusion

In this chapter, we have explored the expertise required to work with young children and how to build it up. The critical thinking exercises will have helped you:

- **consider** the attributes of experts both in general and in working with young children;
- **analyse** the distinctive aspects of the teacher's role and the implications for your own;
- **identify** ways of building up expertise, emphasising relatively small changes but with a focus on your relationships and interactions with children;
- **imagine** how CPD can become an integral part of professional life.

In the final chapter, you are invited to pull together the different strands raised throughout the book by imagining future challenges and opportunities and reflecting on the key lessons about pedagogy, with a focus on what is distinctive about this when working with young children.

Further reading

Alexander, R (ed) (2010) *Children, their World, their Education – Final report and recommendations of the Cambridge Primary Review.* Abingdon: Routledge
For those studying to be teachers, especially, Chapter 21 (pages 406–436) is excellent though complicated, with pages 416–419 particularly good on expertise.

Leeson, C (2007) In Praise of Reflective Practice. Pages 171–181 of Willan, J, Parker-Rees, R and Savage, J (eds) *Early Childhood Studies.* Exeter: Learning Matters
A well-argued and practical discussion of reflection, with a focus on the Early Years but applicable more widely.

---

11 Facing the challenge of an unknown future

Chapter Focus

The critical thinking exercises in this chapter focus on:

⊙ **imagining** future changes to education policy and practice;
⊙ **articulating** the values which underlie your understanding of education;
⊙ **synthesising** the main ideas of the whole book;
⊙ **considering** the implications for you as an educator.

The key ideas discussed are: **knowledge society, technology, school improvement, values, relationships**

This chapter is particularly relevant to QTS Standards: **2**, **5**, **7a**, **8** and to Knowledge and Understanding, Application and Reflection (*Education Studies*) and Subject knowledge and Subject skills (*Early Childhood Studies*)

Introduction

In this book, I have drawn on the traditions described in Chapter 2, the insights of research and my own experience to try to shine a light on the complexity and fascination of pedagogy when working with young children; and to suggest that what seems like common sense or is recommended as good practice may not be what most enhances children's learning. The approach was described as like assembling the pieces of a jigsaw or diving for important but hidden truths about pedagogy, like submerged pearls. Each person's jigsaw will be at different stages of completeness, depending on your own prior experience, interests and role. This chapter tries to synthesise key points, and discover some pearls, though inevitably the implications will vary according to your role and context. I hope that you will have found others for yourself in the search.

The critical thinking exercises start by imagining possible changes in the next 30 to 40 years, to help you think through how your role may change; and what matters most, emphasising principles and values. The last two exercises invite you to consider key points about young children, learning and pedagogy; and to what extent the general principles apply to children of different ages. The book ends by emphasising that, whatever your level of experience, success depends on how well you enhance children's learning; and this on continuing to think through your pedagogy.

CASE STUDY

As a deputy head, I took a Year 6 class skating on an end-of-year outing, and was persuaded onto the ice for only the second time ever. I was scared, but hardly anyone took my fears seriously. The competent skaters who said how easy it was were no help at all. The most valuable support came from the least likely source, David, a child who found school life difficult and was constantly in trouble. He literally took me by the hand, and led me round. He gave me simple, one-at-a-time instructions. He told me to experiment, he skated alongside, encouraging me. He let me make mistakes without bombarding me with advice; and he got me to skate on my own, returning from time to time to see how I was getting on. Though I remained very tentative, I could just about skate round the rink on my own by the end.

Before reading on, pause to think about my behaviour, how other children responded and what David did to help me; and try to relate this to what a young child needs most when feeling vulnerable, as I did. I love this story because it describes an adult in the position of the child; and the most unlikely child showing many attributes associated with effective pedagogy. We shall return to these shortly.

Key ideas: **Knowledge society and technology**

What are the key challenges facing educators in the next 30 to 40 years?

It is hard to recognise that what seems 'normal' is, often, relatively recent and may change in the future. When I started teaching in 1976, changes now taken for granted were unimaginable, literally in relation to technology, with others such as the National Curriculum and Ofsted almost impossible to foresee. Equally, many assumptions widely shared then no longer apply, such as the teacher working alone with a class of children for most of the week, uninterrupted but with very little assistance. However, most settings where young children go to school or nursery in 2011 are remarkably similar to those of 1911, as are those in England or in New England. They spend most of the week in a class with children of much the same age, usually with the same teacher, with a curriculum which has many similarities across cultures and societies. Although the style of teaching in many primary schools changed during the period from the 1960s to the 1980s, what and how teachers taught changed less than is often assumed. So, change is always occurring, but schools, classrooms and pedagogy remain remarkably similar from generation to generation. Similarly, despite many changes, the purposes of

/continued

Key idea: **Knowledge society and technology – continued**

education and how its success is measured show considerable continuities and seem likely to continue to do so. For example, the demand from parents and carers for young children to be looked after while adults are at work; or from politicians for results which provide easily collected measures of success are likely to remain constant. The assumptions which dominate the education system may change, but these are more likely (sadly) to be influenced by social, cultural or political, rather than educational, considerations.

Critical thinking exercise 1: looking into the future

Four factors likely to affect the world, and education, significantly in the next 30 years or so are:

- globalisation;
- changing work patterns and the requirements of employers;
- knowledge of the brain;
- technological change.

A **Consider** and **discuss** how, if at all, the first two may affect young children. their learning and the role of educators. Be creative and adventurous, as this is largely a matter of speculation.

B **Imagine** how changes to knowledge of the brain and technology may alter our view of how best young children should learn. Again, take a few risks but also be sceptical of, and challenge, what is claimed in these respects.

C Try to **identify** possible implications for how young children will, or should, be taught.

Comment

It is often asserted that economic and social trends such as globalisation and changes in the world of work will alter education fundamentally, especially for older students. As we saw in Chapter 2, the policy changes in the last 20 years have been based, in part, on the perceived need to prepare children better for such trends. For example, the rationale for the emphasis on standards of literacy and numeracy and the (long overdue) extension of modern foreign languages into primary school relates to international competitiveness. Globalisation is usually seen in terms of economics, but Hargreaves (2003, page xix) cites George Soros' view that it can lead to fragmentation and a reduced sense of belonging to a wider community and that *state education is in a pole position to teach a set of values, dispositions and senses of global responsibility that extend beyond the bounds of the knowledge economy.*

Hargreaves (2003, page xviii) argues that teaching for the 'knowledge society':

 involves cultivating these capacities in young people – developing deep cognitive learning, creativity and ingenuity among pupils; drawing on research, working in networks and teams, and pursuing continuous professional learning as teachers; and promoting problem-solving, risk-taking, trust in the collaborative process, ability to cope with change and commitment to continuous improvement as organizations.

These capacities are similar to those we have explored; and which the current climate tends to inhibit in its desire for conformity and standardisation.

Knowledge about how the brain works is often seen as offering the key to children's future learning needs. Growing knowledge of the plasticity of young children's brains and of how particular activities help to strengthen neural connections supports the view that early experience matters profoundly. But translating these findings into specific teaching programmes is more problematic. Claims about many commercial schemes and ideas such as children needing to drink water regularly or eating particular foods are often said to be backed by brain research. However, Tommerdahl (2010, page 107) writes of *the impossibility of moving straight from the laboratory into the classroom*, arguing that classroom practices need to be based on educational theory, which must take account of psychological mechanisms. These, in turn, need to recognise the insights of cognitive neuroscience on brain function and architecture, which is distinct from neuroscience itself. So, classroom strategies need to be evaluated, but even then making the link to brain function will be difficult. For example, Tommerdahl (2010, page 107) recognises that neuroscience may provide insights especially in relation to special educational needs; but emphasises the level of variation between how typically developing individuals learn means that one should be cautious, saying that *it cannot be overemphasised what early days we are in.*

The claim that technology will change both learning and teaching significantly is commonly made. The internet, more sophisticated mobile phones, e-books and other inventions not yet imagined are likely to make the access to information much easier and communication quicker. Therefore, learners will have less need to memorise, and more to critique which information is most useful or to be trusted; and instant communication may reduce the opportunities for slower, more analytical thinking. New technologies may change learning by broadening our, and children's, ideas of creating music and visual art, for instance, and using these to present work in original, interesting ways. More radical changes are possible, for example children creating their own computer programs and applications and linking with children in other countries, as a matter of course.

Despite these possibilities, there is a danger of:

- technology leading to an increasingly individualised engagement with the world and, unless used interactively, to a transmissive mode of teaching;

- lessons in ICT being used to teach low-level skills which even very young children can learn easily and quickly more informally;
- those who are most disadvantaged having least access to new technologies.

It is worth recalling how little pedagogy has changed despite previous technological changes. In Noss and Pachler's words (1999, page 195), *as each technological innovation (radio, television, video etc.) has come and gone, it has left education with a feeling that something good had happened but that nothing fundamental has changed.* You may think that this is too cautious and that the future holds all sorts of exciting possibilities for transforming how children learn; for example, that computers can replace people, as, in some respects, no doubt they can; or that neuroscience will help identify improved ways of learning to decode text or of teaching spelling, as, no doubt, they will. However, remember the TLRP's emphasis on learning relationships and the social nature of learning. Interaction with people is irreplaceable, especially for young children.

An uncertain future means that we all, children and adults, must learn to navigate through unfamiliar territory. Adults have to prepare children for, and be prepared for, uncertainty. Hargreaves (2003) describes a triangle of competing interests where teachers have the potential to be:

- catalysts of the knowledge society and the opportunity it promises;
- counterpoints to the threats which the knowledge society brings in terms of inclusiveness;

but risk being

- casualties where higher expectations are often met with standardised solutions, provided at minimum cost.

From his analysis, I highlight that teachers should act as listed in Table 4:

Table 4

As **catalysts**	<ul><li>promote deep cognitive learning;</li><li>learn to teach in ways they were not taught;</li><li>treat parents as partners in learning;</li><li>build a capacity for change and risk;</li><li>foster trust in processes.</li></ul>
As **counterpoints**	<ul><li>promote social and emotional learning, commitment and character;</li><li>develop cosmopolitan identity;</li><li>work and learn in collaborative groups;</li><li>forge relationships with parents and communities;</li><li>preserve continuity and security.</li></ul>
As **casualties**, avoid the temptation to:	<ul><li>coach children to memorise standardised learning;</li><li>learn to teach as they are told;</li><li>work harder and learn alone;</li><li>treat parents as consumers and complainers;</li><li>respond to imposed change with fearful compliance.</li></ul>

(drawn from Hargreaves, 2003, pages 15, 45 and 59 respectively)

Educators must see themselves both as catalysts and as counterpoints, partly to avoid becoming casualties themselves but mainly because professionalism involves prioritising the welfare of the children. There seems little doubt that the role of teachers and other educators will continue to change. For example, the number of adults who work with children – both professionals and parents – with differing expertises may result in class teachers being more like managers of a group of educators, planning programmes, with less direct interaction with a whole class. So the role as a generalist, especially in Key Stage 2, may alter, with implications for the type of expertise required. Already, many class teachers in primary schools concentrate mainly on literacy and numeracy, and spend little time on the foundation subjects. If children are taught more by specialists, the class teacher's main expertise may be less in relation to subject knowledge than in assessment, to decide what additional support is required.

The Standards for QTS and QAA Benchmark Standards highlight knowledge and understanding, skills and attributes as the main components of professional competence. This reflects the distinction made in Chapter 3 between knowledge *that*, knowledge *how* and knowledge *of.* These elements are all intertwined, though particular lessons or contexts may require a greater emphasis on one or more of these. The content knowledge, and especially how this is accessed, seems certain to change rapidly. The pedagogical skills required are likely to be more constant, though there are so many that the challenge will be to decide which to develop. The attributes, or qualities, necessary to work with young children, discussed in Chapter 10, such as equity, empathy and expertise, especially those based on principles, are the most enduring. As Hargreaves (2003, page 161) states, *teachers are not deliverers but developers of learning. Those who focus only on teaching techniques and curriculum standards…promote a diminished view of teaching and teacher professionalism that has no place in a sophisticated knowledge society.*

Key idea: **School improvement**

What matters most in enhancing children's learning?

There is a huge amount of research on school improvement. The rationale of frequent policy changes in the last 20 years has been to improve schools. This has included the introduction of, and regular changes to, the National Curriculum, the creation of Ofsted, the National Literacy and Numeracy Strategies and an unprecedented stream of guidance. School leadership has also been emphasised as vital to school improvement. Most of these approaches are structural and their success, or otherwise, a matter of debate. The structures within which educators work and the quality of school leadership affect profoundly how and what children are expected to learn and adults to teach. However, there is a broad

/continued

Key idea: **School improvement – continued**

consensus on the centrality of the interaction between learners and teachers. Consider the following statements.

- *the quality of an education cannot exceed the quality of its teachers* and *a curriculum is only as good as those who teach it,* from the Rose Report (DCSF, 2009, page 10 and Recommendation 9).
- *the quality of an education system cannot exceed the quality of its teachers,* from a McKinsey Report on the world's best-performing school systems (2007, page 3).
- *educational change depends on what teachers do and think. It's as simple and complex as that,* from the Canadian academic, Fullan (1991, page 117).

If, and when, you doubt that you are making a difference to young children's lives, remember how important you are. Your expertise, your judgement and your values matter.

Critical thinking exercise 2: working out what matters most

Jackson et al. (1993, page 277) write:

> *we do not say that opinions, decisions, and outlooks of other [people] count for nothing, or deny that the teacher's freedom to act on what he or she believes and desires may be greatly constrained by both institutional and social forces, some of them emanating from outside the school itself. But we do insist that within such limits teachers must be seen and see themselves as occupying key roles in classrooms – not simply as technicians who know how to run good discussions or teach encoding skills to beginning readers but as persons whose view of life, which includes all that goes on in classrooms, promises to be as influential in the long run as any of their technical skills. It is this extended view of a teacher's responsibility that makes it appropriate to speak of teaching as a moral enterprise.*

A **Identify** what sorts of knowledge and understanding, skills and attributes you would wish the children you have taught to have.

B **Analyse** what is most important and enduring about a good teacher in the light of the quotation above.

C **Illustrate** how you show respect or honesty (or another personal value) in your interactions with children and what makes this difficult.

Thinking Through Pedagogy for Primary and Early Years

Comment

You will, surely, wish that the children in your care will have gained many different types of knowledge and skills by the time that they move on to the next class or school. It would be strange if you did not wish them to be literate and numerate. I should be surprised if you did not want them to have an understanding and enjoyment of music and science, of history and art, of physical education and geography. The importance we ascribe to these will vary, partly because of what we value most, our enthusiasms and our prejudices. However, important as these are, a continued engagement with, and probably enjoyment of, learning and the attributes of successful learning such as resilience and reciprocity, co-operation and confidence will be even more so, not only in the next phase of schooling, but throughout life. It may be useful to know the formula to calculate the radius of a circle or the colours of the rainbow; but more so how to apply, or discover more, knowledge or relate to people different from oneself.

Schools have a duty to promote community cohesion. This is a more complex idea than may appear on the surface. Putnam (2000) distinguishes between two types of capital – bonding, which helps groups to cohere, and bridging, which provides the glue across social and cultural divides. One challenge in cultural development is to enable children to learn about both similarity and difference, about what binds as well as what separates, for adults both to recognise and value children's culture and to broaden their horizons and, especially for older children, challenge their assumptions. Empowering children to think critically, debate and negotiate is essential to citizenship in a democratic society. So, learning to listen and understand, to discuss and debate is not just about academic learning, but fundamental to spiritual, moral, social and cultural development. Moreover, community cohesion refers not only to ethnicity and faith, but to class and age (see Eaude, 2009b). It is a challenge for every school, although the nature of the challenge will be very different in a village school and a large multicultural children's centre.

We have seen that young children, especially, learn by example, in relation to reading or listening, to questioning or wondering, to holding doors open to resolving disagreements. If one wishes children to be respectful, they need to be shown respect. To learn to be honest, or empathetic, children need to experience adults showing these attributes. Authentic action is worth more than any amount of moralising. However, this does not relate only to character. As Alexander (2010, page 308) states *pupils will not learn to think for themselves if their teachers are expected to do as they are told*. More widely, in Bruner's (1996, page 15) words, *an education enterprise that fails to take the risks involved becomes stagnant and eventually alienating.*

Key idea: **Values**

I have tried to strike a balance between the influence of the environment in which you work and your own principles and values. Hart et al. (2004, page 264), in describing their alternative model of pedagogy which is not based on judgements of ability, express the hope that this *will provide a stimulus for teachers to review their values and reconsider their choices.* Halstead (1996, page 5) defines values as *principles, fundamental convictions, ideals, standards or life stances which act as general guides to behaviour or as points of reference in decision-making or the evaluation of beliefs or action and which are closely connected to personal integrity and personal identity.* Values are often seen as vague statements of intent rather than principles and fundamental convictions, but values are expressed most clearly in actions. They can be expressed in personal terms, such as equity, respect or honesty, or in institutional terms, such as a mission statement which sets out principles, such as 'success for all' or 'fulfilling each individual's potential'. Values can be descriptive of what we do and aspirational in helping to influence beliefs and actions. But either way, they guide behaviour, whether consciously or not, and are linked to what matters most to us.

Remember how Moyles (2004), in Chapter 1, argued that the paradoxes of pedagogy could easily dampen the passion and undermine the professionalism necessary to work with young children. One of the hardest aspects of being an educator is deciding which 'voice' to listen to when one's personal values clash with external expectations; for example, if there is pressure for a child to write but you believe that they need more opportunity to play, or to paint; or if you have targets to meet but feel that this entails restricting the curriculum.

This is also difficult when the values of a child or a family do not match with your own or those of the school. The most obvious is when a child, reprimanded for hitting back, replies that their mum or dad have told them to do so – and you have to show that this is unacceptable without devaluing their home background. Working with Muslim families provides a more subtle example. They value especially two qualities which most adults in Western society either do not see as important or do not understand – modesty and *izzat* (roughly translated as honour or reputation). Recognising the importance of this requires an attunement to parents' and children's wishes, in aspects such as changing for PE or diet, to be sensitive without overemphasising difference. As Bruner (1990, page 30) writes, *open-mindedness is the keystone of what we call a democratic culture*, arguing that this implies *a willingness to construe knowledge and values from multiple perspectives, without loss of commitment to one's own values.*

Schools are, for many children, beacons of hope and bastions of security in an often-confusing and sometimes harsh world. However, many of the structures and expectations associated with schooling inhibit the attributes of successful, lifelong learning which young children exhibit. Instead, they encourage or reinforce limited or inappropriate aspirations and undermine some children's identities as learners. While individual educators cannot change the system, they can, through their own pedagogy, help to avoid these results and provide the springboard for lifelong learning.

Critical thinking exercise 3: the key messages for pedagogy

Noddings (1991, page 161) writes:

Schools should become places in which teachers and students live together, talk to each other, reason together, take delight in each others' company. Like good parents, teachers should be concerned first and foremost with the kind of people their charges are becoming. My guess is that when schools focus on what really matters in life, the cognitive ends we are now striving towards in such painful and artificial ways will be met as natural culminations of the means we have widely chosen.

A **Identify:**
- three key messages about young children's learning raised in this book;
- three main lessons about your role as an educator.

B **Comparing** the developmental tradition and the standards agenda, **articulate** which elements of each you believe most enhance successful learning.

C **Discuss** what we can learn from interactions between adults and children before they start, and outside school.

Comment

It may seem strange that I have warned you to be wary of generalisations and simple solutions and then invited you to highlight a few key messages. Of course, your own background and role will mean that some messages will have resonated more for you than others; and the tacitness of expertise that you may return to others in the future. However, in this section, I reflect on what I believe to be the most important and surprising lessons I have learned as a teacher and in writing this book.

The vast majority of young children come to school having learned, in the most remarkable way, to walk, to talk, to relate to others. Most show many of the attributes of successful learners, at least in the right situation. Yet, too often schools encourage an attitude of 'learned helplessness'. This seems to result from adults' (both educators' and parents'):

- desire for conformity and suspicion of creativity;

- emphasis on surface knowledge and short-term performance;
- focus on ability and intelligence.

We have discussed the first two. In terms of the third, Dweck (1999, page 96) writes, *intelligence…gains importance over the school years, as children pursue their academic studies, experience successes and failures, observe the successes and failures of their peers, and observe the reactions of their own parents to their academic efforts.* Even more forcefully, Hart et al. (2005, page 22) cite Nash's comment *whatever else children learn or fail to learn in school, they learn to measure themselves against their classmates…Schools teach hierarchical levels of personal worth more successfully than anything else.* Many children succeed because of, or despite, this, but a minority become disengaged, because schools take too little account of their experience and knowledge out of school and different ways of learning. As a result, the range of activities is often too narrow and children's emotional needs and their stage of cognitive development are not considered in enough depth, leading to a loss of a sense of agency and engagement. So, while education has the potential to enhance the lives of all children, and the years up to the age of 11 are vital in enabling this, this happens too infrequently. Put more simply, too many children become bored and disengaged because they do not see the point of what they are asked to do.

In reflecting on the traditions described in Chapter 2, and the subsequent argument, it seems that:

- the developmental tradition tended to overemphasise individual activity and to provide too little challenge but that its emphasis on the 'whole child' and breadth of experience reflected what young children need;
- the standards agenda tends to overemphasise a narrow range of skills and outcomes, leading to many children not developing the attributes of successful learners, but that the focus on entitlement and inclusion has helped raise expectations of many children, parents and educators.

Tharp and Gallimore (1988, page 27) suggest that *the principles of good teaching are not different for school than for home and community. When true teaching is found in schools it observes the same principles that teaching exhibits in informal settings.* We have seen that the knowledge to be learned at school is in some respects distinct from that outside; and working with a class makes the interaction and dialogue possible at home or in a small group more difficult. An approach based on instruction may make (most) educators more comfortable, but it is not the best way to enable conceptual development in young children or enhance the attributes of successful learners. Children need more of the types of interaction, activity and experience described in this book – play, first-hand experience, the arts and dialogue – than they currently receive if they are to flourish.

Your pedagogy will, inevitably, be affected by the expectations that others have of you. However, young children's learning depends strongly on their own expectations of themselves, which you can help to create and sustain by:

- encouraging a sense of agency rather than learned helplessness;
- believing that children can succeed, whatever their circumstances;
- celebrating children's varying interests and successes.

All of these entail thousands of small steps and interactions, which come more naturally to those who are attuned to children rather than worried about covering every detail of what is supposed to be taught.

Thinking back to David teaching me to skate, we can see that he took seriously my worries (rather than telling me that it was easy), he held my hand, and gave me advice, he encouraged me, but empowered me to try on my own. In more academic language, this can be seen as:

- being attuned to how my prior experience affected my self-concept (as a skater);
- assessing my ability, not to compare me with others, but to decide on what I needed to do to improve;
- providing different types of support and feedback while staying alongside and paying attention to my struggle;
- leaving me to work out how to practise and assimilate new experience, relying on my own attributes as a learner, even if I was not very resilient in that context.

Despite all the complexity of pedagogy, these are qualities we can all, to some extent, develop. But it requires a deep understanding of the wide range of how young children learn and the factors which influence this; and, which is especially hard, a recognition that a direct focus on outcomes may not be the best way to achieve these. Children need a broad range of experience and of support not only to become rounded individuals, but to achieve academic success. Remembering Noddings' words above, schools and educators trying too hard may be part of the problem.

Key idea: **Relationships**

To what extent are there general principles of effective pedagogy?

Throughout the book, we have considered the general principles of effective pedagogy set out by the TLRP. However, I have suggested that, as educators, we should take particular account of how very young children learn and models of Early Years practice. So, this section explores in what ways Early Years pedagogy is distinctive and what lessons this holds for those working with older children.

Critical thinking exercise 4: to what extent is there a specific pedagogy for Early Years?

Effective pedagogy in the early years was found to involve both the kind of interaction traditionally associated with… 'teaching' and also the provision of instructive learning environments and routines… Good outcomes were linked to settings that:

- *viewed cognitive and social development… as complementary;*
- *provided children with a mixture of practitioner initiated group work and learning through freely chosen play;*
- *provided adult-child interactions that involve 'sustained shared thinking' and open ended questioning;*
- *had practitioners with good curriculum knowledge combined with knowledge and understanding of how young children learn;*
- *had strong parental involvement, especially in terms of shared educational aims;*
- *provided formative feedback to children during activities and… regular reporting and discussion with parents;*
- *ensured behaviour policies in which staff supported children in rationalising and talking through their conflicts;*
- *provided differentiated learning opportunities that met the needs of particular individuals and groups of children.*

(selected from Sylva et al., 2010, pages 161–162)

A **Compare** the key differences between pedagogy in an Early Years setting and a Key Stage 2 class.

B **Identify** the implications for you, as an educator, of the TLRP's view that *more prominence needs to be given to the importance of learning relationships.*

C **Articulate** what lessons there may be for those working in Early Years settings from those working with older children – and vice versa.

Comment

To suggest that ideas from Early Years practice should be applied directly to the different situation of a Year 6 class – or vice versa – would be unhelpful; just as it is to imply that those teaching in areas of acute social disadvantage should copy practice in the 'leafy suburbs'. Judgement is required to decide on the most appropriate activities and experiences, bearing in mind a wide range of factors – among them, governmental, parental and school expectations, the dynamics and motivation of the group and children's prior experience and interests. Every sector and phase has some wonderful teachers and others who are not so good; which makes generalisations about primary or secondary education very hazardous. However, the TLRP's suggestion that the processes and the conditions required to encourage deep learning and embedded skills are broadly similar for everyone prompts a search for some general principles as part of your repertoire.

One obvious difference between a Year 5 or 6 class and those in Early Years settings is the types of activity and focus. Early Years pedagogy is concerned more with style than content, providing breadth of experience and starting from how children develop and learn rather than curriculum coverage. While older children will need more specific knowledge, a curriculum and assessment system based on outcomes privileges knowledge *that* (factual) over knowledge *how* and knowledge *of* oneself and other people. This tends to lead towards an emphasis on:

- a narrow range of curriculum, which favours children from certain types of background;
- a limited range of assessment, too often not starting from what the child already knows;
- a culture of short-term performance and comparisons of ability, which too often discourages relatively low achievers and may do little to encourage high achievers to adopt the attributes of successful learners.

The number of adults present in Early Years settings enables more discussion with small groups or on a one-to-one basis, making it easier to encourage the sorts of interaction which are familiar at home. In contrast, the deployment of teaching assistants to work out of the class with small groups has the benefit of reducing the size of the main group, but risks children being labelled as of lower ability and missing out on the dialogue which helps build up metacognitive strategies. So, it is worth considering how other adults can be used in varying ways, for instance by joining in class discussions and providing a second adult voice.

The more obvious needs of very young children for nurture as well as challenge make emotional attunement a priority for Early Years educators, but this remains relevant with older children (and adults); especially so for those who are finding learning difficult, as we all do, at times, like me skating, or some children much of the time. For example, many children with special educational needs, especially those with emotional and behavioural difficulties, may need security and continuity of relationship at least as much as extra tuition or being told how to behave. Yet, too often, a focus on the skills they find hard to acquire, or the lack of predictability by working with a variety of adults, may reinforce failure and patterns of inappropriate behaviour, despite the best of intentions.

Those who educate young children have long known of the importance of learning relationships. As we have seen, cognition is closely tied up with emotion and learning involves social interaction as well as individual endeavour. Adults modelling how to act, to interact and to think, from welcoming someone new to dealing with frustration, from listening to new ideas to telling a story, from working out what to do when one does not know to sharing one's own knowledge, provides one of the vital mechanisms by which children learn. So, the types of relationships formed, and sustained, are vital in valuing and affirming children's self-concept, in raising their aspirations and encouraging the attributes of successful learners.

Learning relationships are too personal for it to be appropriate to specify exactly what such relationships should be like. The nature of a group, and individual children, will affect what sorts of relationship are possible. Adult–child relationships will, and should, not be equal, because adults have a responsibility of care and a role which determines the boundaries of the relationship. However, children's emotional and cognitive needs will be met best when adults are:

- authoritative without being controlling, to allow freedom and creativity;
- attuned to individual children's own backgrounds, interests and responses;
- reciprocal, trusting the child as well as engendering trust;
- supportive without being over-protective, to provide the security which enables risk-taking.

The TLRP has identified general principles about effective pedagogy, though these always need to be related and applied to the particular situation and to what is to be achieved. Individuals have to work within the culture and expectations of their own school or class; but they can also help to create a richer culture and higher expectations. In doing so, many lessons can be learned from the pedagogy practised in the Early Years, especially in relation to the three fundamental changes identified by the TLRP, which are:

- interventions being based more on how learners are learning;
- the conception of what is to be learned being broadened;
- learning relationships being given more prominence.

Conclusion

This chapter has tried to synthesise some key messages about pedagogy. The critical thinking exercises will have helped you to:

- ◉ **imagine** possible challenges and opportunities in the next 30 to 40 years and the implications for both children and educators;
- ◉ **consider** how knowledge and understanding, attributes and skills are interconnected and the enduring importance of values;
- ◉ **articulate** general principles about learning and pedagogy, reflecting on those set out in the TLRP;
- ◉ **identify** to what extent there is a specific pedagogy for the Early Years and the lessons to be learned from this phase.

Structures, curricula, resources, school culture, external expectations – and much else besides – all affect how young children learn. But, in Alexander's words (2010, page 307), *pedagogy is at the heart of the enterprise*. Pedagogy is both complicated and yet embedded in the millions of ordinary, everyday actions and interactions which a child has with other children and adults, with books and toys, with ideas and experiences. These will vary both because each person's prior experience and approach to learning is different. So, enhancing and building on the attributes of young children as successful learners involves forming the relationships, establishing the environments and setting the expectations which engage and inspire them. This requires a deep knowledge of children and of oneself and passion and expertise, which, as we saw in Chapter 10, are hard both to articulate and to develop. Such expertise consists of a repertoire of professional skills, knowledge and understanding and attributes, on which to draw in making informed judgements depending on the circumstances and needs of specific groups and individuals. So, thinking through pedagogy is a never-ending search; but immensely worthwhile both personally and in enhancing children's lives.

Further reading

Alexander, R (ed) (2010) *Children, their World, their Education – Final report and recommendations of the Cambridge Primary Review*. Abingdon: Routledge
The chapter 'Re-thinking pedagogy' (pages 279–310) is very thought-provoking, although focused on primary rather than Early Years education, and mainly on cognitive learning.

Anning, A (1991) *The First Years At School*. Buckingham: Open University Press
Chapters 2 and 3 contain accessible summaries of key ideas about children learning and teachers teaching in the Early Years.

Siraj-Blatchford, I (1999) Early Childhood Pedagogy: Practice, Principles and Research. Pages 20–45 of Mortimore, P (ed) *Understanding Pedagogy and its Impact on Learning*. London: Paul Chapman Publishing
A wide-ranging discussion identifying key features to be considered in Early Years pedagogy.

References

Alexander, R (2000) *Culture and Pedagogy: International comparisons in primary education.* Oxford: Blackwell

Alexander, RJ (2004) Still No Pedagogy? Principle, pragmatism and compliance in primary education. *Cambridge Journal of Education,* 34 (1): 7-33

Alexander, R (2008) *Essays on Pedagogy.* Abingdon: Routledge

Alexander, R (ed) (2010) *Children, their World, their Education - Final report and recommendations of the Cambridge Primary Review.* Abingdon: Routledge

Alexander, R, Rose, J and Woodhead, C (1992) *Curriculum Organisation and Classroom Practice in Primary Schools - A discussion paper.* London: Department of Education and Science

Anning, A (1991) *The First Years At School.* Buckingham: Open University Press

Baldwin, J (1961) *Nobody Knows My Name.* New York: Dial Press

Ball, C (1994) *Start Right; The importance of early learning.* London: Royal Society for the Encouragement of Arts, Manufacture and Commerce

Barber, M (2005) Informed Professionalism: Realising the potential. Presentation to a conference of the Association of Teachers and Lecturers, London

Bateson, G and Bateson, MC (1988) *Where Angels Fear.* New York: Bantam

Bekoff, M (2001) Social Play Behaviour. *Journal of Consciousness Studies,* 8 (2): 81-90

Benjamin, W (1999) *Illuminations.* London: Pimlico

Black, P (1999) Assessment, Learning Theories and Testing Systems. Pages 118-134 of Murphy, P (ed) *Learners, Learning and Assessment.* London: Paul Chapman Publishing

Black, P (2001) Dreams, Strategies and Systems: Portraits of assessment past, present and future. *Assessment in Education,* 8 (1): 65-85

Black, P and Harrison, C (2004) *Science Inside the Black Box.* London: nferNelson

Black, P and Wiliam, D (1998) Assessment and Classroom Learning. *Assessment in Education: Principles, Policy and Practice,* 5 (1): 7-74

Bliss, J, Askew, M and Macrae, S (1996) Effective Teaching and Learning: Scaffolding revisited. *Oxford Review of Education,* 22 (1): 37-61

Bloom, BS (1956) *Taxonomy of Educational Objectives, Handbook 1: The Cognitive Domain.* New York: David McKay Co Inc.

Blyth, WAL (1998) *English Primary Education* (2 volumes). London: Routledge

Bowlby, J (1965) *Child Care and the Growth of Love.* London: Penguin

Brantlinger, E (2003) *Dividing Classes: How the middle class negotiates and rationalizes school advantage.* London: Routledge Falmer

Brooker, L (2002) *Starting School – Young children learning cultures.* Buckingham: Open University Press

Bruner, JS (1963) *The Process of Education.* Cambridge, Mass.: Harvard University Press

Bruner, JS (1990) *Acts of Meaning.* Cambridge, Mass.: Harvard University Press

Bruner, JS (1996) *The Culture of Education.* Cambridge, Mass.: Harvard University Press

Bruner, JS (2006) *In Search of Pedagogy – The selected work of Jerome S Bruner* (2 volumes). London: Routledge

Cambridge Primary Review (Summary) (2010) *Introducing the Cambridge Primary Review.* www.routledge.com

Campbell, RJ and Kyriakides, L (2000) The National Curriculum and Standards in Primary Schools. *Comparative Education,* 36 (4): 383–395

Carr, W and Kemmis, S (1989) *Becoming Critical: Education, knowledge and action research.* Lewes: Falmer

Chitty, C (2010) Brian Simon and FORUM. *Forum for 3-19 Comprehensive Education,* 52 (2): 255–259

Claxton, G (1997) *Hare Brain, Tortoise Mind – Why intelligence increases when you think less.* London: Fourth Estate

Claxton, G (2002) *Building Learning Power.* Bristol: TLO Ltd

Claxton, G (2005) *An Intelligent Look at Emotional Intelligence.* London: Association of Teachers and Lecturers

Craft, A (2009) Changes in the Landscape for Creativity in Education. Pages 5–21 of Wilson, A (ed) *Creativity in Primary Education.* Exeter: Learning Matters

Craft, A, Jeffrey, B and Leibling, M (eds) (2001) *Creativity in Education.* London: Continuum

Cupitt, D (1995) *What is a Story?* London: SCM Press

Daniels, H, Cole, M and Werstch, JV (eds) (2007) *The Cambridge Companion to Vygotsky.* Cambridge: Cambridge University Press

David, T (2001) Curriculum in the Early Years. Pages 55–66 of Pugh, G (ed) *Contemporary Issues in the Early Years – Working collaboratively for children.* London: Paul Chapman Publishing

Day, C (1999) *Developing Teachers – The challenge of lifelong learning.* London: Falmer

DCSF (2004) www.dcsf.gov.uk/everychildmatters/ accessed 31 August 2010

DCSF (2009) *Independent Review of the Primary Curriculum: Final Report* (the Report of Sir Jim Rose). http://search.publications.education.gov.uk accessed 24 August 2010

Demie, F (2001) Ethnic and Gender Differences in Educational Achievement and Implications for School Improvement Strategies (short report). *Educational Research,* 43 (1): 91–106

DES (1985) *Education for All* (The Swann Report). London: Department of Education and Science

DES (1990) *Starting with Quality* (The Rumbold Report of the Committee of Inquiry into the Quality of the Educational Experience Offered to 3- and 4-year olds). London: HMSO

Desforges, C (1995) *An Introduction to Teaching: Psychological perspectives.* Oxford: Blackwell

DfES (2003) *Excellence and Enjoyment* (summary). www.globalgateway.org.uk/Default.aspx?page=2074)

DfES (2005a) *Social and Emotional Aspects of Learning (SEAL): Improving behaviour, improving learning.* http://nationalstrategies.standards.dcsf.gov.uk/primary/publications/banda/seal accessed 24 August 2010

DfES (2005b) *Learning Behaviour: The report of the practitioners' group on school behaviour and discipline.* London: DfES

DfES (2006) *Independent Review of the Teaching of Early Reading* (the Rose Review). London: DfES

Donaldson, M (1982) *Children's Minds.* Glasgow: Fontana

Donaldson, M (1992) *Human Minds – An exploration.* London: Allen Lane

Dowling, M (2010) *Young Children's Personal, Social and Emotional Development.* London: SAGE

Drury, R (2007) *Young Bilingual Learners at Home and School – Researching multilingual voices.* Stoke-on-Trent: Trentham

Dweck, CS (1999) *Self Theories: Their role in motivation, personality and development.* Philadelphia: Psychology Press

Eagleton, T (2000) *The Idea of Culture.* Oxford: Blackwell

Eaude, T (2008) *Children's Spiritual, Moral, Social and Cultural Development – Primary and Early Years.* Exeter: Learning Matters

Eaude, T (2009a) Creativity and Spiritual, Moral, Social and Cultural Development. Pages 58–67 of Wilson, A (ed) *Creativity in Primary Education.* Exeter: Learning Matters

Eaude, T (2009b) *Bowling Alone? What can schools do to promote cohesive communities?* London: National Education Trust

Ecclestone, K and Hayes, D (2009) *The Dangerous Rise of Therapeutic Education.* London: Routledge

Erricker, C (1998) Journeys Through the Heart: The effect of death, loss and conflict on children's worldviews. *Journal of Beliefs and Values*, 19 (1): 107–118

Eyre, D (2009) The English Model of Gifted Education. Pages 1045–1059 of Shavinina, LV (ed) *International Handbook on Giftedness* (2 volumes). Dordrecht: Springer

Eyre, D (2010) Gifted and Talented. Pages 388–401 of Arthur, J and Cremin, T (eds) *Learning to Teach in the Primary School* (2nd edition). Abingdon: Routledge

EYFS (Early Years Foundation Stage) www.teachernet.gov.uk/teachingandlearning/eyfs accessed 16 August 2010

Fox, R (2005) *Teaching and Learning: Lessons from psychology.* Oxford: Blackwell

Fullan, M (1991) *The New Meaning of Educational Change*. London: Cassell

Gallagher, JJ (2009) Gifted Education in the 21st Century. Pages 122–134 of Eyre, D (ed) *Gifted and Talented Education* (volume 1). London: Routledge

Galton, M, Simon, B and Croll, P (1980) *Inside the Primary Classroom*. London: Routledge, and Kegan Paul

Gardner, H (1993) *Frames of Mind: The theory of multiple intelligences*. London: Fontana

Gardner, H (1999) Assessment in Context. Pages 90–117 of Murphy, P (ed) *Learners, Learning and Assessment*. London: Paul Chapman Publishing

Geertz, C (2001) Imbalancing Act: Jerome Bruner's cultural psychology. Pages 19–30 of Bakhurst, D and Shanker, SG (eds) *Jerome Bruner: Language, Culture, Self*. London: SAGE

Gerhardt, S (2004) *Why Love Matters: How affection shapes a baby's brain*. Hove: Routledge

Gillborn, D and Mirza, HS (2000) *Educational Inequality: Mapping race, class and gender: A synthesis of research evidence*. London: Ofsted

Gipps, C (1994) What We Know About Effective Primary Teaching. Pages 22–39 of Bourne, J (ed) *Thinking Through Primary Practice*. London: Routledge

Gipps, C and MacGilchrist, B (1999) Primary School Learners. Pages 46–67 of Mortimore, P (ed) *Understanding Pedagogy and its Impact on Learning*. London: Paul Chapman Publishing

Goldberg, S (2000) *Attachment and Development*. London: Hodder Arnold

Goleman, D (1996) *Emotional Intelligence: Why it can matter more than IQ*. New York: Bloomsbury

Gregory, E and Williams, A (2000) *City Literacies: Learning to read across generations and cultures*. London: Routledge

GTCE (2010) *Making CPD Better: Bringing together research about CPD*. London: General Teaching Council for England

Hadow Report (1931) www.educationengland.org.uk/documents/hadow1931/index.html accessed 19 August 2010

Halstead, JM (1996) Values and Values Education. Pages 3–14 of Halstead, JM and Taylor, MJ (eds) *Values in Education and Education in Values*. London: Falmer

Hare, D (2008) *David Hare: Plays 3* (Skylight). London: Faber and Faber

Hargreaves, A (2003) *Teaching in the Knowledge Society – Education in the age of insecurity*. Maidenhead: Open University Press

Hargreaves, DH (1999) The Knowledge-Creating School. *British Journal of Educational Studies*, 47(2): 122–44

Harlen, W (2010) The Quality of Learning – Assessment Alternatives for Primary Education. Pages 484–529 of Alexander R (ed) *The Cambridge Primary Review Research Surveys*. Abingdon: Routledge

Hart, S, Dixon, A, Drummond, MJ and McIntyre, D (2004) *Learning without Limits*. Maidenhead: Open University Press

Hay, D with Nye, R (1998) *The Spirit of the Child*. London: Fount

Hiebert, J, Carpenter, TP, Fennema, E, Fuson, K, Human, P, Murray, H, Olivier, A and Wearne, D (1999) Problem Solving as a Basis for Reform in Curriculum and Instruction: The case of mathematics. Pages 151–170 of Murphy, P (ed) (1999) *Learners, Learning and Assessment.* London: Paul Chapman Publishing

HMSO (1967) *Children and their Primary Schools: A report of the Central Advisory Council for Education (England)* (The Plowden Report). London: HMSO

Hobsbaum, A, Peters, S and Sylva, K (1996) Scaffolding in Reading Recovery. *Oxford Review of Education,* 22 (1): 17–35.

House of Commons (2009) *National Curriculum: Fourth Report of Session (of Children, Schools and Families Committee) 2008–09.* London: The Stationery Office

Hubbard, T (2002) http://news.bbc.co.uk/1/hi/education/1844620.stm accessed 3 September 2010

Ireson, J, Mortimore, P and Hallam, S (1999) The Common Strands of Pedagogy and Their Implications. Pages 212–232 of Mortimore, P (ed) *Understanding Pedagogy and its Impact on Learning.* London: Paul Chapman Publishing

Isaacs, S (1970) *The Children We Teach.* London: University of London Press

Jackson, PW, Boostrom, RE, and Hansen, DJ (1993) *The Moral Life of Schools.* San Francisco: Jossey Bass

John, P (2008) The Predicament of the Teaching Profession and the Revival of Professional Authority: A Parsonian Perspective. Pages 11–24 of Johnson, D and Maclean, R (eds) *Teaching: Professionalization, Development and Leadership.* Dordrecht: Springer

Kagan, J (1994) *Galen's Prophecy.* London: Free Association Books

Kelly, G (1991) *The Psychology of Personal Constructs.* London: Routledge

Kimes Myers, B (1997) *Young Children and Spirituality.* London: Routledge

Layard, R (2005) *Happiness.* London: Allen Lane

Layard, R and Dunn, J (2009) *A Good Childhood – Searching for values in a competitive age.* London: Penguin

Leadbeater, C (2005) *The Shape of Things to Come: Personalised learning through collaboration.* www.standards.dfes.gov.uk/sie/documents/shape.pdf accessed 27 July 2010

Leeson, C (2007) In Praise of Reflective Practice. Pages 171–181 of Willan, J, Parker-Rees, R and Savage, J (eds) (2007) *Early Childhood Studies.* Exeter: Learning Matters

Lohman, DF and Korb, K (2006) Gifted Today but not Tomorrow? Longitudinal changes in ITBS and CogAT scores during elementary school. *Journal for the Education of the Gifted,* 29: 451–484

Lovat, T and Toomey, R (eds) (2009) *Values Education and Quality Teaching: The Double Helix Effect.* Dordrecht: Springer

Macintyre, A (1999) *After Virtue.* London: Duckworth

McKinsey and Company (2007) How the world's best-performing school systems come out on top. www.mckinsey.com accessed 16 August 2010

McMahon, L (1992) *The Handbook of Play Therapy.* London: Routledge

Maslow, A (1998) *Toward a Psychology of Being.* New York: Wiley

Mayall, B (2010) Children's Lives Outside School and Their Educational Impact. Pages 49–82 of Alexander, R (ed) *The Cambridge Primary Review Research Surveys.* Abingdon: Routledge

Mortimore, P (ed) (1999) *Understanding Pedagogy and its Impact on Learning.* London: Paul Chapman Publishing

Moyles, J (2004) Passion, Paradox and Professionalism in Early Years Education. Pages 9–24 of Wragg, EC (ed) *The RoutledgeFalmer Reader in Teaching and Learning.* London: RoutledgeFalmer

Myhill, D, Jones, S and Hopper, R (2006) *Talking, Listening, Learning – Effective Talk in the Primary Classroom.* Maidenhead: Open University Press

NACCCE (National Advisory Committee on Creative and Cultural Education) (1999) *All Our Futures: Creativity, Culture and Education.* Sudbury: DfEE

NCC (National Curriculum Council) (1993) Spiritual and Moral Development: A discussion paper. York: NCC

Noddings, N (1991) Stories in Dialogue: Caring and interpersonal reasoning. Pages 157–70 of Witherell, C and Noddings, N (eds) *Stories Lives Tell: Narrative and dialogue in education.* New York: Teachers' College Press

Noss, R and Pachler, N (1999) The Challenge of New Technologies: Doing old things in a new way, or doing new things? Pages 195–211 of Mortimore, P (ed) *Understanding Pedagogy and its Impact on Learning.* London: Paul Chapman Publishing

Nutbrown, C (2001) Watching and Learning; The tools of assessment. Pages 66–77 of Pugh, G (ed) *Contemporary Issues in the Early Years – Working collaboratively for children.* London: Paul Chapman Publishing

Ofsted (2002) *The Curriculum in Successful Primary Schools.* London: Ofsted

Ofsted (2003) *The Education of Six Year Olds in England, Denmark and Finland: An international comparative study.* London: Ofsted

Ofsted (2009) *Twenty outstanding primary schools – Excelling against the odds in challenging circumstances.* www.ofsted.gov.uk/Ofsted-home/Publications-and-research accessed 5 September 2010

Ofsted (2010) *Learning: Creative approaches that raise standards.* www.ofsted.gov.uk/Ofsted-home/Publications-and-research accessed 5 September 2010

Olson, DR (2001) Education – The bridge from culture to mind. Pages 104–115 of Bakhurst, D and Shanker, SG (eds) *Jerome Bruner: Language, Culture, Self.* London: SAGE

Osborn, M (2008) Teacher Professional Identity Under Conditions of Constraint. Pages 67–81 of Johnson, D and Maclean, R (eds) *Teaching: Professionalization, Development and Leadership.* Dordrecht: Springer

Osborn, M, McNess, E, Planel, C and Triggs, C (2003) Culture, Context and Policy Comparing Learners in Three European countries. Pages 35–57 of Sutherland, R, Claxton, G and Pollard, A (eds) *Learning and Teaching Where World Views Meet.* Stoke-on-Trent: Trentham Books

Thinking Through Pedagogy for Primary and Early Years

Palmer, S (2006) *Toxic Childhood*. London: Orion Books

Papert, S (1999) www.papert.org/articles/Papertonpiaget accessed 21 July 2010

Passey, D (no date) *Higher Order Thinking Skills: An exploration of aspects of learning and thinking and how ICT can be used to support these processes.* www.northerngrid.org/ngflwebsite/hots/HOTSintro.pdf accessed 25 August 2010

Putnam, RD (2000) *Bowling Alone: The collapse and revival of American community.* New York: Simon and Schuster

QAA (Quality Assurance Agency for Higher Education) (2007a) Education Studies Benchmark Statement. www.qaa.ac.uk/academicinfrastructure/benchmark/honours/Education07.pdf accessed 22 July 2010

QAA (Quality Assurance Agency for Higher Education) (2007b) Early Childhood Studies Benchmark Statement. www.qaa.ac.uk/academicinfrastructure/benchmark/statements/EarlyChildhoodStudies07.pdf accessed 22 July 2010

QCDA (Qualifications and Curriculum Development Agency) (1999) http://curriculum.qcda.gov.uk/key-stages-1-and-2/inclusion/nonstatutory guidance/index.aspx

Reed, ES (2001) Towards a Cultural Ecology of Instruction. Pages 116–126 of Bakhurst, D and Shanker, SG (eds) *Jerome Bruner: Language, Culture, Self.* London: SAGE

Resnick, L (1999) Making America Smarter. *Education Week Century Series*, 18 (40): 38–40

Salmon, P (1995) *Psychology in the Classroom – Reconstructing teachers and learners.* London: Cassell

SCAA (School Curriculum and Assessment Authority) (1996) *Education for Adult Life: The spiritual and moral development of young people: A summary report.* London: SCAA

Schön, D (1987) *Educating the Reflective Practitioner.* San Francisco: Jossey Bass

Simon, B (1981) Why No Pedagogy in England? Pages 124–145 of Simon, B and Taylor, W (eds) *Education in the Eighties: The central issues.* London: Batsford

Siraj-Blatchford, I (1999) Early Childhood Pedagogy: Practice, principles and research. Pages 20–45 of Mortimore, P (ed) *Understanding Pedagogy and its Impact on Learning.* London: Paul Chapman Publishing

Speed, PF (1983) *Learning and Teaching in Victorian Times.* Harlow: Longman

Sternberg, RJ (2004) Individual Differences in Cognitive Development. Pages 600–619 of Goswami, U (ed) *Blackwell Handbook of Cognitive Childhood Development.* Oxford: Blackwell

Sternberg, RJ (2007) Culture, Instruction and Assessment. *Comparative Education*, 43 (1): 5–22

Suggate, S (2010) *Nursery World*, January 2010, or www.nurseryworld.co.uk accessed 26 August 2010

Sylva, K, Melhuish, E, Sammons, P, Siraj-Blatchford, I and Taggart, B (eds) (2010) *Early Childhood Matters – Evidence from the Effective Pre-school and Primary Education project.* Abingdon: Routledge

Tassoni, P and Hucker, K (2005) *Planning Play and the Early Years.* Oxford: Heinemann

Tharp, RG and Gallimore, R (1988) *Rousing Minds to Life.* Cambridge: Cambridge University Press

Thomson, P and Hall, C (2008) Opportunities Missed and/or Thwarted? 'Funds of knowledge' meet the English National Curriculum. *The Curriculum Journal,* 19 (2): 87–103

Tizard, B and Hughes M (1984) *Young Children Learning – Talking and Thinking at Home and at School.* London: Fontana

TLRP (Teaching and Learning Research Programme) (2006) *Improving Teaching and Learning in Schools.* London: TLRP (see www.tlrp.org)

Tommerdahl, J (2010) A Model for Bridging the Gap Between Neuroscience and Education. *Oxford Review of Education,* 36 (1): 97–109

Training and Development Agency (TDA) (2007) Professional Standards for Teachers – Qualified Teacher Status. www.tda.gov.uk/upload/resources/pdf/s/standards_qts.pdf accessed 22 July 2010

UN (no date) www.un.org/millenniumgoals/education.shtml accessed 22 July 2010

UNESCO (1994) www.unesco.org/education/pdf/salama_e.pdf accessed 31 August 2010

UNICEF (no date) www.unicef.org/crc/ accessed 22 July 2010

UNICEF (2007) Child Poverty in Perspective: An overview of child well-being in rich countries. *Innocenti Report Card* 7. Florence: Innocenti Research Centre

Watkins, C (2005) *Classrooms as Learning Communities.* Abingdon: Routledge

Watkins, C and Mortimore, P (1999) Pedagogy: What do we know? Pages 1–19 of Mortimore, P (ed) *Understanding Pedagogy and its Impact on Learning.* London: Paul Chapman Publishing

West-Burnham, J. and Huws-Jones, V (2007) *Spiritual and Moral Development in Schools.* London: Continuum

White, J (2010) Aims as Policy in English Primary Education. Pages 282–305 of Alexander, R (ed) *The Cambridge Primary Review Research Surveys.* Abingdon: Routledge

Wilkinson, R and Pickett, K (2009) *The Spirit Level – Why more equal societies almost always do better.* London: Allen Lane

Willan, J, Parker-Rees, R and Savage, J (eds) (2007) *Early Childhood Studies.* Exeter: Learning Matters

Williams, R (2003) *Silence and Honey Cakes – The wisdom of the desert.* Oxford: Lion

Winnicott, DW (1980) *Playing and Reality.* Harmondsworth: Penguin

Wragg, EC (2004) The Two Rs – Rules and relationships. Pages 60–71 of Wragg, EC (ed) *The RoutledgeFalmer Reader in Teaching and Learning.* London: RoutledgeFalmer

Index

Added to a page number 'f' denotes a figure and 't' denotes a table.

Thinking Through Pedagogy for Primary and Early Years